ENGLISH LEGAL SYSTEM

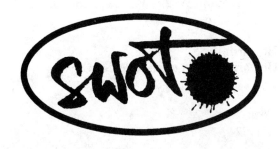

ENGLISH LEGAL SYSTEM

Third Edition

Stephen R. Wilson

Principal Lecturer in Law,
University of Northumbria at Newcastle

Series Editor: C.J. Carr, MA, BCL

First published in Great Britain 1988 by Blackstone Press Limited,
9–15 Aldine Street, London W12 8AW. Telephone 0181-740 1173.

© David A. Howarth, 1988
© David A. Howarth and Stephen R. Wilson, 1996

First edition, 1988
Second edition, 1992
Third edition, 1996

ISBN: 1 85431 479 3

British Library Cataloguing in Publication Data
A CIP catalogue record for this book is available from the British Library

Typeset by Montage Studios Limited, Tonbridge, Kent
Printed by Bell and Bain Limited, Glasgow

CONTENTS

PREFACE

David Howarth's death in 1993 was a loss not only to his colleagues but also to the wider academic community. He is greatly missed. The necessary task of updating his text I have undertaken with sadness.

David's sentiments, expressed in the preface to the second edition of this book, hold good. Once again there have been substantial changes in the English legal system and changes continue apace in teaching and assessment methods.

Students, even during their year of studying this area, cannot escape the fact that almost inevitably there will be changes or initiatives which will require detailed consideration. This edition seeks to reflect the seemingly never-ending changes to the English legal system that have occurred since 1992. Prominent amongst these are: the Report of the Royal Commission on Criminal Justice; the Criminal Justice and Public Order Act 1994, which, *inter alia*, abolishes committal proceedings and alters the consequences of a defendant's right to silence; the Criminal Appeal Act 1995; the 1995 Green Paper on Legal Aid; the Conditional Fee Agreements Order; the granting of rights of audience in the superior courts to solicitors; the use of Hansard as an aid to statutory interpretation; and Lord Woolf's consideration of access to justice. A note of caution should be sounded concerning the abolition of committal proceedings. Whilst the 1994 Act provides for abolition and the introduction of transfer of proceedings, as yet this change has not been brought into force. The text, therefore, contains comments on both systems.

Many universities have moved to a semesterised and modularised or unitised system of course delivery, with a consequent greater emphasis on coursework, and in some cases different forms of assessment. I have sought to reflect this change with an expanded section on coursework and the introduction of hints on oral presentation in chapter 2.

Largely this work remains David's, and I have left in place his numerous anecdotes and observations which continue to illuminate the text. It only remains for me to say thank you to David's wife Margaret and to Alistair MacQueen of Blackstone Press for entrusting this task to me. The law in this book is accurate up to September 1995.

Steve Wilson
December 1995

PREFACE TO THE SECOND EDITION

To be told that a second edition is required of a book one has written is instantly gratifying whilst at the same time a reminder of the need for the expenditure of some effort. In the present case, there are two compelling reasons for the preparation of a new edition: substantial changes in the subject matter and substantial changes in teaching, that have occurred since the publication of the first edition.

Within the limits of the space available I have tried to reflect these two types of change. In the first place, more emphasis is given throughout to the European Community's impact on our legal system as well as incorporating material arising out of the events leading up to and the passing of the Courts and Legal Services Act 1990. Further changes in the law have entailed a review of legal aid and the whole area of 'access to justice'.

On the teaching side, account has been taken of the awakening of the professions and academics to the need to teach skills appropriate to the needs of lawyers, and reference has been made to the increasing volume of literature geared to that end.

As with the preface to the first edition, I believe it is right to record my personal vote of confidence in the future of the English legal system, especially in the light of the present doubts raised in some quarters and currently being articulated through the work of the Royal Commission on Criminal Justice.

Once again I should like to record my thanks to my publishers and the encouragement of my family.

David A. Howarth
The Hemmel, Newton
January 1992

PREFACE TO THE FIRST EDITION

Prefaces are as various as the courses for which this book has been written. Some are expressions of gratitude, some are self-deprecatory, some are expressions of modesty and some are defiant challenges to the reader.

The wise, but dull, course is to stick to a factual introduction to the book and conclude with a series of acknowledgments. In this case, there is a special reason for doing just that. A recurring theme throughout the book is its emphasis on the need to be well informed before daring to be critical. On reading through what I have written about our legal system in England and Wales, I have discovered that, like Blackstone, I believe there is much of great value in our legal system. There are two reasons why this is appropriate. One is that this book is appearing under the imprint of the Blackstone Press and the other is that I believe students should be reminded occasionally that a 'critical study' involves fair minded judgment and is not solely concerned with disapproving comment.

My enquiries into the teaching of the English legal system in contemporary law schools showed me how many different approaches to the subject there are. The selection of topics and their treatment is intended to reflect that which is common to most courses. As stated in the text, the subject is a fast moving one. It has been possible to include some references to the Legal Aid Bill, but the material in chapter 10 does not take into account the findings of the Marre committee on the future of the legal professions, which are being 'trailed' in the press as this preface is being written. That committee's findings promise to be more far reaching than those of the Ormrod committee in the early seventies and to have a good chance of being implemented. The working lives of students who read this book may well be profoundly affected by the report of the Marre committee.

My own work too has been affected by the writing of this book. In daring to tell students how to achieve success I have acquired a new sympathy for students labouring under the expectations that tutors have of them. Also, I feel bound to look again at the way in which I manage the business of teaching and learning.

During the preparation of this book I have received much encouragement from Heather Saward and Jonathan Harris in spite of their preoccupation with other more weighty matters. The book would never have been completed without the typing skills of Lesley, Mary and my daughter Sally, and the tolerance and patience of my wife who is still waiting for that bit of decorating and that . . . and that . . .

David A. Howarth
The Hemmel, Newton
March 1988

TABLE OF CASES

1 THE 'ENGLISH LEGAL SYSTEM' IN THE LAW CURRICULUM

The phrase 'English legal system' in the title of this book and as it occurs in the heading of this chapter is used as a convenient term to refer to a body of knowledge that, to some extent, appears as part of the first-year curriculum of nearly all first degree courses in law, in English universities. As such a study, however, the 'English legal system' has become a 'broad church' embracing a variety of approaches to teaching the aspects of the law to be considered here, and some disagreement between institutions about what should be included in this subject. This is reflected in the different titles given to courses by different institutions at the present time. Also, there has been and continues to be change in the content and approach to the subject, to an extent not necessitated by changes in the law from year to year.

This chapter is intended to help you to overcome the first obstacle to success in this subject. That is, to know and understand what type, of several, is the legal system course in the curriculum that your degree course has adopted. Even where a degree course has only a brief introductory element devoted to an explanation of the courts and their working, matters which other courses deal with as part of a legal system course counting as a whole first-year examined subject will be found glinting through the 'interstices' of substantive subjects such as criminal law and contract law.

Indeed, there is a sound argument for this integrative approach, for one of the main purposes of teaching you about the legal system is to provide the necessary background and method to learning the substantive law; and when 'legal system' is taught as a separate subject students are tempted and want to compartmentalise the knowledge and techniques acquired in the legal system course and not to apply it in the context of other subjects such as contract, criminal law and property. You will find that your 'legal sytem' tutor is only too well aware of this problem, for his colleagues teaching other subjects will be constantly complaining that he does not appear to be teaching you and your fellow students anything at all, because it will seem sometimes, in, say, contract classes, that you have never heard of the different courts in which contract cases may be heard or whether judgments of the House of Lords are more important than judgments of a circuit judge sitting in a county court.

So, lesson one is that, whatever the nature and name of your 'legal system' course, it must not be treated as a separate compartment of knowledge, because this part of the curriculum of the law student, more than any other, is interdependent with other parts, and to a large extent is the faithful servant of the student seeking to come to grips with any other legal subject taught within the compass of a degree in law.

It was not always so. In the preface to the first edition (1939) of his book, *The Machinery of Justice in England*, R.M. Jackson made the following comments:

> In the past the administration of justice has hardly been considered a 'subject'.... law books are apt to assume that the reader is acquainted with the subject. Thought about law has changed a good deal in the last twenty years.

That can equally be said of the years from 1971 to 1991.

> The best introduction to law is a study of the institutions and environment in which lawyers work.... in some law schools ... academic tradition has ... succeeded in imposing a mass of historical study to satisfy the idea that it is cultural to know what happened in the middle ages and not cultural to know what happens in the 20th century.

And, for the present generation of students, what might happen until well into the 21st century.

The following brief note of the development of 'legal systems' teaching and courses is offered as an aid to understanding contemporary influences on 'legal systems' courses and their structure and objectives. Most legal subjects used to be taught in a strong historical framework. That worked perfectly well so long as nearly all law students had studied history to at least GCSE standard and many to A level equivalent (and O level Latin was an entry requirement to many law degree courses) and the law itself was contained within the compass of such a work as *Stephen's Commentaries on the Laws of*

England, which was the staple academic diet of students studying for the first part of the solicitors' examinations. The development of 'new' subjects such as company law, and Dicey's 'non-subject' of administrative law, industrial law and many others, made the historical perspective in the 'old' subjects of crime, contract, property (and so on) seem less compelling and relevant: and perhaps the 1925 property legislation ultimately was to have the same effect.

In spite of these changes in law teaching, the attitude to culture referred to in Jackson's preface still prevailed, and many degree schemes introduced a compulsory course in 'English legal history', but history stopped safely short of the present, perhaps with the 'perfection' of the legal system on the passing of the 1873–5 Judicature Acts.

Subsequently, legal history was transformed into 'English legal system'. For a long time such courses were descriptive of the contemporary court systems and the role of lawyers, together with a historical study of the sources of law and the development of the major branches of common law and equity. This was an era when the student who needed to be or chose to be an examination question spotter could always rely upon being asked the following question, based on a statement in Maitland's classic work, *The Forms of Action at Common Law:*

'The forms of action we have buried but they still rule us from their graves.' Discuss.

That strong historical element in the syllabus of an English legal system course has subsequently declined, almost to the point of extinction, under the combined impact of the sociological perspective on law and a perceived need amongst law teachers to give students an insight into legal method at an early stage of their course. At the present time, therefore, all of these influences clamour and jostle to make themselves a part of the contents of that amorphous, rubber-like subject known as the 'English legal system'.

Today's student of the English legal system must not only meet Jackson's criteria of knowing the institutions (of the law) and the environment in which lawyers work, but also must be able to offer a social critique of those institutions and be skilled in the handling of cases, the finding of *'rationes decidendi'* and the interpretation of statutes. Which of these aspects of study receives most emphasis in a particular course at a particular institution may be reflected in the title of the course, because academics generally believe, contrary to Shakespeare, that there is a great deal in a name. Much effort goes into a choice of name for a subject so as to make clear to other academics, and perhaps to students, the objectives of the course, and maybe the prejudices of those who devised the course. More will be said later about the significance of particular course titles.

The development of courses is closely related to the availability of suitable course materials. In the past, and to a considerable extent it is still true, that has meant the availability of one or more recognised standard textbooks. Whether or not the emergence of a 'standard' text is a good or bad thing from the point of view of students' scholarly development is beside the point in a work such as this, designed to give help to students, first in meeting the requirements of their course and, secondly, in developing a deeper interest in their subject. That is not possible unless the first and basic level of achievement in mastering the basic requirements of a course has been attained. So, as with other subjects and branches of law, such as contract and tort, where a number of outstanding books in the 19th century influenced the practical development of the law in those areas as well as the pedagogic treatment of those subjects, the study of the English legal system has been much influenced by a number of outstanding textbooks, which have appeared on the reading lists of English legal system courses of many schools and departments of law. We are probably still too close to the developments in the structure and operation of our courts and tribunals over the past 40 years to say whether or not the exposition and critique of that structure and its operation through the use of these books has been influential in guiding and moulding those developments.

It is true to say, however, that in the successive generations of law students over that period of time, there can be few who, in their own generation, have not become acquainted with *Potter's Historical Introduction to English Law and Its Institutions*, Jackson's *The Machinery of Justice in England*, Kiralfy's *The English Legal System*, Walker and Walker's *The English Legal System*, and now Smith and Bailey's *The Modern English Legal System*. The first edition of each of these books represents a stage in the development of academic thinking about our legal system. Such books represent, as it were, the mainstream concern with a descriptive and mildly critical treatment of contemporary court structures and the personnel connected with them, prefaced with a larger or smaller historical introduction, including in some cases an explanation of the place of equity in English law. There is also discernible in the developments of this subject as exemplified by the early editions of the standard texts, a shift towards a treatment of the subject as a study of the law in action.

It has been stated already that present-day courses on the English legal system include, in most cases, a study of legal 'method' and legal technique. The origins of this go back to a descriptive and historical treatment of the 'sources' of English law as part of English legal history courses and early English legal system courses. Contemporary theoretical studies of legal systems as related bodies of rules, concepts and principles have also stimulated interest and teaching in 'legal method' as part of the teaching of 'legal systems'. This development has also produced its own standard texts such as Farrar and Dugdale's *Introduction to Legal Method*, Zander's *Cases and Materials on the English Legal System* and the delightful and stimulating *How to Do Things with Rules* by Twining and Miers. These and other books have appeared in response not only to the needs of students on existing courses but also, in many cases, the appearance of a book has stimulated other academics' thinking and led in turn to the adaptation of existing courses and the development of new courses. A further development is the addition of skills teaching. This too has become part of a legal system course and is catered for by new books such as *Learning Legal Rules* by Holland and Webb and *Learning Legal Skills* by Lee and Fox.

Therefore, if one takes the books and their authors as representative of thinking about the subject, referred to in this book for convenience as 'The English legal system', a brief perusal of all or some of them will show the student the various angles from which the subject may be approached. A particular angle or approach may be quite apparent from the list of contents, and it is instructive to compare the topics which are included or excluded by different authors, the arrangements of topics into themes, and the extent of the treatment accorded to a topic.

For example, the topics dealt with in Farrar and Dugdale's *Introduction to Legal Method* are quite different from those making up the contents of Ingman's *The English Legal Process*.

Equally, and perhaps more striking, are the differences in the arrangement of Walker and Walker, *The English Legal System*, 6th ed., and the first edition of Smith and Bailey's *The Modern English Legal System*, dated within nine months of each other. The former still had almost 90 pages of historical introduction, whilst Smith and Bailey adopt a thematic approach to the subject, setting the solving of legal problems at the heart of their work in a framework of rules and institutions.

Each approach has its own value and is equally valid on its own terms. What matters to students is to know which of many approaches to this subject they are being invited to adopt in their own course. It is also important for students to know that there are other ways of looking at the English legal system. Nor should students expect a course to follow closely and precisely the order of treatment in any particular textbook, even when it is prescribed reading for a particular course. For this reason every student would be well advised to read at least one book on the legal system written from a standpoint other than that adopted on the course being studied, and to read it as literature and not as a text to be pored over, analysed, digested and eventually learned for the immediate purpose of passing an examination.

References to the variety to be found amongst textbooks written for this subject lead on to a consideration of how this subject relates to the law curriculum as a whole. Why do we study 'the legal system' separately, and what do other subject teachers expect the student to learn in the legal system course that is essential for the learning and study of other subjects such as contract law or criminal law? At least one university department of law has changed its collective mind on this matter, twice within the past 12 years, and is at present integrating much of the material that forms part of a traditional legal systems course into other substantive subjects. Many other departments retain separate courses. When those courses contain a sizeable element of 'legal method', relating to the handling of case law and statutes, there is undoubtedly a logistical problem to be faced. If your course is of this kind, you must appreciate as soon as possible that, at any rate at first-year level, 'method' cannot be studied in isolation.

The problem referred to just now is, of course, how to teach 'method' without any materials in the shape of knowledge of a substantive branch of law ready to hand. It is a familiar 'chicken and egg' problem. How can one solve a 'contract' problem without knowing both the rules of contract and the correct method of applying those rules. So, courses which attempt to teach 'method' as such must rely for their examples on material from other subjects. This requires a degree of cooperation between the teachers of different subjects. It also means that when it is done well students should more readily appreciate that law cannot be studied in completely separate and watertight compartments. This is a lesson that teachers of this subject will be stressing throughout the course, and, hopefully, students will learn and apply in their work as a whole, whether it is in preparation for seminar discussion, a written assignment or in an examination.

OBJECTIVES OF COURSES

It has been suggested so far that different 'legal systems' courses represent different 'mixes' of the objectives to be pursued in teaching a legal system course at all. What then are those different objectives? If they are made explicit, then you, the student, will be able to judge how to approach your own 'legal system' course and, if need be, adopt a variety of ways of looking at the subject and the ways in which you will be assessed as part of the course. Succeeding chapters in this book are arranged so as to make plain not only the variety of courses currently being taught in English departments of law, but also the variety of objectives that may be combined within a single course, demanding a flexible approach to methods of learning and assessment.

The six main objectives that may be separated out from a consideration of many of the courses now being taught are the following:

(a)   acquisition of necessary background knowledge of the system and how it works,

(b)   understanding of the historical development of the English legal system,

(c)   an analytical treatment of contemporary legal institutions,

(d)   an introduction to legal techniques, legal method and legal reasoning,

(e)   a critique of the 'law in action',
(f)   an introduction to lawyers' skills.

In any one course, all or some of these objectives may be found with varying emphases. Some material that is included in a 'legal system' course at one institution may be found in a course with a quite different title at another institution. Thus, for example, (e), above, may appear as a separate course or as part of the separate course with a title such as 'law in society'. However, the present book is based on the premise that the reader is faced with a first-year course with a combination of all or some of the above objectives, and probably a variety of types of assessment. Within such a course different topics lend themselves more or less readily to a particular type of treatment. The principal chapters on the different parts and aspects of the course are presented so as to indicate the approach to a topic that may be most commonly found in a legal system course which is a foundation course.

However, the reader is warned that the approach to a topic used for the sake of example, in this book, will be by no means the only valid approach that may be adopted in the reader's own course.

You must seek to develop sensitive antennae to pick up the nuances within the teaching you receive on your own course so that you may enter into a dialogue with those teaching and examining you on shared and common terms of reference. To do that is not to compromise your own academic integrity nor does it entail simply following the known 'party line' when it comes to examinations. There is a great difference between an answer simply setting out, for example, the terms and conditions of judicial appointments in response to a question about the social and education background of judicial appointees, and an answer arguing cogently and with facts to back up the argument, that Griffith's view as expressed in his book, *The Politics of the Judiciary,* is far too pessimistic about the likelihood of judicial impartiality in politically sensitive cases. The first answer can never score good marks, because it does not answer the question asked. The second answer may score very good marks even though the person marking the answer has shown in his previous teaching that he accepts Griffith's standpoint in this matter.

It is now time to say something in more detail about the six objectives set out above and the way in which they may affect the structure of your own course.

Background Knowledge

It seems that all degree courses, either as part of an induction course or as an integrated part of a 'legal systems' course, require students to acquire a working knowledge of the contemporary architecture of the English legal system. This will consist of a knowledge of which are the courts with criminal and civil jurisdiction and the provisions for appeals, including the provision made in each case for the exercise of the judicial function. Essential background knowledge also includes usually an outline knowledge of the doctrine of *'stare decisis'* as it relates to the hierarchies of the courts and a knowledge of how law reports are set out and the arrangement of the different parts of a statute. This background knowledge is the basic requirement for beginning a study of the legal system and also for a study of substantive branches of the law. If your own degree scheme has a separate short course containing roughly the foregoing items, then it is likely that it will be compulsory to attend classes in that short course. Different institutions, however, have different ideas about whether such a short course, usually lasting six to eight weeks, should be assessed, and if so, how it should be assessed. In any event, do not neglect this vital part of your studies. The sooner you know the difference between the Queen's Bench Division of the High Court and the Civil Division of the Court of Appeal the sooner you will stop making silly mistakes in the law of contract, which have nothing to do with your knowledge of the rules of contract law, but everything to do with knowing when a case is no longer 'good' law because it has been overruled.

Equally, little progress can be made in any substantive subject until you are able to find your way around the case reports and statutes.

Historical Development

Many courses retain a historical section, even if it is only a nominal one in some cases. The emphasis at the present time will be on the development of the court system. In some cases there will be an outline given of the development of the common law courts and their jurisdictions from the time of the Conquest. Such a treatment can produce in some students a distorted historical perspective, with the impression taking root that Henry II's establishment of the assize system was closely followed by the Judicature Acts of 1873–5, and the whole lot was put right just yesterday by the Beeching Royal Commission, which resulted in the Courts Act 1971. In order to avoid such bizarre thoughts forming in the student's mind and because of the limited time available in a crowded syllabus, courses now concentrate very much on the reform of the court system in the 19th century. When this historical survey of the courts reaches the 20th century it shades off into the analytical treatment of the problems presented by our contemporary legal institutions.

There is one other major question which continues to receive some attention in 'legal systems' courses from the historical standpoint. That is, the origins and development of equity both as a source of law and as the foundation of a separate jurisdiction throughout most of our legal history. Equity, as a topic within a legal systems course can include a comparison of general and particular equity and the need that all legal systems have for a means of alleviating hardship caused by the inflexible application of fixed rules. It will also, generally, entail a study of the struggle between the courts of common law and the Court of Chancery and a look at the subsequent development of equitable doctrines following the end of that struggle brought about by the decision of James I in favour of the Court of Chancery.

It may be also that a course will include references to the 'forms of action' and their influence on the development of the law, perhaps dealing with the development of the law of contract.

If there is a historical component in your English legal system course, whatever topics are chosen, these topics will figure generally in the examinations in the form of essay questions of a type to which most students will be well accustomed. The justification for continuing to teach the elements of legal history is twofold. Even such a limited insight into our rich and varied legal history as is possible within the compass of a one-year comprehensive course on the English legal system will demonstrate the dynamic and changing nature of English law and its institutions, and the student will be, therefore, better prepared to study the present rapidly changing law. Furthermore, some knowledge of how we got to where we are today helps in understanding some of our present problems and may explain, although not excuse, some of the presently perceived defects in our law and its institutions. This will continue to be the case so long as we continue to reject a wholesale legal revolution as the basis of change and reform. So, dear reader, in your probable state of passive resistance to learning legal history as part of the legal system course, be assured that only exceptionally, in present-day first-year courses, will legal history be taught as an end in itself. At least some of you, the author hopes, will develop a liking for the history of our common law heritage and go on to study it as another part of your course of studies or maybe develop it as an interest which will illuminate your future professional life.

Analytical Study of Legal Institutions

If, in the future, you intend to practise in the courts in connection with criminal litigation or any branch of law involving civil litigation, a detailed knowledge of the courts and their working will be essential. In a first-year legal system course you can lay down a sure foundation for such practice by acquiring the skill of knowing which is the most appropriate forum in which to bring or defend your client's claim and what, if anything, can be done about a case that initially has an unsatisfactory outcome. The study of legal institutions must be much more than merely descriptive for this purpose. Indeed, if for no other reason than extreme tedium for lecturers and students, a straightforward exposition of legal institutions is to be avoided as part of the teaching of the course. There are many more effective ways of getting over information of that kind than attempting to teach it in class. Of course, it may well be that you will be examined on this factual knowledge in order that your teachers may be sure that you have acquired the information as part of the 'background knowledge' objective. How then can you expect to be taught and assessed with respect to an analytical treatment of legal institutions? One way of dealing with this part of the syllabus is first of all to expect students to acquire for themselves factual knowledge of the system at a specified level of particularity and detail, suited to the needs of the individual course. This knowledge may or may not be tested objectively at an early stage. If there is time it is a good idea to do so in order to reinforce the knowledge gained. Even if there is no formal testing arranged as part of the course, students benefit from informal self-testing, alone or in groups.

Once it can be assumed that the knowledge base exists, the course can proceed to the analytical stage. This may take the form of establishing a number of themes, maybe in the form of questions to be posed and considered. No final answer will ever be given to many of these questions. Typically, the questions take the following form: What is a court? What is an appeal and how does it differ from a review? Why do we have two tiers of appellate courts? And so on. Those are some of the broader themes and questions. Each can be further broken down into smaller parts. For example, why shouldn't the prosecution be allowed to appeal against acquittal of the accused or the imposition of a too lenient sentence following conviction? Two matters in particular are to be noted about the way in which this important and central part of any English legal system syllabus is presented here. First, whenever a topic is presented in the form of a question always work out the significance of knowing the answer to the question posed, and if careful thought produces no significant reason why you should want to know the answer to a question, ask your teacher why a topic is being included and why it is being presented in that particular way. Secondly, this method of treating the study of legal institutions facilitates the inclusion of matters of topical interest as and when appropriate. Students should be ready to respond in these cases by showing at least the level of awareness of the well-informed person in the street, before coming to classes. Thus, whilst the jury and the question of appeals will always provide material for analysis and discussion, the change to the accused's right to silence in criminal proceedings is a matter of a controversial nature and will no doubt provide the basis for essay titles and examination questions in forthcoming examinations.

Legal Technique and Legal Method

This forms a large and sometimes dominant part of the present-day legal system syllabus on many degree courses. As mentioned earlier in this chapter, this part of the syllabus arose out of the study of 'sources of law' in a previous generation of English legal system courses. Students are now expected as part of their first-year studies, on many courses, to attain a level of sophistication in handling cases and statutes formerly attained after three years study of the law including a third-year jurisprudence course that contained a sizeable element devoted to the study of the sources of law.

Again, within the context of a present-day course combining at least background knowledge and legal technique and legal method it must be apparent that just as the analytical study of institutions arises naturally out of the background knowledge so the technique and method element in the course also arises out of the required background knowledge of cases, the hierarchy of the courts and the structure of statutes. Once again, therefore, you will find that you are expected to come to 'method' classes knowing in outline the doctrine of *stare decisis*, and such matters in relation to statutes as the significance of short titles, schedules and the structure of section numbering, with subsections and paragraphs. Again, this knowledge may or may not be tested formally. Rest assured, those concerned will think themselves entitled to assume that you have this knowledge and can apply it to order.

Under the broad heading of 'technique' and 'method', there is found a variable approach by different courses. The differences between courses lie mainly in the depth to which students are required to go as a formal part of a first course on the English legal system. However, it is possible to give some general guidance about this part of the syllabus that may be appropriate and useful to all students whose courses have a separate component dealing with 'technique' and 'method'.

In so far as there is a requirement to study method as such and not as part of, say, contract or tort, it is nevertheless necessary to acquire some knowledge of substantive law in order to be able to demonstrate the 'method' being studied. This knowledge of the substantive law may be given in encapsulated form as a set of principles or in some cases students will be expected to appreciate the context of cases they are asked to read as a 'method' study, in the substantive subject from which they are taken. Thus, there is a convenient group of cases on *Rylands v Fletcher* (strict liability) which Cross uses in the first edition of his book, *Precedent in English Law*, to show how the rule in *Rylands v Fletcher* was developed and subtly changed by the judges over a number of decisions, whilst leaving certain aspects of the rule still in a state of uncertainty after the last case in the series. In using such a group of cases, the teacher has to ensure that the student knows at least that *Rylands v Fletcher* is a form of liability in tort that is strict and not based on negligence and that, in origin at any rate, it was a form of tort liability concerned with the use of land and the escape of things from the land. Thereafter, in reading the cases, teacher and student must both bear in mind that they are primarily concerned with legal method; that is, in this case, the application of the doctrine of precedent and the connected reasoning processes of the judges, and not with expounding and criticising the rule in *Rylands* v *Fletcher* as a tort doctrine. Finally, students are expected to draw the conclusion that the techniques and methods discovered by work on this set of cases can be applied to other cases and sets of cases in other subjects.

A further point of guidance appropriate to all courses containing a 'method' component is that it is in this part of the syllabus that the examiner has most scope for devising problem questions and students can expect to be set problems and exercises in both case method and in handling statutes at all stages of the course.

Statutes have begun to receive much more attention in recent years, not only as sources of law and the way in which they are classified as amending, consolidating and codifying statutes, but also as part of legal method. The study of statutes has now developed in some courses to the stage where statutes are studied as an integrated whole, from their inception and production through to their application and interpretation by the courts. This is one of those topics where there has been recent interaction between the production of new literature on the subject (such as Miers and Page, *Legislation*) and what is being taught on undergraduate courses. Students may now expect therefore to be asked to do relatively traditional exercises on statutory interpretation alongside somewhat more innovatory exercises in drafting clauses or even short statutes. In quite a few cases students are asked to work with fictitious statutes designed to illustrate a particular point, and care should be taken never to confuse a fictitious statute, produced to illustrate a teaching point, with either a real statute or proposals which may have been made (perhaps by the Law Commission in the form of a draft statute) for actual legislation in the foreseeable future.

Law in Action

This approach to the subject is concerned with the relationship between law and society. The law in action approach deals with the 'actual' effects the law has on people and the purposes which the law serves or the purposes which the law claims, on its own terms, to serve. On examination the two sometimes do not correspond. 'Law in action' also deals with the social structures of the law, including the judiciary, the magistracy, juries, lawyers and clients. The whole course can be presented from the 'law in action' standpoint and several courses in English departments of law place a strong emphasis on this approach throughout the syllabus for the English legal system course. Such a thoroughgoing sociological approach is quite valid. It is more usual, however, to find some parts of the subject singled out for this sort of treatment, leaving a more extensive study of the sociology of law until later in the degree curriculum; very often as an option or as part of a legal theory programme. Once again, however, students should accustom themselves to thinking about the legal system in terms of its overall purposes and its impact on the life of society. In the study of law in action students must come to terms with the presentation of facts through quantitative and statistical means. Comparatively few law students have studied mathematics beyond O level and not a few law students are refugees from studying anything involving numbers. A little effort devoted to understanding statistical tables, charts and graphs will be well repaid in terms of both understanding and the ability to present arguments in a concise and accurate form. Good examples of the way in which numbers are used in connection with the study of 'law in society' may be found in Zander's *Cases and Materials on the English Legal System*. From there, students can go on to study at first hand the official statistical records of the legal system published by Her Majesty's Stationery Office.

Matters commonly selected for treatment in this way, within a particular course, include studies of the types of case brought before the courts, the impact of legal aid, and the social make-up of the judiciary and legal profession, with the consequences this has for the sort of law that is produced for society.

The title of the course you are studying will often give an indication of the dominant approach adopted. Courses with the straightforward title 'English legal system' will tend to be eclectic and to attempt to combine all six approaches, with the main emphasis on an analytical treatment of legal institutions, with only slightly less emphasis on legal method; whereas courses with the words 'legal process' or 'legal method' in their title will place most emphasis on legal institutions and the handling of legal materials respectively. Courses with a reference to 'society' in their title can be expected to deal with the material almost exclusively in accordance with the 'law in action' approach.

An Introduction to Lawyers' Skills

At the present time both academics and the legal professions are concerned that students should develop from an early stage those skills which lawyers need in practice. The Law Society has identified five such skills, represented by the acronym DRAIN. They are drafting, research, advocacy, interviewing and negotiation. This development is recognised and aided by the appearance of books such as *Learning Legal Rules* by J.A. Holland and J.S. Webb and *Learning Legal Skills* by S. Lee and M. Fox.

Many topics within a legal system course lend themselves to teaching which incorporates an element of skills teaching. Drafting statutory provisions has been a feature of some courses for a considerable time. New developments include the use of role-playing exercises to develop interviewing and negotiation skills, especially in relation to work in the courts. The work of the small claims court is an ideal topic for this sort of treatment.

TYPES OF ASSESSMENT

Course titles and their corresponding approaches to courses may or may not indicate the types of assessment involved in the course and the weighting to be given to each type of assessment. Historical and institutional topics readily lend themselves to traditional essay questions and 'method' topics are an appropriate vehicle for problem questions. The law in action approach may produce essay questions of a different sort, requiring the arguing of a case for change in the law to meet actual deficiencies in the current state of the law. Judicious use of statistics and quantitative arguments is always well received in answering questions of the law in society type. You must be prepared, however, in all courses at the present time, to answer a variety of types of question. You can expect to be told what weighting is given to examinations and assessed coursework. If you are not told, ask! You need that information to enable you to assess the importance of individual pieces of work and to help you in achieving a properly balanced approach to your study of the subject. This theme will be developed further in the next chapter.

ARRANGEMENT OF THIS BOOK

To conclude this survey of the place of 'legal system' courses in the law curriculum the pattern adopted in the rest of this book is set out and explained in Table 1.1, with reference once again to the six main objectives of the various courses. The pattern of the rest of the book, after a second chapter on study methods and preparation for examinations and assessments, does not represent or replicate any one actual course on the English legal system. Instead it sets out the main topics found in most such courses and divides them up under the six main objectives selected. The division is based on what seems a natural approach to adopt to a particular topic but it must be stressed that this is simply one teacher's method of selection which may or may not be shared by your teachers or reflected in the way in which your course is presented. As pointed out previously there is more than one way of studying the judiciary.

It is hoped that this pattern will be of use to as many students as possible and at the same time encourage flexibility of thought in the application of knowledge.

Table 1.1

Objective

Acquisition of essential background knowledge	A short treatment of the court structure in outline and guidance on the setting out of case reports and the structure of statutes.
Historical understanding	The reform of the courts in the 19th and 20th centuries: the development of law and equity in a common law jurisdiction.
Analytical study of legal institutions	A thematic and problem-based review of the courts of civil and criminal jurisdiction, a comparison with other institutional methods of settling disputes, other matters relating to the legal process, e.g., contempt, legal aid.
An introduction to legal method	A more detailed study of the doctrine of precedent, legislation, computer-based retrieval systems, law reform.
A critique of the law in action	A study of the working of small claims courts, the system of compensation for accidents, the work of the legal profession; the judiciary and the magistracy; access to legal services.
An introduction to lawyers' skills	The use of interactive methods of learning.

TEXTBOOKS AND READING

At the time of writing there are several standard student textbooks available for courses on the English legal system. Some of these books arose out of the student needs in connection with a particular course. Often a quick look at the preface will disclose this fact. Teachers responsible for courses will give advice on the most suitable books for their course. This is a fast-moving subject and sometimes you will have to make a choice between the most up-to-date text on the subject and the book that is best suited to your own course. Unless the course is one that is almost exclusively based on, say, legal method, or law in action, it is probably wiser to choose the most up-to-date edition of a standard work as a personally owned resource and rely on the library for special materials in the nature of monographs and periodical articles on the aspects of the subject which are peculiar to your own course. Do not overlook the fact that many news items reported in the columns of the daily press will also provide up-to-the-minute information about the developments in the administration of justice and other aspects of this subject. Earlier in this chapter you were recommended to read, as literature, an account of the legal system. The following is a short selection of works of this sort. Some of them may be out of print but obtainable from your library.

(a)   Cecil, H., *The English Judge* (Hamlyn Lectures).
(b)   David, R., *Major Legal Systems in the World Today*, transl. J.E.C. Brierley, part 3.
(c)   Harding, A., *A Social History of English Law* (Penguin, 1966).
(d)   Kiralfy, A.K.R., 'English law' in J.D.M. Derrett (ed.), *An Introduction to Legal Systems*.
(e)   Stein, P., *Legal Institutions* (Butterworths, 1984).

2 STUDYING EFFECTIVELY

ASPIRATION, INSPIRATION AND PERSPIRATION AMOUNT TO SWOT!

These three things are the ingredients of success. Aspiration, or a desire to succeed, you have shown by buying this book. Everyone has some small spark of inspiration. Unfortunately, few people can rely upon inspiration alone in order to achieve success. That leaves perspiration. In his book, *The Rise of the Meritocracy*, Michael Young produced the equation, IQ + effort = merit. The key to success lies not in intelligence alone, nor in effort or hard work alone but in the intelligent expenditure of energy, designed to maximise the effect of your efforts.

This chapter is about maximising the effects of your efforts in learning about the English legal system in the way in which *your* course requires. One of the saddest things about teaching is to see students working hard and expending great efforts but ineffectively. Often, the first inkling one has of this situation is the submission of a long piece of work which comprehensively relates material, some relevant and some irrelevant, but not an answer to the question asked. Questions in examinations and other pieces of work rarely take the form 'Write all you know about . . .' but many answers take the form, 'This is all I know, kindly select the material you want'.

To escape from the 'write all you know' syndrome requires confidence and a flexible and almost fluid approach to writing. To reach that stage of development takes time. For most of you law is a new subject with a new language all of its own and its own conventions of learning and discourse. For that reason I am going to suggest that in your early studies you adopt a framework within which to work out answers to problems and write essays, but your framework must be sufficiently open and supple to enable you to grow in confidence so that eventually your work will cease to be angular and rigid and become rounded and supple in texture. Take encouragement from the way in which judges like Lord Denning impose a structure on their judgments, so that you can follow the development of their reasoning and argument.

OBJECTIVES

In order to prevent your voyage of discovery becoming an odyssey, your first requirement is to identify your goals and to map out the stages of your work. Chapter 1 was about the different sorts of goals sought by a wide variety of first-year courses, but all with the common theme of 'the English legal system'. This is the time to read carefully the syllabus for your course and to decide what sort of course it is. It may fall into any one of the following categories and may combine two or more of the categories:

(a) a study of legal institutions and sources of law,
(b) a study of the legal process, including procedure,
(c) a study of legal method,
(d) a study of the law in its social and economic context.

You do not have to rely on the printed syllabus alone. By the time you are reading this, your course will probably be well advanced and it should be apparent to you whether your course comes into one or other of the categories set out above. You may also identify course objectives from the books recommended; e.g., the very title of Dr Ingman's book, *The English Legal Process*, proclaims its objective. In many cases you will have to study carefully the list of contents in order to decide for which sort of course an author is writing. The course will set aims and objectives in terms of what you, the student, will know and be able to do at the end of the course. You yourself will set other objectives. If there is an examination, one of your objectives will be to complete your preparation for the examination in good time and to have your knowledge base ready a few days before the date of the examination, leaving time for final reflections. If you have coursework during the year, whether assessed or not, your objective will be to produce an even burden of work, balanced between the preparation and submission of specific pieces of work and your general reading and consolidation of the subject.

YOUR WORK AND COURSE OBJECTIVES

In the rest of this chapter I am going to suggest what your work should be in terms of meeting course objectives. You will have identified the type of course on which you are embarked. I am going to describe a pattern of work designed to achieve success on a course which combines the following objectives:

(a)   a detailed knowledge of the main institutions of the English legal system (this may be an end in itself and also a prerequisite for the study of substantive law),
(b)   an ability to apply the elementary rules of legal method, and
(c)   a critical awareness of the strengths and weaknesses of English legal institutions and sources of law.

Whether you have attained these objectives may be tested in a number of ways: by an end-of-course examination, by assessed coursework or by monitoring of your performance throughout the course. Your attendance record and contributions to discussion in tutorials and seminars are ways in which performance may be monitored. I am not going to suggest any strict timetabling or apportioning of your time within this subject or between this subject and others. Suffice it to say that such timetabling is invaluable. In the case of English legal system courses the key to preparing a successful timetable of work is to study your syllabus in terms of the weighting given to the categories set out in the previous section. If, for example, your course was limited to a study of the criminal and civil processes in English courts, you should take account of the following factors in arranging a timetable of work:

(a)   Each process, criminal and civil can be studied separately.
(b)   There are common themes with problematic issues, e.g.:

(i)   methods of beginning cases,
(ii)   choice of mode of trial between serious and non-serious cases,
(iii)   arrangements for appeals, whether unrestricted or with leave.

(c)   On balance, the criminal process is more complex than the civil.

Thus I would divide my time up in three ways; between separate studies of the criminal and civil process and a third part devoted to issues relating to the English legal process as a whole, including its foundation in the adversary system and comparative points between criminal and civil processes. This might result in a 40 : 30 : 30 apportionment of the time available.

It is what happens within each of those amounts of study time in relation to the objectives of the course with which I am concerned. From the beginning of the course the nature of your work will grow in its scope and depth and the pattern will be repeated within each major topic. The growth in scope is represented by the following stages, each one of which is added to the previous one, not simply succeeding it. The stages are: preliminary exploration of the subject topic, learning, application, testing. These stages are represented in a teaching programme which consists of lectures, tutorials and assessments in the following way. Preliminary exploration is based on the syllabus you are given and the recommendations it contains about reading; learning is based on lectures and your own reading; application is the work you do for tutorials and seminars and also the use you make of this subject as essential knowledge in your work in the substantive subjects; and testing may take a number of forms: self-testing, assessed pieces of work and examinations, which may include mid-sessional examinations.

Let us look now at the details of what is to be done at these different stages in relation to the different parts of the teaching programme. The work to be done can be broken down into activities relating to the progress of the course:

(a)   Preliminary work.
(b)   Work during lectures.
(c)   Work after lectures.
(d)   The tutorial and after.
(e)   Preparation of coursework and examinations.

PRELIMINARY WORK

The first chapter in this book said something about the development of the study of the English legal system as part of law degree courses. It also dealt with the way in which textbooks reflected different stages of that development. Your first piece of preliminary work is to see where your course fits into that pattern of development and to choose from amongst the range of books purporting to cover the English legal system the one that is most appropriate for your course. Certain books will be recommended and some books may even be prescribed reading. Students who have done the course before you may be a good source of advice. They will have their own perspectives on the usefulness of different books. Remember, however, in this regard that newly fledged second-year students may be as unscrupulous as second-hand car dealers are supposed to be. They may want to get rid of an old out-of-date edition or simply an unwise purchase. Do not neglect your own advice. Study the different books carefully before buying one. A lot may be gleaned about a book from seeing how frequently it has gone into new editions, reading the preface and studying the layout of the book as exemplified in the list of contents. These things alone will tell you about the book's general reliability and approach to the subject.

As you are probably a newcomer to the study of law, you should become aware of the different types of book that you may use. There are textbooks, such as Ingman's *The English Legal Process* and Smith and Bailey's *The Modern*

English Legal System, which are expositions of a coherent body of knowledge about a stated subject. In one sense, they are the embodiment of that subject. For example, the law of tort was for many years a combination of the textbooks now known as *Salmond and Heuston on the Law of Torts* and *Winfield and Jolowicz on Tort.* No good student relies on a textbook alone. Good students go to the original authorities, the statutes, cases and periodical and other writings that together make up the subject. The subject of the English legal system is no exception. It is not just a book-work subject. This will become apparent shortly.

Secondly, there are books which are often called 'Cases and Materials', such as the two books by Professor Zander. These are valuable source books. They consist of original source materials on a number of set themes, either connected by a commentary by the author, setting the scene, or simply containing questions of a problematic nature at the end of each section; the questions arise out of the points made and opinions expressed in the extracts preceding the questions. For most courses, such books are an invaluable aid as an entrée to materials you might otherwise miss, but they are not usually a substitute for a textbook covering the course as a whole.

Thirdly, there are monographs on particular aspects of the subject. Professor Griffith's *The Politics of the Judiciary* is one such work. You will refer to these works during the preparation of essays, when more detail is needed than is contained in the standard textbooks. The footnotes in your textbook will guide you to relevant works of this sort as well as to other materials to be mentioned. The note on legal method, preceding chapter 8 of this book, contains advice on the specialist books covering legal method syllabuses and parts of syllabuses.

The 'other materials' referred to above are periodical articles and, in this subject, a number of government publications such as reports of Royal Commissions and departmental committees. You will be referred also to publications of the law reform agencies, particularly those of the Law Commissions.

As English legal system courses often include a section on the literature of the law generally, it is probably convenient for you in this preliminary work to become acquainted with the major reference works in English law such as *Halsbury's Laws of England.*

The first stage of your preliminary work, to be done in those sometimes dull waiting days after registration and before the full lecture and tutorial programme begins, is to discover the different sorts of literature that you will come across in studying the subject and make a careful choice of a textbook you will buy. Maybe you will buy as well a cases and materials book and decide also whether you need a specialist book on legal method.

Having made your choice of books and bought them, begin to get acquainted with them. If you have been given a course programme it should be easy enough to work out which parts of your textbook you can begin to read so as to be a little ahead in your preliminary reading when you attend lectures.

During the course of your study you are going to have to find a variety of materials for reference. Accordingly, the other sort of preliminary work you should do is to get acquainted with the layout of the library. In an English legal system course you will need to be able to find quickly the following materials on a regular basis:

(a)   Acts of Parliament. Find out if your library has all the different series of statutes so that in case of need you can find an alternative to your first preference.

(b)   Law reports. Know where the principal series of reports are shelved and where recent unbound parts are kept.

(c)   Periodicals. Get to know whether volumes of previous years are kept on the open shelves or not. If they are not kept on the open shelves, what system is there for gaining access to previous years' volumes?

(d)   Government publications. Discover how extensive is the collection of these in your library .

This would be an ideal time to study chapters 2 and 3, on finding and reading the law, in *Learning Legal Rules* by J.A. Holland and J.S. Webb.

Finally, enquire of the library staff whether there are any systems for short-term loans or for limited-time reading of certain books in the library.

WORK DURING LECTURES

What happens during lectures by way of teaching and learning is open to doubt. I remember attending a series of lectures on political economy, given by a lecturer who was known as the 'Economic Danny Kaye'. Today he would be known probably as the 'Economic Ben Elton'. He was fascinating, fast in delivery and totally bewildering in the lack of structure in his material. Fortunately there was a good book on which the examination was set. Attending lectures is a difficult method of learning. They are, however, still relied upon heavily as the principal means of teaching on many courses.

Some lecturers are on an ego trip, some are genuinely entertaining, some read a book aloud, some dictate endlessly. I am assuming that you experience none of these types *in extremis,* and that the lecturer informs, presents different points of view and gives guidance on the evaluation of the information he gives.

In response, you are to receive impressions, some more lasting than others, and to record information. The information you record is not to be regarded as the sum total of knowledge of what you must learn. It is the foundation of that knowledge. On the impressionistic side, you may receive views about the virtues and vices of textbooks, about established opinion, about the way in which practising lawyers think about the legal system. When conveying impressions, lecturers paint pictures in words, use colourful metaphors and sometimes express things in common parlance. Beware of being carried away by such behaviour to the extent of recording it verbatim in your notes. Colourful and graphic explanations in the lecture room may sound well and make a point strongly — they do not translate well into the more sober prose required in the writing of essays and examination answers.

As to the recording of information, you should develop the ability to listen to what is being said and to record a note of what has been said in the pauses in the lecturer's delivery. Make notes rather than attempt to record verbatim the whole of what is said. Every lecturer's style is different but it is possible to become accustomed to knowing when the lecturer expects items to be recorded in student notes. Either there will be a direct statement or instruction that a passage is being dictated or a change in the pace and emphasis in delivery will clearly signal that IMPORTANT POINTS are being made. A lecturer will usually begin by saying what material is to be covered and the main points or themes that will be developed during the course of the lecture. This will enable you to make a note at once of the headings under which you will make your notes. It may be that you will be told simply that there will be, say, five points to cover. This will help you to keep track of the lecture and to know when a section is completed.

Prepare your notes with plenty of headings. During the lecture, leave space for later amendments and additions. You should record carefully all references to cases, statutes, passages in books and periodicals. If not provided in advance these will often be written up on a blackboard. It is not always possible during a lecture to ask the lecturer to repeat all references made and this makes necessary one of the most important follow-up pieces of work, checking references.

In all parts of the legal system syllabus there are at least two objectives:

(a) To describe and analyse the system as it is. In so far as the system is presented as a set of propositions of law, make a note of the proposition as set forth in the lecture and any authority which is cited in support. In a lecture on precedent, for example, when dealing with the extent to which courts are bound by their own previous decisions, your notes might simply record:

COURTS BOUND BY OWN DECISIONS (EXTENT OF)
House of Lords: from 1898 to 1966, H of L regarded itself as bound by its own decisions. *London Street Tramways Co. Ltd* v *London County Council* [1898] AC 375. In years leading up to 1966, need felt for more flexibility. Several examples where rule found inconvenient, working injustice, e.g.,

occupiers' liability, duties owed to invitees, licensees became almost indistinguishable.

Also: Parliament found little time for law reform of 'lawyers' law'. *Practice Statement 1966* cautious in its terms. Relaxed the rule. Exceptions.

(b)   To evaluate the legal system in a critical way. Evaluative comments fall into two categories. Each should appear in your notes and be distinguishable:

(i)   A rule of law or an institution or procedure may be criticised because it does not achieve its stated objective. For example, it might be said that the rules under the Bail Act 1976 are not working as intended because they are applied too strictly or liberally as the case may be.

(ii)   On the other hand, the criticism may be of the rule of law, institution or procedure as such. For example, it might be said to be wrong in principle for anyone accused of murder ever to be allowed bail.

Try to arrange your notes in such a way that the two types of evaluative comment may be picked out immediately when you are reading your notes subsequently, and perhaps selecting material for other treatment at the time of examination preparation.

At the end of a lecture you should have:

(a)   positive impressions of the subject-matter,

(b)   a record of the factual content of the lecture, broken down into parts under subheadings,

(c)   a note of the references to the authorities (statutes and cases) that have been cited for the propositions upon which statements were based, and

(d)   comment on the effectiveness of the rule or institution, if such comment was made, and possibly

(e)   comment concerned with the desirability of changing some aspect of the legal system.

Comments under (d) and (e) should also be supported by reference to argument and evidence for the case being made.

WORK AFTER LECTURES

The work you do after a lecture as a follow-up is the link between the teaching you receive and the learning you do for yourself. This work falls into a number of categories but first come one or two routine tasks to be done *as soon as possible* after a lecture:

(a)   Check any doubtful statements of a factual nature, which you may have noted, against an original source. Discrepancies between what is said in a lecture and what appears in a textbook will not always be accounted for by error on the lecturer's part. There may have been changes since the book was last published. The lecturer may even have said so specifically but you did not hear. If doubts remain after a check, ask the lecturer about it or check it out in a recent source such as *Current Law*, or the noter up in the *New Law Journal*.

(b)   Check references you have been given. In the case of both references and other statements made in the course of a lecture, mistakes can arise through mishearing what is said. Not all lecturers stand still. Some wander about, talking all the time at all angles to the class, sometimes with consequent bizarre effects on the acoustics of the lecture room. Another reason for the need to check references, which is particularly important in English legal system courses, is to develop a proper sense of chronology. The law depends upon two principles which make a sense of chronology vital, the doctrine of precedent and the repeal of legislation by subsequent inconsistent legislation. You must know the order of events in order to say what the law is now. With respect to statutory references it is especially important in studying the English legal system to ascribe the right rule or provision to the correct statute. This requires you to take considerable care because there are several statutes of the same name, but passed in different years. They all might be important for some aspect of the legal system. Be sure that you can distinguish Criminal Justice Acts of 1967 and 1982 from Administration of Justice Acts 1960, 1970 and 1982.

There is also more than one Law Reform (   ) Act.

Two other pairs you should beware of confusing are: Supreme Court Act 1981 and Courts Act 1971, and Justices of the Peace Act 1979 and Magistrates' Courts Act 1980.

Before relying on a Court of Appeal decision make sure that it has not been overruled by the House of Lords.

(c)   Make a note of the cases and passages in statutes that you intend to look up later, with a view to making summaries of the points contained in them for inclusion in your notes. Remember that the proposition of law for which a case is cited as authority is more important than the facts of the case. For example, the factual dispute between the parties in *Young v Bristol Aeroplane Co. Ltd* [1944] KB 718 is rarely mentioned. (It was a workmen's compensation case.) Yet the case is still one of high importance.

Having carried out these tasks of a ministerial nature find a time when you can spend sufficient time to read the cases and statutes and complete your notes.

Then you should compare the views and attitudes which will by now be reflected from your notes with corresponding passages in your textbooks.

This is probably the best stage in your work to read articles which have been referred to or which you have discovered by reading the footnotes in your textbooks. Prepare summaries of articles which you read and file these with your main notes, making cross-references to the points in your notes which the article amplifies or illustrates. This attitudinal or critical work may form the basis of an argument to be put forward in a tutorial discussion.

Finally, read your completed notes and the corresponding passages in your textbook or textbooks for *reflection,* so that you may make a final note of links between the topic you are dealing with and other topics within the syllabus. These notes, in skeletal but not cryptic form, will come in useful when the time for revision comes round before examinations or you have to write an essay or produce some other piece of work.

If the topic on which you were working was, for example, the extent to which both the House of Lords and the Court of Appeal are bound by their own decisions, you would have first of all a set of lecture notes. The work which I have described above could be achieved in this example by working from chapter 7 of Farrar and Dugdale's *Introduction to Legal Method* and going systematically through footnotes 41 to 66, set out on pp. 114 and 115 of the 3rd edition. Substantially the same results could be achieved by using any of the standard English legal system textbooks in the same way.

TUTORIALS

Tutorials and seminars are occasions when meeting in a small group enables you to strengthen and deepen your understanding of a relatively small part of the syllabus. They are also occasions on which you may carry out a process of self-appraisal. It is *unfair* to your fellow students to go to a tutorial meeting not properly prepared. These are occasions on which you will be called on to make a contribution to a discussion. Tutors make special efforts to prevent students hiding away in the anonymity of a group. Tutorial methods vary. Sometimes you will be told in advance that you will be called upon to make a specific contribution and that the other members of the group will have to make a constructive comment on your presentation. In other cases the discussion will be more free-ranging. In every case, however, at the end of the tutorial meeting, either a student or a tutor should summarise the main points of the discussion and any conclusions that have been drawn.

Tutorials in an English legal system course will take one of two basic forms: a discussion of some aspect of the legal system or an exercise in applying legal rules or demonstrating legal method. The first of these corresponds to the essay-type question on an examination paper. If the subject set is too broad or too large there are unfortunate consequences for both tutor and student. Tutors find it difficult to control and structure a discussion. Instead of a dialogue developing, the tutorial may become a series of unconnected and random remarks. Equally, students will find it difficult to know where to begin and how to impose a structure on their preparation for the tutorial. The fact that there is limited time available for the discussion of all the topics within the syllabus is no excuse for attempting to raise a discussion on, e.g., 'magistrates' courts'. The only rational response to such a tutorial topic would be to produce a précis of what is written in the textbooks.

Tutors are well aware of this problem so they set topics for discussion which by their titles disclose an angle for discussion. In the case of discussions about 'magistrates' courts', the topic might be presented as 'the quality of justice administered by lay justices in magistrates' courts'. This is at once a smaller topic and by its very title indicates a number of points for discussion. These would include: what is expected of decisions in magistrates' courts in order for them to be seen as just? That in turn leads on to a discussion about the nature of the work in magistrates' courts and the fact that they are based in a definite locality. Justice in this context might depend upon the type of case as much as the quality of the decision-making, according to principles of consistency, equality of treatment and adherence to the law. Having determined the criteria for deciding whether decisions in magistrates' courts are acceptable, you would turn to the other side of the question and ask whether there is any reason to suppose lay justices cannot meet those criteria. The only disabling factor which is inherent in the fact of the justices being lay people is their lack of detailed knowledge of the law. Other desirable qualities in a judge, of even handedness, consistency etc., are shared by lay and professional alike. In conclusion, you might say that the quality of justice in magistrates' courts depends partly upon the sort of cases given to the justices to decide and the expectations of the system in terms of the number of cases to be handled in a given time. Partly it will depend upon a careful selection of people for appointment as justices who may be expected to share all the qualities of a professional judge apart from a knowledge of the law, and that deficiency can be overcome by providing expert advice and guidance to the justices on points of law. When making a point during a tutorial discussion, try to give apposite examples and to cite evidence in support of statements which you make. For example, if you were making a point that some benches of magistrates are less than fully representative of all sections of a community you could say that Lord Chancellors have remarked in the past on the difficulty of finding sufficient active trade unionists for appointment to the bench in places like Eastbourne and Cheltenham.

That sort of tutorial subject is an enduring one which comes up time after time and is always fresh. An alternative way of presenting such topics for discussion is to state the subject-matter and then to set out a number of specific points for consideration. In such a case it is usual to give clear directions about reading and sources of information generally. There is another sort of tutorial subject. That is the 'single issue' subject, where there is a problem area within the law. One such subject might be 'the failure of the Crown Prosecution Service to live up to expectations of it'. If no detailed instructions were given about how to tackle this or any other 'single issue' subject you would have to impose a structure on it for yourself, preparing to discuss the subject under a number of headings. You would then be prepared to make a sensible contribution to the discussion at whatever stage it became your turn to do so, because you would always have a point of reference. The 'single issue' subjects that come up for discussion in English legal system tutorials may generally be analysed in the following way:

(a)   a consideration of the history of the problem, in order to determine the origins of the problem,

(b)   a full description of the nature of the problem,

(c)   a diagnosis of the causes of the problem (this may be implicit in the description),

(d)   a consideration of proposals for the alleviation of the problem,

(e)   an attempt to evaluate those proposals in terms of their likely effects.

In the case of the question about the failure of expectations relating to the Crown Prosecution Service, this would entail preparing material on the following points, *inter alia:*

(a)   At least the immediate prehistory of the Prosecution of Offences Act 1985 and the idea that there should be greater uniformity in decisions to prosecute.

(b)   An imbalance between the distribution of staff and the incidence of the heaviest case loads, the organisational problems of any new organisation formed from many existing and previously independent organisations.

(c)   Unexpectedly heavy case loads in some parts of the country, low morale amongst the staff, lack of a satisfying career structure.

(d)   Redistribution of work between professionally qualified and non-professional staff, reclassification of offences, extended rights of audience in the Crown Court, better pay and career structure for professionally qualified staff.

(e)   A change in the nature of the decision to prosecute if left to non-professional staff, expected better flow of cases through the courts, some saving in costs and time and better coordinated preparation of cases for trial, improved morale amongst the staff leading to greater efficiency.

Virtually all questions that you can be asked in a tutorial of this sort can be answered by reference to one of these headings. If you have prepared, say three points under heading (d) and they have all been mentioned by the time that you are asked to say what you would do about the problem, say straightforwardly that all measures that you would take have already been mentioned. You will be surprised how often you will be able to go on and amplify what your fellow students have to say.

Before leaving the question of tutorials I must include a few words on exercises in legal method which form the other common subject-matter of tutorials in English legal system courses. These are exercises in statutory interpretation or in determining the *ratio decidendi* of a case or cases. In the latter type of exercise you may be asked to apply your findings to additional situations. In general terms, these exercises are similar to the problem-type questions that are set in substantive areas of law, such as contract or tort. There are examples of this type of question in chapters 8 and 9. Special things to look out for in preparation for tutorials based on these exercises are as follows:

(a)   Remember that they are exercises in legal method. Concentrate on showing, for example, *why* you think a particular proposition represents the *ratio* of a case rather than showing *what* proposition represents the *ratio* of the case given.

(b)   Accept as facts, which need not be proved or discussed, those things and statements in the exercise or problem which are presented as facts.

(c)   Take careful note of the operative words in the instructions you are given. Are you asked to explain, to discuss or to comment?

Finally, if you have done the follow-up work to your lectures you will discover the benefits when it comes to preparing tutorial questions. You will have acquired already a knowledge base relevant to most tutorial questions, because tutorials and seminars arise out of the teaching programme in most cases. Therefore, you will have more time available for thinking about the tutorial problem itself, instead of having to treat it as a completely new and isolated piece of work for which you have to start acquiring background knowledge before you can tackle the tutorial work itself.

After the tutorial session has taken place you should conduct a personal review of the tutorial as a whole. The things which you should review are:

(a)   The general response to the question set which seemed to gain general acceptance by the tutor and your fellow students.

(b)   Your own response to the question set, in comparison with the general response.

(c)   The differences between (a) and (b).

If you discover that there are significant differences between your own response and the generally accepted response you must consider the reasons for it, and if necessary do something about them. In any case, you should make notes of the differences and the reasons for them. The reasons for the differences may be any one or more of the following:

(a)   Inadequate preparation (perhaps you did not look at all the material to which you were directed).

(b)   Misunderstanding of the whole or part of what was set as the tutorial work. (Misunderstanding can sometimes arise out of the fact that words, phrases and sentences can bear more than one meaning. If faced with such a situation always make plain in any written work the meaning you are assuming and on which you are basing your answer.)

(c)   Alternative explanations that had not occurred to you, of aspects of a question or applications of a rule. (This may be an indication that you should note an additional point to make in future work on the topic. One of the major benefits of tutorial work is the opportunity to pool your knowledge and ideas with those of your fellow students.)

COURSEWORK AND EXAMINATIONS

Courses devoted to the English legal system are increasingly assessed by an element of coursework as well as an examination. For effective performance on a course as a whole, if it is assessed partly by coursework, you must pay proper attention to the coursework that counts towards the final assessment of the course. The first thing to do is to make sure that you know:

(a)   how many pieces of work count in that way, and
(b)   when they are to be submitted.

It is then up to you to ensure that you submit the required pieces of work at the right time. Failure to submit a piece of work on time may result in the imposition of a penalty in terms of overall course assessment. The instructions given with work will be quite explicit. In particular, if the work is to be submitted in the form of an essay, guidance about the length of the essay will be given. In writing up your coursework stick to the guidelines you are given. Inordinate length will not earn extra marks, and indeed excess length may disqualify a coursework submission. If the coursework takes the form of a written exercise in, say, statutory interpretation or the working of a precedent, do not submit an essay on the subject, but proceed directly to the work in hand. A brief introductory paragraph setting the problem in its context will be sufficient. In too many cases, answers to the actual questions set are submerged beneath the weight of an overpowering narrative surge, setting out the whole of the topic from beginning to end.

The following advice is relevant not only to the preparation and writing of coursework, but also, in a slightly modified form, to examination questions.

Part of the problem that students face in presenting work on law degrees is that they do not know what is expected of them and how such expectations are to be satisfied. The first year of legal studies is a time when you should be 'tuning in' to what tutors expect of you. Time spent on this process at this early stage will reap rich rewards not only in year one, but more importantly in later years. So what is expected of you?

The key to this is an obvious point: coursework, or examinations or other assessments are all designed, either wholly or in part, to allow you to demonstrate that you *understand* the topic under consideration. So within the constraints of the exercise, usually a piece of written work, you must show your understanding; there will be no opportunity to explain orally any assumptions of knowledge you have made.

A first consideration in seeking to show your understanding of a legal area is to consider for whom you are writing. The usual standard is that your answer should be comprehensible to a reasonably intelligent lay person. This is useful as it prevents students from falling into the trap of assuming that the tutor marking the work knows or understands this or that and that therefore no explanation is required. Remember, it is your understanding, not the lecturer's, that is being assessed. Failure to explain relevant legal concepts will necessarily mean that you will not achieve the marks allocated to the explanation of such concepts.

The starting point in preparing an answer is a careful analysis of the question asked. It is important to note the limits of the question and to include only information relevant to that question. Listing the issues or requirements raised by the terms of the question is a useful beginning. As you read more widely the list may be revised or supplemented. A vital task is to do what you are asked to do, hence you must clearly grasp the instruction.

The most usual instructions found on an English legal system coursework or examination paper are 'explain', 'comment', and 'discuss'. The quality of your answer will depend upon an appropriate response.

Explain
An explanation requires more than a 'description' or an 'account' of something. Explanations require you to give reasons for things which you describe. For example, if you are asked to 'Explain the procedures for the choice of mode of trial in criminal cases', you should approach the question in this way:

(a)   Refer to the rules as set out in the Magistrates' Courts Act 1980.
(b)   State the reasons why you think there are two different modes of trial.
(c)   Show how the rules in the Magistrates' Courts Act 1980 lead to choices of mode of trial in accordance with those reasons you have set out.

Questions which require you to explain are generally but not always on less controversial topics.

Comment
This instruction often stands alone at the end of a question set in the form of a statement or quotation. If the statement refers to an event, then the answer which you give should seek to put the event into its context and to show what influence it had on the subsequent development of the law. Sometimes the statement refers to a state of affairs. In this case it will usually be controversial or at least open to argument and challenge. An example of a question requiring you to comment, might be:

'The interests of the taxpayer who provides the funds for legal aid are as important as the interests of the applicant for legal aid when an application is being considered'. Comment.

Such a question requires an evaluation of the arguments for and against making economy and efficiency the dominant values in the administration of the legal aid fund. (See chapter 8.)

Discuss
In the case of both essay-type questions and problem questions, this instruction is reserved for those situations where choices are still open and you are required to show the strengths and weaknesses of alternative points of view. This instruction is most appropriate in problem-type questions where the set of facts provided is incomplete or where there is doubt remaining over the effect of a decision. So, immediately after the case of *Rondel* v *Worsley* questions were set which were designed to provoke discussion of when, if ever, barristers might be liable for professional negligence. Opinions needed to be based on judging how the speeches in that case in the House of Lords might be applied in other situations involving a barrister's competence as adviser rather than as advocate.

It is clear from the foregoing that explaining, commenting and discussing involve higher-order skills than describing.
Essay-type questions often produce student answers that invite the tutor to select the relevant information from the whole. Clearly such an 'answer' does not demonstrate the understanding expected of the student. You must be selective in the material you present. The key is the relevance of the material to the question. You must constantly judge the relevance of what you write against the question asked. If you cannot explain the link between the material you wish to use and the question then you should be reading further to see if you fully understand the question, or leave the material out of your answer. What is relevant is determined by the terms of the question.

Having selected the correct material, the next step is to structure your answer. At a basic level your essay should have an introduction, a middle section, and a conclusion. The purpose of an introduction is to allow you to outline the issues you will address in the body of your answer. The middle section then explores the issues raised. This is where careful consideration of the instruction in the question comes into play, as this determines the presentation of the substance of the middle section of your answer. For example, you may have to evaluate arguments for and against a particular point of view. In attempting to formulate the arguments, the following description of critical thinking, taken from Harry Maddox, *How To Study*, may be of assistance:

(i)   Definition of the problem or issue;
(ii) Formulation of hypotheses and possible solutions;
(iii) The search for evidence or relevant facts;
(iv) Drawing inferences from the facts; and
(v)   Drawing conclusions and verifying them from evidence already presented and considered.

As a part of your answer you must cite authority for the rules you state or the information you provide. It is essential that you are able to back up any views you express by reference to evidence. Such evidence may be found, *inter alia*, in cases, statutes, reports (e.g., of Royal Commissions), articles and statistical surveys.

The development of your answer must be explicitly related to the issues raised by the question. This is an aspect of essay presentation where students often lose marks. Some students expect material to be self-explanatory. The onus is upon you to spell out the connection with the question asked. By doing this you are demonstrating that you understand.

Students often fail to present a conclusion. It is essential for a conclusion to be provided as it draws together the material already discussed. Note that it should not introduce new material.

A good piece of coursework will acknowledge the sources used. Footnotes may be used and your answer should include a bibliography. If you quote directly from any source this too must be acknowledged. In a bibliography, references to books should include: the author's name; the title of the book; where it is published; the publisher and the date of publication. References to articles should include: the name of the author; the title of the article; the journal; the date and volume number; and lastly the page reference. To save yourself a frustrating task, always take a full reference note of sources as you read them.

In writing your answer remember the constraints placed upon you: for coursework, there will usually be a word limit; and for examinations, a time limit. You must tailor your answer accordingly. Ensure that all relevant issues are addressed.

Lastly, as the English legal system is dynamic, particularly at this time with an innovative Lord Chancellor, watch for reports of developments in the quality daily newspapers. Inclusion of such information, where relevant, will demonstrate initiative on your part and an understanding that the law and legal system are not static.

In relation to examinations much of the above advice still holds good. The expectations of the examiner, however, have to be slightly different in that you are subject to a time limit and therefore cannot write as much as you would for a piece of coursework.

Examinations have other special problems. Your preparation for an examination should be designed to enable you to manage the examination time itself to your best advantage.

You cannot expect to be able to impose your will and your terms of engagement on the examination itself. The examiner has the initiative and the examination takes place on the examiner's terms. The examination only becomes a fair contest if students learn the rules of the game and examiners keep to the rules. The principal rules followed include:

(a)   Examinations are set within the boundaries of a published syllabus.

(b)   Clear instructions are given about the length of time allowed for the examination and the number of questions to be attempted.

(c)   Different weightings may be given to questions on the same examination paper.

Your examination preparation should be designed so that you can deploy your knowledge within the scope of these very general rules in the examination itself.

For the purposes of illustration *only* in this section of this chapter I am going to assume that your English legal system syllabus is made up in the following way:

I   The English legal system as a member of the family of world legal systems.

II   English legal institutions.

III   Legal method.

I shall also assume that two thirds of the time available is devoted to parts I and II and that one third of the time available is devoted to part III.

What are the consequences for your preparation of each of the three principal rules set out above?

Within the Boundaries of a Published Syllabus

'Question spotting' is an inevitable feature in preparation for an examination on a known syllabus but, there is intelligent question spotting and there is lazy and potentially disastrous question spotting. We all know what the latter is! Selection of four or five topics which are 'mugged up' as set pieces to the exclusion of all else.

What, then, do I mean by intelligent question spotting? Let me begin by making two statements. They are both true of all examinations on set syllabuses.

(a) Some topics are so important a part of the syllabus that there will always be a question on them.

(b) Every topic within the syllabus may be examined at some time or another.

Bearing these two statements in mind, you will see at once the need for basic coverage of the whole of the syllabus as part of your work programme in connection with lectures, reading and tutorials as set out earlier in this chapter.

It is a question of how to select topics for extra in-depth treatment. In the first place, taking my sample outline syllabus, it might be possible to identify some topics coming within the first statement made above. For example, there has got to be a question about legislation and a question about case law on any paper set on that syllabus. Similarly, there must be certain topics which will always provide examination questions on legal institutions. This sort of 'obvious' question cannot be relied upon to the exclusion of all others. For this reason, if your examination paper requires you to do, say, five questions out of nine set, there will usually be only four questions that come into the 'obvious' category, leaving you one short of the required number. Therefore, you must always have prepared some of the topics coming within the scope of the second statement as well. How do you select between these 'second-tier' topics? There is no guaranteed way of knowing when a topic will appear in an examination. Two guidelines may be of assistance:

(a) The frequency with which a topic has appeared on past examination papers.

(b) The emphasis given to a topic during the teaching of your course. Perhaps it was very topical, e.g., distribution of business in the civil courts, in 1991–2, or it was used as an example of a larger theme, e.g., classification of offences in connection with a study of the efficiency of the courts.

Before moving on to the second general rule I must give you some warnings about what has been said here. The selection of topics is selection of topics for special in-depth treatment. I am assuming that you will have an adequate knowledge of the whole of the syllabus to ensure a pass standard, whatever the questions may be. Although the course may be presented as a number of discrete topics you must take account of themes and problems that are common to more than one topic, so that you may expect questions relating to an aspect of the legal process as a whole, and not limited to the civil or criminal process. That is why I have put a list of possible topics of this sort at the end of the chapters on the civil and criminal process,

Finally, do not be tempted to prepare set answers. Prepare topics within a flexible framework so that you can cope adequately with different sorts of question on the same topic. You will find examples of this later on in the book.

Clear Instructions About Time Allowed and Number of Questions

Always allow time at the beginning to read over the paper as a whole and to select the questions you intend to attempt. Allow time at the end as well, so that you can read what you have written and put right obvious errors. Out of a three-hour examination, this will leave you with approximately two and a half hours. If you have to answer five questions you will have between 20 and 25 minutes continuous writing time. Before the examination practise writing complete answers to questions within the amount of time permitted. It is essential that you learn to adjust your rate of work so that you do not run out of time before or during your last question. It is impossible for markers to compensate the lack of a fifth answer by taking into account that there are four good but rather lengthy answers. Completing a last answer in note form is a measure to be adopted only as a last resort.

If you know that one of your answers is likely to be more lengthy than the others, do not do it first. To do so entails the risk of spending so much time on it that all your other answers will suffer by comparison. These suggested timings will need adjustment if your examination is to last two hours only or you have to answer four questions only. The comments in this section are to be read subject to the possibility of questions having different weightings.

Only by seeing how much you can write in a stated amount of time will you be able to judge the depth of treatment and amount of detail required in relation to different questions.

Questions may be Given Different Weightings

Unless the contrary is stated you may assume that all the questions on a paper carry equal marks. That being so, you should be able to gauge the amount of detail required in an answer. The same topic may sometimes stand by itself as a question, and sometimes form part of a longer question. The approach which you adopt and the amount of detail you include in an answer will vary accordingly. Compare, for example, the answers you would give to the following two questions:

(a)   Explain the extent to which courts are bound by their own previous decisions.
(b)   Comment on the decision in *Young* v *Bristol Aeroplane Co. Ltd* (1944).

See chapter 8 on these points, but note also the different ways in which you might use your material to (a) *explain* the position of the Court of Appeal and (b) to *comment* on the position of the Court of Appeal.

Finally, you should note the possibility that examinations in some courses will include compulsory questions. Do not forget to do these questions, especially as they usually carry more marks than the other questions. Sometimes you are told how long to spend on such questions. Follow the instructions.

ORAL PRESENTATION

With the advent of skills development on law courses, especially on the Legal Practice course, you may be assessed not only on the content of your material but also on your ability to present it. Several points need to be borne in mind in approaching such a task. First, you must ensure that your material is structured in a way that is easy to follow and that the language used is appropriate. In relation to this second point, you must identify what you are expected to do, e.g., an argument before a court will have to be presented differently from a seminar with a group of advice workers on current developments in relation to dispute resolution. Ensure that your presentation is not too detailed; concentrate instead on the main points of the relevant subject-matter.

Secondly, your performance will largely depend upon the amount of preparatory work you do. The more knowledge and understanding you acquire in relation to the relevant subject-matter, the more relaxed you can be about your presentation.

Thirdly, in presenting material, maintain eye-contact with your 'audience'. By doing this you can gauge if your points are being understood. In order to maintain this eye-contact, avoid reading from notes. If you need notes, put them on postcards rather than on pieces of paper which tend to be cumbersome and distracting if waved about.

Fourthly, try for a well-placed delivery of material; too fast and your audience will be lost, too slow and they may doze off. Allied to this is the need to vary your delivery, emphasising certain points by altering the tone and pace of speech.

Lastly, if appropriate use visual aids, such as over-head projection slides, for setting out the structure of your presentation, or, for example, for displaying statistics or other technical information.

AFTER THE EXAMINATION

You will not need advice about what to do after the examination but here is a piece of advice for those of you who are susceptible or of a nervous disposition. Avoid the company of those of your fellow students who are bolstering their own tottering egos by conducting a public post-mortem on the examination. In conclusion, here is a variation on that theme.

Two students were discussing an examination question in a public house. Let us say the question was one of criminal jurisdiction over oil rigs. 'Well', said one of the students, 'I don't think bloody X and Y', referring to the authors of a well-known textbook, 'could answer that question'. Unknown to the students, X was visiting the town and was sitting nearby in the public house. Without disclosing his identity, X asked to see the question. Having studied the question at some length, X said at last, 'I cannot speak for Y, but bloody X cannot do the question'.

FURTHER READING

Clinch, P., *Using a Law Library* (Blackstone Press, 1992).
Kenny, P.H., *Studying Law* (3rd edn., Butterworths, 1994).

3   *BASIC TOOLS FOR THE JOB*

The 'job' referred to in the chapter heading is the understanding of the English legal system and the ability to criticise it analytically. At the core of the system at the present day is a group of institutions, the ordinary courts, making decisions in a judicial manner according to law. That law is based in modern times, on previous decisions of the courts themselves, known as case law or precedent, and legislation.

In this chapter, then, I intend to set out the fundamentals of that system, which will, when you have learned them, become your tools for the job described above. The material in this chapter is intended to be factual and as far as possible, without controversy. It is material which you will have to keep referring back to in the course of preparing for seminars, writing essays and preparing for examinations, until it becomes part of your everyday thinking about the legal system.

Moreover, it is material that forms the essential framework of analytical and problem-based work set on the criminal and civil process. It is also the knowledge base upon which it is essential for you to found critical studies of the legal system or 'law in action'. Critical study must be based on empirical knowledge. I believe that the material in this chapter is the minimum core of such empirical knowledge of the legal system that is needed by first-year students of the English legal system. My belief is founded on the fact that first-year legal system courses centre around a study of the courts and the sources of the law applied in those courts in the context of an introduction to the study of legal method. The rest of the chapter is divided into three parts:

(a)   The courts and the judiciary.

(b)   Cases as a source of law.

(c)   Legislation as a source of law.

THE COURTS AND THE JUDICIARY

The material is arranged in two forms. First, there is a statement setting out the names of the courts, their composition and an indication of their principal jurisdiction. Secondly, there is a table setting out the details of the judiciary under a number of headings, followed by certain supplementary statements about the judges and their office. Except at the highest level, the House of Lords, the English legal system has separate civil and criminal courts. For more detail concerning the courts and the judiciary, see T. Ingman, *The English Legal Process*, chapters 1 and 2.

Two distinctions are important:

(a)   Between superior courts, with an inherent and unlimited jurisdiction, and inferior courts. The former have now got a statutory foundation, but they were originally courts acting directly in the name of the Crown. The Court of Appeal and the Crown Court are superior courts. Although superior courts exercise the judicial function of the royal prerogative, the Crown Court is anomalous in that, like inferior courts, it is sometimes subject to control by the supervisory jurisdiction of the High Court.

(b)   Between courts of record and courts not of record. A court of record's proceedings are part of the records kept by the Public Record Office.

The statute establishing a court will enact that the court is or is not a superior or inferior court and enact also whether it is a court of record. A court may be an inferior court of record, such as the county courts.

The Courts

House of Lords

The Appellate Committee of the House of Lords, part of the High Court of Parliament.

Composition: the Lord Chancellor and the Lords of Appeal in Ordinary, and any peer who holds or has held high judicial office. There are usually one or two Scottish Law Lords.

Jurisdiction: almost exclusively appellate; it's the final appeal court for England and Wales and Northern Ireland in civil and criminal cases, and for Scotland in civil cases only.

Supreme Court

Constituted by s. 1 of the Supreme Court Act 1981, and consisting of the Court of Appeal, the High Court and the Crown Court. The Lord Chancellor is president of the Supreme Court.

Court of Appeal

Since 1966 the Court of Appeal has consisted of a Civil Division and a Criminal Division. The latter was formed to take over the work of the Court of Criminal Appeal. It is constituted under s. 3 of the Supreme Court Act 1981.

Composition: the Lord Chancellor is an ex officio member. The normal composition of the court is that the Master of Rolls is president of the Civil Division and the Lord Chief Justice is president of the Criminal Division. The president of the Family Division and the Vice-Chancellor of the Chancery Division are ex officio members. There are also up to 29 Lords Justices of Appeal. (Be careful to distinguish a Lord of Appeal in Ordinary from a Lord Justice of Appeal.)

Jurisdiction: Civil Division: the hearing of appeals from the High Court and the county courts. (It is possible to 'leap-frog' the Court of Appeal and take appeals direct to the House of Lords from the High Court.) Appeals are normally heard by three judges but in some cases two judges may sit: see Supreme Court Act 1981, s. 54, Court of Appeal (Civil Division) Order 1982 (SI 1982 No. 543).

Jurisdiction: Criminal Division: hears appeals from persons convicted at the Crown Court. Note that the Criminal Division also reviews sentences imposed in the Crown Court, if the Attorney-General refers them as being unduly lenient.

High Court

It is a constituent part of the Supreme Court and comprises three divisions: the Chancery Division, the Queen's Bench Division and the Family Division. By s. 71 of the Supreme Court Act 1981, the High Court may sit at any place in England and Wales. Standing directions provide for the regular sitting of the court at a number of towns based on the circuit system.

Composition: the Lord Chancellor is an ex-officio member and is also president of the Chancery Division. The Lord Chief Justice presides over the Queen's Bench Division, there is a vice-president of the Chancery Division and a President of the Family Division. There are also up to 98 ordinary High Court judges sometimes known as 'puisne' judges (Supreme Court Act 1981, s. 4).

Jurisdiction: the High Court is mainly a civil court with an inherent jurisdiction. The business is distributed between the three divisions by the provisions of the Supreme Court Act 1981, sch. 1, in accordance with administrative convenience and the traditions of the divisions. The

Commercial Court and the Admiralty Court are specialist functions of the Queen's Bench Division, authorised by the Supreme Court Act 1981, s. 6. Each division of the High Court may sit as a Divisional Court when exercising a supervisory or appellate jurisdiction. Such court consists of two or more judges.

Crown Court

A constituent part of the Supreme Court. The Crown Court was established by the Courts Act 1971 following the report of the Royal Commission on Assizes and Quarter Sessions (the Beeching Report). It is now constituted by the Supreme Court Act 1981, s. 1(1).

Composition: the Supreme Court Act 1981, s. 8(1), declares that the Crown Court judges are the High Court judges, circuit judges, recorders and justices of the peace. It is a court that sits at any place in England and Wales. Its sittings are arranged in accordance with the circuit system at first, second or third-tier centres.

Jurisdiction: under the Supreme Court Act 1981, s. 46, the Crown Court has exclusive jurisdiction over trials on indictment. In this respect it is *not* subject to the supervisory jurisdiction of the High Court. It hears appeals from persons convicted summarily in the magistrates' courts. It also has powers of sentencing in the case of persons committed for sentence by the magistrates.

County courts

Local courts established in modern form in 1846 and currently regulated by the County Courts Act 1984.

Composition: in addition to circuit judges assigned to each county court district by the Lord Chancellor under the County Courts Act 1984, s. 5, the district judges appointed under s. 9 of the same Act are minor judicial office holders.

Jurisdiction: the county courts have a general jurisdiction regulated by the County Courts Act 1984 and the High Court and County Courts Jurisdiction Order 1991 (SI 1991 No. 724), and special jurisdiction under other statutes. The most important of these is the divorce jurisdiction under the Matrimonial and Family Proceedings Act 1984 exercised by courts designated as divorce county courts by the Lord Chancellor. The county courts also have the very important small claims arbitration scheme for virtually all matters involving not more than £1,000. The Lord Chancellor has indicated an intention, in line with Lord Woolf's interim report on *Access to Justice*, to raise this limit to £3,000.

Magistrates' courts

The courts in which the ancient office of Justice of the Peace is exercised. These courts are currently regulated by the Magistrates' Courts Act 1980. They sit locally and frequently.

Composition: in addition to the lay magistrates there are about 80 stipendiary magistrates throughout the country.

Jurisdiction: the jurisdiction of the magistrates' courts is entirely statutory. Their functions are:

(a)   To conduct summary criminal trials.

(b)   To act as examining magistrates during committal proceedings/ transfer proceedings for trial to the Crown Court, where a person is accused of committing an indictable offence.

(c)   To exercise some minor civil jurisdiction.

Table 3.1   Holders of judicial office in the ordinary courts of the English legal system
Abbreviations:

App Jur A 1876 & 1947	Appellate Jurisdiction Acts 1876 and 1947
CA 1971	Courts Act 1971
AJA 1977	Administration of Justice Act 1977
JPA 1979	Justices of the Peace Act 1979
SCA 1981	Supreme Court Act 1981
AJA 1982	Administration of Justice Act 1982
CCA 1984	County Courts Act 1984
CLSA 1990	Courts and Legal Services Act 1990
CJPOA 1994	Criminal Justice and Public Order Act 1994

Title of Office and qualification	By whom appointed	Tenure	Court to which assigned	Other courts in which may sit. See note 5
Lord Chancellor. Barrister.	Queen on advice of Prime Minister.	During pleasure of the Crown	House of Lords (App Jur A 1947).	President of Supreme Court (SCA 1981, s. 1). Ex officio in Court of Appeal (SCA 1981, s. 2(2)). Ex officio in High Court (SCA 1981, s. 4(a)).
Lord Chief Justice. As for Lord Justice of Appeal (SCA 1981, s. 10(3)).	Queen on advice of Prime Minister.	During good behaviour (SCA 1981, s. 11).	House of Lords if a peer holding high judicial office (App Jur A 1876). Court of Appeal (SCA 1981, s. 2(2)). President of Criminal Division (SCA 1981, s. 3(2)).	High Court. President of QBD (SCA 1981, s. 4). On directions of Lord Chancellor may sit as county court judge (CCA 1984, s. 20).
Master of the Rolls. As for Lord Justice of Appeal (SCA 1981, s. 10(3)).	Queen on advice of Prime Minister.	During good behaviour (SCA 1981, s. 11).	President of Civil Division of Court of Appeal 1981, s. 3(2)). House of Lords if a peer.	As for other judges of the Court of Appeal.
Lord of Appeal in Ordinary. Two years' high judicial office or Supreme Court right of audience for 15 years (App Jur A 1876, s. 6 as amended by CLSA 1990, sch. 10).	Queen on advice of Prime Minister.	During good behaviour (App Jur A 1876).	House of Lords.	Court of Appeal ex officio (SCA 1981, s. 2(2)). Only sits with consent at direction of Lord Chancelor.

Vice-Chancellor. High Court judge or judge of Court of Appeal or general rights of audience in any part of the High Court for 10 years (SCA 1981, s. 10 as amended by CLSA 1990, s. 71).	Queen on advice of Prime Minister.	During good behaviour (SCA 1981, s. 11).	High Court. Vice-president of Chancery Division (SCA 1981, ss. 4&5).	Court of Appeal ex officio (SCA 1981, s. 2) (and as for High Court judge).
President of Family Division. As for Vice-Chancellor.	Queen on advice of Prime Minister.	During good behaviour (SCA 1981, s. 11).	High Court, President of Family Division (SCA 1981, ss. 4&5).	Court of Appeal ex officio (SCA 1981, s. 2) (and as for High Court judge).
Lord Justice of Appeal. General rights of audience in any part of the High Court for 10 years or a judge of High Court (SCA 1981, s. 10 as amended by CLSA 1990, s. 71).	Queen on advice of Prime Minister	During good behaviour (SCA 1981, s. 11).	Court of Appeal.	House of Lords (App Jur A 1947). High Court, Crown Court (SCA 1981, s. 9). County courts (CCA 1984, s. 5).
Puisine judge of High Court. General rights of audience in the High Court for 10 years or a circuit judge for two years (SCA 1981, s. 10 as amended by CLSA 1990, s. 71).	Queen on advice of Prime Minister.	During good behaviour.	High Court. Assigned to a division by Lord Chancellor. Crown Court.	Court of Appeal (SCA 1981, s. 9). County courts (CCA 1984, s. 5).
Circuit judge. A Crown Court qualification for 10 years or a county court qualification for 10 years or a recorder (CA 1971, s. 16 as amended by CLSA 1990, s. 71).	Queen on advice of Lord Chancellor.	May be removed by Lord Chancellor for misbe-haviour or incapacity (CA 1971, s. 16(4)).	Crown Court. County Courts (CA 1971, s. 26(1)).	High Court on directions of Lord Chancellor (SCA 1981, s. 9). Court of Appeal (Criminal Division) (SCA 1981, s. 9 as amended by CJPOA 1994, s. 52).

Recorder. As for circuit judge.	Queen on advice of Lord Chancellor.	May be removed by Lord Chancellor for non-compliance with conditions, misbe-haviour or incapacity (CA 1971, s. 21(6)).	Crown Court.	County courts (CCA 1984, s. 5). High Court (SCA 1981, s. 9).
District judge, master of Supreme Court. A general qualification for seven years (CLSA 1990, s. 71).	Lord Chancellor.		County court.	
Stipendiary magistrate. A general qualification for seven years (JPA 1979, s. 13 as amended by CLSA 1990, s. 71).	Queen on recom-mendation of Lord Chancellor.	During her Majesty's pleasure.	Magistrates' courts.	
Justice of the peace. Any person of full age and capacity (JPA 1979).	Lord Chancellor on behalf of Queen in consultation with advisory committee (JPA 1979, s. 6(1)).	May be removed for misbe-haviour.	Magistrates' courts.	

Notes to the table

1   Section 71 of the Courts and Legal Services Act 1990, together with sch. 10 to the Act, provides a new scheme of eligibility for judicial appointments; making them open to *all*, barristers, solicitors and others, who have the necessary qualifications, defined in s. 71(3) of the Act in terms of 'rights of audience'. Cases transferred from the High Court to the county court should be heard by a circuit judge and not by a recorder.

2   Judges of the Supreme Court and Lords of Appeal in Ordinary retire at age 70 unless appointed before 1959 (Judicial Pensions and Retirement Act 1993).

3   Circuit judges retire at age 70 (CA 1971, s. 17(1)). Lord Chancellor may continue them in office until age 75 (CA 1971, s. 17(2)).

4 Stipendiary magistrates normally retire at age 70, but may be continued in office by the Lord Chancellor until age 72 (JPA 1979). Lay magistrates do not retire but are placed on the supplemental list at age 70.

5 SCA 1981, s. 9, sets out the rules relating to the transfer of judges between different parts of the Supreme Court.

6 SCA 1981, s. 11(8) (which applies to all judges of the Supreme Court except the Lord Chancellor) provides machinery for the removal of judges of the Supreme Court who become permanently incapable of performing the duties of their office.

CASES AS A SOURCE OF LAW

A system of case law depends upon the principle that like cases should be treated alike.

The system of case law or precedent in the English legal system depends upon two elements:

(a) The application to the instant case of the *ratio decidendi* of a relevant previous case.

(b) The doctrine of *stare decisis* according to a hierarchy of the courts. This is the doctrine whereby courts are bound by the decisions *(rationes decidendi)* of all courts higher than themselves in the hierarchy. In some cases courts are bound also by their own decisions (see below).

Some necessary terminology

Ratio(nes) decidendi: the binding part of a decision. There is neither an agreed definition of the *ratio decidendi* nor an agreed way of discovering the *ratio decidendi* of a case. The definition given by Cross and Harris in *Precedent in English Law*, is a good working definition:

> The *ratio decidendi* of a case is any rule of law expressly or impliedly treated by the judge as a necessary step in reaching his conclusion, having regard to the line of reasoning adopted by him, or a necessary part of his direction to the jury.

It follows that a case may have more than one *ratio decidendi*.

Obiter dictum: an *obiter dictum* is any expression of law pronounced in the course of a judgment that does not from part of the *ratio decidendi*. *Obiter dicta* (the plural of *dictum*) may be persuasive but not binding authority.

Reversing: occurs when a court higher in the hierarchy overturns the decision of a lower court on appeal in the same case.

Overruling: is where a principle laid down in one case is overturned by a court in a different, later case. Overruling is subject to the doctrine of *stare decisis*.

Distinguishing: the principle of law from a previous case need not be applied if the case before the court is sufficiently different, either on the facts or on a point of law. This enables judges to avoid the consequences of a decision that would be binding on them otherwise.

Precedent in the Courts

House of Lords
Between 1898 (*London Street Tramways Co. Ltd* v *London County Council* [1898] AC 375) and 1966 (*Practice Statement* [1966] 1 WLR 1234), the House of Lords regarded itself as bound by its own previous decisions. Within the bounds of the *Practice Statement* this is no longer so. The House of Lords binds all lower courts.

Court of Appeal, Civil Division
As a result of the decision in *Young* v *Bristol Aeroplane Co. Ltd* [1944] KB 718, the Civil Division is generally bound by its own previous decisions. It is bound by the House of Lords. There are well-defined but limited exceptions to the rule which are set out in *Young's* case and *Boys* v *Chaplin* [1968] 2 QB 1. See also the case of *Davis* v *Johnson* [1979] AC 264 for unsuccessful attempts to extend the exceptions.

Court of Appeal, Criminal Division
In principle the Criminal Division is bound by itself and its predecessors, the Court of Criminal Appeal and the Court for Crown Cases Reserved. In practice, where the liberty of the subject is involved, precedents are not strictly followed. In *R* v *Gould* [1968] 2 QB 65, the court adopted the practice formerly followed by the Court of Criminal Appeal.

Divisional Courts
A Divisional Court is bound by previous decisions of a Divisional Court in the same way as the Court of Appeal is bound by its own previous decisions (*Police Authority for Huddersfield* v *Watson* [1947] KB 842), subject to the exceptions in *Young's* case, and its decisions are binding on a High Court judge sitting alone. In turn, Divisional Courts are bound by the Court of Appeal and the House of Lords.

High Court
A decision of a High Court judge is binding on inferior courts, but not technically speaking on another High Court judge. In the interests of judicial

comity it is rare for one High Court judge knowingly to disagree with the decision of one of his colleagues.

Magistrates' courts and county courts
Decisions of these courts are not binding. However, there is expected to be consistency in decision-making. Occasionally a decision of a county court is reported in *Current Law*.

Privy Council
Normally, decisions of the Privy Council are not part of English law and therefore are not binding precedents. The decisions of the Privy Council may nevertheless be highly persuasive, as in *Overseas Tankship (UK) Ltd* v *Morts Dock & Engineering Co., the Wagon Mound* [1961] AC 388.

Court of Justice of the European Communities
The decisions of the European Court of Justice are binding on all English courts (European Communities Act 1972, s. 3). The court does not regard itself as bound by its own previous decisions.

LEGISLATION AS A SOURCE OF LAW

At the present day legislation is the most important source of new law in our legal system. As such it is extremely important for you to get used to handling legislation as a source of law as soon as possible in your studies. Many of you will have had introductory courses intended to get you acquainted with using a law library. Try to make sure that the impetus imparted by an introductory course is maintained by regular use of the library and in particular by referring to statutes in their various series. Those of you who have not had the benefit of an introductory course should begin by discovering in your own library which series of statutes are held by the library. You should then become accustomed to the methods by which statutes are given references. That means being able to find statutes by reference to their short titles and their year and chapter number. With pre–1963 statutes you have to come to terms with citation by reference to the regnal years and the appropriate session of Parliament.

Much of the legislation passed today is in the form of delegated or subordinate legislation. The first thing to grasp here is the fact that most but not all delegated legislation is in the form of statutory instruments with a regular system of citation of their own.

In looking at legislation systematically for the first time, you should take note of the following points about legislation in general and individual statutes in particular. Once you are clear on these matters your life as a law student will become more straightforward and you will find that you will have more time to spend on reading and understanding the law rather than simply finding an applicable statute or section of a statute.

Classification of Legislation

Statutes are classified in a number of ways:

(a) as public general Acts or private Acts, to indicate the scope and applicability of the Act;

(b) as amending, consolidating or codifying statutes, indicating both the methods and procedures by which the Act was passed and also the current approach to interpretation of the particular statute.

Consolidating and codifying statutes will usually declare themselves as such in the long title to the Act.

Validity of Legislation

In accordance with the doctrine of Parliamentary sovereignty a statute that can be shown to have been passed in due form and to have received the royal assent cannot be challenged in the courts (*British Railways Board* v *Pickin* [1974] AC 765). In the case of subordinate legislation this is not the case (see next paragraph).

Subordinate Legislation

This form of legislation is subject to the control of the courts under the *ultra vires* rule. Challenges under the *ultra vires* rule are comparatively rare. Nevertheless you must be aware of the principal forms of subordinate legislation, especially with reference to their coming into force and the consequent validity of acts done under them. At this early stage you should be able to distinguish those statutory instruments with immediate effect but subject to a negative resolution within 40 days, from those which only come into force when there is an affirmative resolution implementing them, having been made in draft form. Subordinate legislation is not subject to amendment by Parliament. Amendments can be achieved only by annulment of one instrument and the making of another to replace it.

Commencement

Modern statutes come into force at the date on which they receive royal assent, unless other provision is made for the commencement in a section of the Act. It is usual to provide that different parts of an Act can be brought into force at different dates, by the making of a commencement order by statutory instrument.

Repeals and Amendments

The whole or part of a statute may be repealed by a subsequent statute. If two statutes are in conflict, the later in time prevails. Parts of a statute may be amended by subsequent statutes. It is modern practice to print the amended sections in their amended form as part of the amending statute. HMSO also publishes statutes in their amended form, as *Statutes in Force*.

Parts of a Statute

You should be able to find and know the significance of the following matters relating to the arrangement of a modern public general Act by the end of your first term by the very latest:

(a) The year and chapter number.
(b) The short title. ⎫
(c) The long title. ⎬ Distinguish these two.
(d) The enacting formula.
(e) The sections and schedules. (Look at some representative Acts and make sure that you can find the provisions which bring the schedules in to force.)
(f) The extent of the Act.
(g) The commencement section (if any).
(h) The interpretation section.
(i) Sections amending or repealing other legislation.

CONCLUSION

Only when you have mastered the material in this short chapter will you be able to proceed to explain and discuss the legal system as it exists at the present time. As I said at the beginning; this is the minimum core of knowledge upon which to base any explanation or discussion. Whatever the approach of your particular course these are the basic facts of the system to be applied, explained or discussed. Establish them in your mind wherever possible by reference to the original sources referred to here and in greater detail in the standard textbooks.

There is no specimen question at the end of this chapter for the good reason that no essay and examination question will be limited to the material referred to here. On the other hand few essays can be written or questions answered on the modern English legal system without reference to some of this material. A good source for the material in this chapter would be chapters 2 and 3 of *Learning Legal Rules* by J.A. Holland and J.S. Webb. If you have not already read those chapters in that book, read them now.

FURTHER READING

Ingman, T., *The English Legal Process* (5th edn., Blackstone Press, 1994).
Smith, P.F. and Bailey, S.H., *The Modern English Legal System* by S.H. Bailey and M.J. Gunn (2nd edn., Sweet and Maxwell, 1991).

4 HISTORICAL BACKGROUND

On a summer's day in AD 449, a party of mixed Angles and Jutes beached their ship on the coast of Brittania, and thus began the English legal system, or so I was assured many years ago, by a now eminent academic.

Alas, such certainties are no longer acceptable in treating of the origins and subsequent development of our legal system. As indicated in chapter 1, you will no longer be expected to learn a great deal of legal history as part of a legal system course. However, some awareness of our legal history is essential and this short chapter will select a number of themes from our legal history which continue to be relevant to contemporary issues and which will help to explain some of those features of the present-day legal system which perplex and sometimes irritate us all.

In the second part of the chapter you will find references to material which will assist in placing the legal system in context in our contemporary society.

Even if present-day courses do not often produce examination questions or essays on exclusively historical aspects of the legal system, there are often questions which require answers to include some of the previous history of the topic which is the subject matter of the question. So, for example, in Dr Ingman's book, which aims 'to provide students of the English legal system with a topical and realistic account of some of the more important institutions and practices which form part of our legal process', no fewer than 31 pre-20th century statutes are referred to in the table of statutes.

HISTORICAL THEMES

Origins and Early Development

Every law student should know something of the origins and early development of his legal system. In the case of English law students this means, in practice, some knowledge of the effects of the Norman Conquest on existing Anglo-Saxon law and an outline of the workings of the feudal system. There are two lasting consequences of the Conquest for the English legal system. One is structural and one is to do with the nature of the law itself. The structural legacy is the strong tendency towards centralisation as a result of the overwhelming success of the post-Conquest monarchy in making its 'writ' run throughout the land, with the result that there was eventually established the idea of the 'King's peace'.

Secondly, our law and particularly the law of real property has been moulded from its beginnings on the twin assumptions that all land belongs to the Crown, which then makes grants to its tenants-in-chief, and that those grants once made are heritable according to the rule of primogeniture, i.e., by the first-born son.

Within the limits of the early development of the legal system we may take the following as the starting-points for the themes which in our day find echoes of their very early development:

(a)   The separation of the judicial function from the original comprehensive administrative functions of the Council (Curia Regis).
(b)   The establishment of the system of assizes.
(c)   The control of local and inferior jurisdictions by the King's courts.
(d)   The establishment of the writ system.
(e)   The emerging role of the Chancellor and the beginnings of equity.

To round off our brief historical survey we must add a review of the great changes brought about by the institutional reforms of the 19th century.

The following aspects of our legal history illustrate themes of continuing importance for the workings of English legal institutions as well as for students trying to understand the law and its institutions, and a sound grasp of the salient points and facts will aid understanding and be useful examination and essay material.

THE ROYAL COURTS: THE COURTS OF COMMON LAW

The three great common law courts of Exchequer, Common Pleas and King's Bench became distinct entities with a settled place of sitting, at Westminster, with professional judges and each with its own procedures. These courts continued in existence until the Judicature Acts of 1873-5. With respect to the courts of common law, the salient points to consider are these:

(a)   The small number of judges, who were royal appointees from amongst practising members of the Inns of Court. Barristers came early on to have a monopoly of judicial appointments. That soon-to-disappear and now-criticised monopoly originated in the communal and collegiate life led by members of the Inns of Court. The judges held office at the will of the Crown until the Act of Settlement of 1701 established the modern form of judicial independence.

(b)   The development of the substance of the common law was furthered in the long run by the competition for jurisdiction, over matters originally not within its jurisdiction, by one court at the expense of the other two courts; for example, by the use of legal fictions and the extension of the idea by the King's Bench that the breaking of the King's peace included any act of wrongdoing which could by any stretch of the imagination be said to be done 'by violence and by force of arms', such as the negligent shoeing of a horse.

(c)   The jurisdiction of the royal courts was also enhanced by the decision that a statute forbidding claims for less than 40 shillings in the royal courts, gave the royal courts exclusive jurisdiction over matters involving more than 40 shillings.

(d)   Because these courts acted directly in the name of the Crown this had a drastic effect in curtailing courts of local and private jurisdiction. Local courts with a limited jurisdiction then had later to be revived by statute, experimentally in the 18th century and generally as new-style county courts in the mid 19th century.

(e)   Several factors, however, also placed a limiting effect on the ability of the royal courts of common law to extend their jurisdiction without limit. In a variety of forms these factors have made themselves felt until our own times and need to be taken into account in handling such matters as family law and admiralty law.

These limiting factors included:

(i)   The restrictions placed on the ability of the Chancellor during the 13th century to devise new forms of action (see below).

(ii)   The maintenance of the Church's exclusive jurisdiction over matters relating to succession and the family. This survived the Reformation and lasted until the 19th century.

(iii)   A separate Admiralty jurisdiction.

(These last two had rules based on the civil and canon law rather than common law, and were thus placed together in the 19th-century reforms as the Probate, Divorce and Admiralty Division of the new High Court. A.P.

Herbert, the legal humourist, found a rationale for this odd mixture of jurisdictions when he referred to it as the court dealing with wrecks of wills, marriages and ships.)

(f) The willingness of the Chancellor to act directly in the name of the King, and later in his own name, when he was unable to issue a writ because of the restrictions referred to above, thus giving rise to the development of the Court of Chancery and equity.

THE ASSIZE SYSTEM AND LOCAL JUSTICE

A prevailing concern of those charged with administering the legal system has been to maintain a balance between the claims of uniformity in the law throughout the land and the need to make justice available locally.

Historically, the movement towards uniformity has tended to outweigh the claims of local justice. That can be seen from the days of Henry II onwards, with the establishment of the assize system, which was not reformed fundamentally until the report of the Beeching Royal Commission of 1966 was implemented by the Courts Act 1971. At the same time, the overlap between courts of quarter session and the criminal business (oyer and terminer) of the assizes, as all regular local sittings of the superior courts were known, was sorted out.

The emphasis given to uniformity over locally administered justice can be seen also in the system whereby the assize court hearing was a fact-finding exercise with rulings of law and judgment being reserved for a later hearing at Westminster. The interpretation of the jurisdictional limit of 40 shillings mentioned above, and the decline in the value of money also worked towards the marginalisation of local justice.

On the other hand, because of the limitations of the writ system (see page 58 below) and the limited number of 'pleas of the Crown' or felonies, there was considerable scope left for local courts to develop commercial law and some parts of the criminal law, largely administered in what came to be the courts of quarter session, presided over by the local justices of the peace.

These are the salient points you should bear in mind when considering the historical context of contemporary problems concerning the maintenance of a uniform standard of law and justice throughout the realm and the opposite but related problem of providing justice, both civil and criminal, locally, at the point of need, for the benefit of litigants, their lawyers and the witnesses in the case. Even today, the battle lines over the creation of a single unified civil jurisdiction are drawn up with the judiciary and the Bar on one side (the centralising, uniformity party) and with the solicitors and a variety of client pressure groups on the other side. (At the same time, complaints are heard that no judges of the superior courts are permanently based in the larger centres outside London, such as Birmingham and Manchester.)

CONTROL OF INFERIOR JURISDICTIONS AND APPEALS

During the course of your study of the English legal system you will learn that an 'appeal', by which is meant the substitution of a decision by a higher court for a decision of a lower court, is a comparatively modern innovation, at least outside the realms of Chancery. The reasons for the distinction that is made between appeals and reviews (see Smith and Bailey, *The Modern English Legal System,* chapter 19) lies in our legal history. On the other hand, Dr Ingman in *The English Legal Process* adopts a functional treatment, dividing 'appeals' (chapter 6) from 'reviews' (chapter 11). Dr Ingman thereby emphasises the modern use of judicial review as a means of controlling the executive actions of government; but he concludes by a discussion of the differences between appeals and reviews.

It seems, therefore, that whatever approach your course adopts towards the treatment of the process of judicial review and the appellate process, understanding will be enhanced by a historical appreciation of the reasons why judicial review appeared first in our legal system.

The common law judges act and always have acted directly in the name of the Crown and are not thereby treated as delegates subject to the restrictions of all delegates. They were therefore the obvious agents for the Crown to use in checking the abuses of its delegates, whether those delegates were local courts or other great servants of the Crown. Thus, the common law courts developed the great prerogative writs of *certiorari,* prohibition and *mandamus.* These means of judicial review were effective in controlling inferior jurisdictions but less so in working out a solution to the conflicts between law and equity. At least until the Reformation, disputes between the King's courts and the Church or canon law courts always had to be resolved by political means for the reason that the Church courts did not '*de jure'* accept the Crown as a superior.

This system then was effective to control the acts of courts and jurisdictions inferior to the common law courts but ineffective to control the Chancery (see below) and to put right mistakes made by the common law courts themselves. Those mistakes were kept to a minimum by a system of convening all the judges to deliberate together 'in banc' in important cases. (Today, the Court of Appeal, and the House of Lords, still sometimes sit as a full court of five and seven respectively, e.g., in the case of *Jones* v *Secretary of State for Social Services* [1972] AC 944.) In those cases where it was felt that an obvious error of law had been made, it was possible to obtain a writ of error to bring the case before the House of Lords. Until the mid 19th century lay peers took part in the deliberations of the House. Originally, the Judicature Act arrangements in 1873 would have abolished the appellate function of the House of Lords but their jurisdiction was eventually retained by the Appellate Jurisdiction Act 1876, and provision made for the appointment of salaried 'Law Lords';

they were the first life peers. The form of the modern appeal adopted by the Judicature Act reforms was influenced strongly by the existing procedures in Chancery, which had had a Court of Appeal in Chancery for some 25 years at the date of the Judicature Acts. The Court of Appeal established by those Acts was an appellate court in the sense in which we understand that term today: it was still limited to civil matters and final establishment of a true appellate court for criminal cases had to await the establishment of the Court of Criminal Appeal in 1907. Until that was done, there was a procedure for the review of decisions in criminal cases by the Court for Crown Cases Reserved in which up to 15 judges might sit at a time, although it was usual for fewer judges than the maximum permitted to sit on any one case.

THE FORMS OF ACTION AND THE WRIT SYSTEM

I have said already that the development of the common law was restricted by the limitations of the writ system and the failure of the Crown and the Chancellor to overcome political opposition in the 13th century to the unlimited issue of new forms of writ. The issue of new forms of action was possible again after 1285 but only where they were 'of like case' to existing forms of action. In practice, this Statute of Westminster was used only to develop the writ of trespass into the various branches of 'case', on which much of our modern law of contract and tort is founded. The forms of action, by which a litigant could bring an action only if there was an appropriate writ to cover the facts of his case, were only abolished finally in 1833.

In facing the tasks set by present-day courses on the legal system, with their emphasis on process and method, an awareness of the way in which the forms of action influenced the development of English substantive law is not as important as being able to show, when occasion demands, a knowledge of how the writ system influenced certain other aspects of our legal system, especially as many courses contain elements of the study of procedure and remedies.

There are two major facts about the English legal process which can be better understood by knowing a little of the history of the forms of action. Many of the standard textbooks, such as Walker and Walker, *The English Legal System*, contain sufficient information. But why not read the short classic work, *The Forms of Action at Common Law* by Maitland? Your library is sure to have a copy. You will thereby also gain valuable insight into the origins of our law of tort and contract. The two facts which, as a student of English procedure and remedies you must know, and which depend upon our long adherence to the forms of action are:

(a)   English law is a law of remedies and not of rights. For an up-to-date explanation of the significance of this statement see Atiyah's 1987 Hamlyn lectures, *Pragmatism and Theory in English Law*.

(b)   The continued importance of pleading. Unless the facts alleged by the plaintiff and proved by him (against the contrary adversarial pleading of facts by the defendant) add up to a cause of action known to the law, the plaintiffs' claim will fail. Such was the fate of the plaintiff in the well-known case of *Rondel* v *Worsley* [1969] 1 AC 191.

EQUITY AND OTHER RIVALS

Why are there sometimes two rules: one a common law rule, and one an equitable rule? When you have learned that equitable rules prevail over common law rules, why should you continue to litter your mind with the common law rule?

Such are the questions that may puzzle you and many of your fellow students about equity. Equity is studied as a separate subject in the curriculum of most courses, but it tends to crop up in many subjects such as contract and tort, especially with reference to the availability of equitable as distinct from legal remedies. It is therefore convenient to include something of the origins and role of equity in a legal system course, in order to deal with the institutional aspects of equity.

All systems of law need the discretionary element of an equitable jurisdiction to deal with hard cases caused by the inflexibility of fixed rules. It is the peculiar characteristic of the common law family of legal systems, deriving from the English legal tradition, to have two apparently competing jurisdictions, one legal and one equitable, operating side by side, and at times both claiming jurisdiction over the same matter or case.

In addition to the material on this topic you may find in your recommended textbook, look as well at the summary to the chapter on equity in Allen's book, *Law in the Making,* and the passage in Stein's book, *Legal Institutions,* referred to at the beginning of this chapter. The information about the history and nature of equity that you will find of use in a legal system course may be tabulated in the following way:

History

(a)   Early petitions to the Chancellor, where common law provided no remedy (see page 56 above).

(b)   *Circa* 1475 establishment of Court of Chancery.

(c)   Late 16th, early 17th-century conflicts of jurisdiction between Court of Chancery and courts of common law.

(d)   Settlement by James I in favour of Chancery.

(e)   17th and 18th-century development of modern equitable doctrines by the Chancellors. Equitable maxims.

(f)   19th-century reforms of Chancery procedure.

Nature of Equity

(a) Equity is based on the exercise of discretion according to the dictates of *informed conscience* (quite different from a natural common-sense idea of fair play).

(b) Equity crystalises in the form of the equitable maxims. (See *Snell's Principles of Equity* for examples of how the maxims are applied in substantive subjects.)

(c) Equity is concerned with things of 'fraud, accident and confidence':

(i) Fraud includes many instances of sharp practice whereas the common law idea of fraud is based on the intent to deceive.

(ii) Accident here refers to mistakes: i.e., equity will exercise discretion in correcting documents and agreements so that they reflect the true intentions of the parties to them.

(iii) Confidence refers to all situations, not just that between trustee and beneficiary, where one party relies on the good faith of another, so that equity will intervene to ensure that there is no abuse of that trust or confidence.

Present Scope of Equity

At the present time it is useful to think of the scope of the equitable jurisdiction under the following heads:

(a) All those doctrines and rules of purely equitable origin found in the jurisdiction of the Court of Chancery predating the Judicature Acts.

(b) Equitable remedies, such as injunction and specific performance, available as an alternative to common law remedies but subject to the exercise of equitable discretion.

(c) Certain procedural rules, such as the rules about discovery of documents deriving from the tradition of the Court of Chancery.

These, together with some points from the next section on 19th-century reforms, are the essential foundations of any answer to questions in examination papers about the role of equity in the context of the English legal system.

The heading to this section indicated that equity was not the only rival to the common law. Perhaps 'rival' is too strong a word to use to describe other elements in the English legal system originating in different legal traditions, but which have now been closely assimilated into English law. From the point of view of legal systems courses, that means the separate institutions representing those other traditions which have now been assimilated into the ordinary structure of our institutions, preserving in some instances traces of their different origins through, for example, separate listings of cases and special rules of procedure.

The two principal 'rivals', maintaining for many years exclusive jurisdiction over their own matters, were the ecclesiastical courts and the Court of Admiralty. In so far as the branches of law these institutions represented have become part of English law, the courts administering them have lost their separate existence. I have already mentioned the establishment of the Probate, Divorce and Admiralty Division.

There has, of course, been a further rationalisation on functional lines. This took place in 1971 and is now enshrined in the provisions of the Supreme Court Act 1981, whereby there is a new Family Division of the High Court. Contentious probate matters now come under the Chancery Division and admiralty matters are now the concern of the Queen's Bench Division, with provision being made for separate handling of admiralty matters within the division by an Admiralty Court; as also there is now a Commercial Court both with specially nominated judges.

NINETEENTH-CENTURY AND LATER REFORM OF THE COURTS

There is argument amongst economic historians about when the industrial revolution began. Lawyers avoid fixing lines of demarcation wherever possible, by saying that something is clearly X or is equally clearly not X. (See *Ramsgate Victoria Hotel Co. Ltd* v *Montefiore* (1866) LR 1 Ex 109 on what is a reasonable time.) However, all can agree that by 1800 the industrial revolution was well under way in the United Kingdom. The consequence of that for our legal system was enormous. To cite but three matters: there was a big increase in the size of the population with resulting new kinds of commercial activity; the centres of population had shifted to great new conurbations such as Birmingham, Manchester and Liverpool; the shift away from land as the dominant source and form of holding of wealth. So when, as late as 1966, the Beeching Commission reviewed the assize system, it found that the judges were attending many remote centres, such as Appleby in the then Westmorland, and that only recently a totally fictitious county of Hallamshire had been created so that it could have a high sherriff, so that the assize judges could attend in the county whilst on circuit. (There is no prize for finding out which large English city was thereby entitled to hold an assize.)

That example can be multiplied many times over to demonstrate the immediacy of the reforms in the court system which can be dated, roughly speaking, from the beginning of the 19th century.

I propose, therefore, to pick out several themes arising out of these reforms which may, exceptionally in today's courses, provide material for an examination question or course-work essay, but more likely will provide material for a historical introduction, or side light on, questions of a critical nature about the contemporary legal system. I have selected five. You will no doubt discover more for yourself with the help of such writers as Manchester, Harding (*A Social History of English Law*) and Jackson (*The Machinery of Justice in England*). These are my five themes:

Equity and the Common Law

The opening of Dickens's novel *Bleak House* is set in the actual and metaphorical fog of the Chancellor's court in Lincoln's Inn. Begin by understanding the state of equity and the work of the Court of Chancery in the time of Lord Eldon. Real reforms of equity had to wait until his departure from office. (For a non-lawyer's critical view of Lord Eldon as politician and not as lawyer, see Hazlitt's essay on him in *The Spirit of the Age, or Contemporary Portraits*.) To summarise the situation in equity in the early 1800s we can say:

(a)   The procedure was unduly complex and extremely slow. There was a shortage of judicial manpower.
(b)   Decisions of the Chancellor could be appealed to the Chancellor.
(c)   There was a need to run two sets of proceedings in many cases, because equity could not award common law remedies and vice versa.

The first move was to appoint a Vice-Chancellor. Following the report of a Royal Commission and the departure of Lord Eldon, many sinecures were abolished and the procedures simplified. In the 1850s, courts of common law and equity respectively were empowered to award each other's remedies. Mark particularly the power of the Chancery court to award damages, conferred by Lord Cairns's Act, the Chancery Amendment Act 1858, which appears in modern form in the Supreme Court Act 1981, s. 49. The final move was to fuse the administration of law and equity as a result of the Judicature Acts of 1873 and 1875, with the clear restatement of the principle settled by James I that in case of conflict, rules of equity were to prevail over common law rules.

Beyond this, it is necessary to understand why the question is still raised sometimes as to whether a rule is purely equitable or not. Purists might say that a rule can be exclusively equitable only if it is one that would have been applied in the old Court of Chancery before the Judicature Acts fused the courts of law and equity. It is purists of that kind who would maintain that 'equity is past the age of childbearing', when it seems obvious to a lot of people that equity continues to develop, especially in the field of new and effective remedies to meet today's challenging conditions.

Procedural Reforms

The development of our modern law of contract and tort, as well as a much more flexible form of procedure, depended upon the abolition, in 1833, of the need to plead within the old forms of action. The right of a plaintiff today to amend his writ if he mistakenly sues the wrong defendant (as where a plaintiff might sue the owner of a car when he should sue the driver) dates back to and depends upon this reform. Remember also, however, that it is still necessary to allege facts in a pleading, which if proved add up to a cause of action known to the law. But at least now the plaintiff is permitted to try to convince the court that there should be a remedy, before his action is struck out. (See again, on this point, the lengthy litigation known as *Rondel* v *Worsley*.)

Legal and Equitable Remedies

Many of your legal systems courses will include some material about the remedies available for redress of grievances. The emphasis may, in some courses, be on the alternatives available these days to redress through the courts. It would be unwise, however, to ignore the subject of remedies altogether, especially as I have pointed out that one of the characteristics of English law is that it is a law of remedies, rather than of rights. Indeed, about one quarter of Dr Ingman's *The English Legal Process* is devoted to a study of remedies, with one chapter set aside for private law remedies available through the courts. If historical background is going to be of use, this is an area in which a little effort in learning about the origins and development of private law remedies should pay dividends.

At the present time, interest centres on the development of equitable remedies in the shape of *Mareva* injunctions and *Anton Piller* orders. Another concern of the courts today is to work out rules for the award of damages (e.g., for innocent misrepresentation under the Misrepresentation Act 1967) in substitution for an equitable remedy.

None of this would have been possible without the 19th-century reforms of equity in general and the coordination of the availability of legal and equitable remedies already dealt with (see page 62).

It is worth looking at that material, not just as a history of equitable doctrines and remedies, but also from the especial point of view of the remedies that a court can grant and how the system was brought together and unified during the course of the 19th century.

The Principle of Universality

Enough has been said in this short chapter to indicate that throughout much of the history of English law, the unfortunate litigant has been prone to fail in his quest for justice, either because he sued in the wrong court or brought the wrong form of action.

The principle referred to here is simply my shorthand way of describing how during the course of the 19th century, culminating in the Judicature Acts, the court structure was simplified. It was something to be fought for, against numerous vested interests. Find out why, for example, there were five divisions of the High Court from 1875/76 until 1881. Having learned the details of the reform of the court structures, you should conduct your own analysis of the Supreme Court Act 1981 to try to discover how far the following principles apply. (These are the principles which, with hindsight, can be seen to lie behind many of the 19th-century reforms.)

(a)   Any case, cause or matter, can be brought before any part of the Supreme Court.

(b)   All judges are competent to take any business of the Supreme Court.

(c)   The Supreme Court can sit anywhere in England and Wales.

(d)   If administrative arrangements for the dispatch of business become inconvenient they can be changed with the minimum of delay and legislative interference.

There are limits, as you will find, to all the above four principles. For example, the business of the Supreme Court is divided into Divisions, to which business is referred on the basis of subject-matter, and occasionally it still happens that a particular judge has to decline to take a case in a Division, because on appointment the judge was assigned to a different Division and not given leave to take cases in other Divisions. As to sitting at any place in England and Wales, it is not unknown for the court to sit in a Suffolk churchyard and even to visit a Pacific island in the course of a hearing (see *Tito* v *Waddell* (*No. 2)* [1977] Ch 106).

These matters are trivial in themselves but they are illustrative of the working of the general principles set out above, as they emerged in the work of the 19th-century reformers. The context in which these historical points can be used to effect is by comparing modern proposals for reform with them, and as a yardstick by which to criticise the workings of those parts of our court system not currently subject to proposals for reform. This is the essential historical background to the topics to be dealt with in chapter 6 on the civil process.

The Reform of Criminal Justice

Just as the material in the last section can serve as a historical introduction to the civil process, a brief résumé of the changes in the criminal process during the course of the 19th century can provide a similar introduction and touchstone to chapter 6 on the criminal process. As the title of the chapter indicates I am concerned with procedures and institutions rather than substantive matters. It is still worth noting, in passing, the great changes in the substance of the criminal law between the beginning and end of the 19th century: the massive reduction in the number of capital offences, and the rationalisation of offences against the person in the Act of 1861, to mention but two.

Alongside these substantive reforms there were many reforms in procedure and evidence, although, as already mentioned, a satisfactory system of criminal appeals was not achieved until the opening years of the 20th century with the Criminal Appeal Act 1907.

In the light of contemporary criticisms of criminal justice, about the way in which the system fails to convict the guilty as often as it should, too lenient sentences, procedural and evidential rules weighted in favour of the accused defendant, it will be salutary for you to consider the reforms necessary throughout the 19th century to put the accused into a position accepted as fair by most people today.

The most important reforms can be put under the following heads. Details of the reforms can be found set out in Jackson's *The Machinery of Justice in England*.

(a)   The evolution of fair rules of procedure. For example, rules about who should have the 'last word'.
(b)   The accused's right to representation at his trial.
(c)   The right of the accused to give evidence at his own trial.
(d)   The accused's right to silence.
(e)   The position of the accused's spouse as a witness.
(f)   Rights of appeal, without harsh disincentives.

As stated, some of these reforms, especially (d) above, are now being criticised as representing a position that is too favourable to the accused.

These five themes of reform in the 19th century and after form a useful collection of 'small arms' for use in the war against examiners and assessors. In the concluding section of this chapter I shall make one or two suggestions about how to make good use of the historical knowledge you may acquire as a result of putting the suggestions in this chapter into effect.

USING HISTORY TODAY

Unless your course has a distinct historical section dealing, for example, with English legal history in the 19th century, or the history of equity, it is unlikely that you will be able to answer a complete examination question in the form of a historical essay. Nevertheless, there are opportunities to use your knowledge of legal history by way of a contextual introduction to many questions of a critical nature about the English legal system as it is today.

Look for key words in the question, which invite you to set your answer in a historical context which can go on to develop into a critical examination of the present and conclude by looking into the future. These key words are words which suggest that there has had to be a continuing search and adaptation process, looking for the ideal solution to a problem which will never be solved finally. The words (and they all have equivalents or alternatives) which I should particularly pick out are:

(a) 'Balance', or '(un)fairness'.
(b) 'Present day', or 'present time'.
(c) '(Further) reform' or 'change'.

These words all suggest previous situations or activity, enabling you to select an appropriate historical starting-point for your discussion or comment.

The following areas are ones in which you can expect to be able to make use of this technique both to show evidence of wider reading and to overcome what is always the most difficult part of any answer, producing a good beginning. This predisposes the examiner to thinking that here is a good answer to the question asked; not simply a version combined from a standard text and lecture notes, which more or less relates to the question.

(a) The reforms of the criminal process from 1800 onwards.
(b) The availability of justice (of a high quality) at the local level.
(c) The effect of procedure on the development of substantive law.
(d) The nature and scope of equitable doctrines and remedies.

A question in which these techniques may be used, could appear in this form:

'The (present) (English) rules of criminal procedure and evidence (do not) produce a *fair* trial for both prosecution and accused.' Comment.

My comments on this question for our present purposes are these:

(a) The general form of the question suggests that there is an established body of opinion (not necessarily shared by the examiner) that is sceptical about the validity of the proposition.

(b) The use of the present tense and the key word 'fair' (a 'balance' equivalent) suggests that there may at some time have been different rules of procedure and evidence and that the rules could be changed again.

(c)   The words in brackets: the question is quite different if these words are omitted. For example:

(i)   'Present' — the inclusion of this word is the clearest invitation to consider how the present position was reached and whether or not past changes and reforms have gone too far in trying to secure that the innocent are not convicted.

(ii)   'English' — as this question appears on a paper entitled 'The *English* legal system', this is a clear invitation to include some comparative material: perhaps a comparison with Scots law.

(iii)   'Do not' — the omission or inclusion of these words changes the viewpoint from which the question has to be considered. The inclusion of the words indicates that the maker of the statement places the burden of proof on those who wish to maintain the status quo.

Assuming that the question reads:

'The present rules of criminal procedure and evidence produce a fair trial for both prosecution and accused.' Comment.

Then an opening paragraph in an answer might well make the following points:

(i)   The statement indicates broad satisfaction with the present situation.

(ii)   This has not always been the case.

(iii)   In particular, the accused has in the past been at a disadvantage, compared with the prosecution; in the matters of representation, competence as a witness, protection of previous reputation and character, the right to silence.

(iv)   These matters were dealt with in a series of reforms in the 19th century.

(v)   It is now being suggested in some quarters that the balance has been tipped too far in favour of the accused and that the balance should be redressed by changes in the rules of evidence and procedure.

(vi)   Those suggestions happen to centre on some of the matters referred to above. It is appropriate therefore to consider what evidence there is that changes in those and other areas are needed in order to redress the balance.

In the case of the accused's right to representation . . .

A final word. In purely instrumental terms, if your brief study of the historical background enables you to produce two good introductions to answers on an examination paper of five questions, it will have been worthwhile.

FURTHER READING

Baker, J.H., *An Introduction to English Legal History* (3rd edn., Butterworths, 1990).

Holdsworth, Sir W., *A History of English Law Vol. 1* (7th edn., Methuen, 1956).

Manchester, A.H., *A Modern Legal History of England and Wales 1750–1950* (Butterworths, 1980).

Milsom, S.F.C., *Historical Foundations of the Common Law* (2nd edn., Butterworths, 1981).

Stein, P., *Legal Institutions* (Butterworths, 1984).

5 INTERLUDE — A NOTE ON LEGAL INSTITUTIONS AND LEGAL SYSTEMS

Legal institutions, in the sense of courts and their officials, may be studied from a number of angles. As already indicated in chapter 1, in this book it is assumed that your course will choose to look at legal institutions from an analytical standpoint.

However, before embarking on a review of the elements of a course on civil and criminal process, or as it may be called in some courses, the administration of justice in the civil and criminal courts, let us take the opportunity to set out the way in which this is to be done in the present context and at the same time to point out that the material covered in the next two chapters may be ordered differently in some courses, depending upon the different themes that may be selected for treatment in any one course.

The next two chapters are going to deal respectively with the criminal and civil process. A certain amount of basic knowledge will have been acquired already in the introductory classes which most courses provide. So far as legal institutions are concerned, that basic knowledge will include at least the names of the civil and criminal courts together with the ability to identify which of them are courts of trial with original jurisdiction and the courts to which an appeal may lie.

As a matter of choice and for the purposes of exposition, in the next two chapters, the criminal and civil processes will each be treated as a whole. In each case the history of cases will be traced from inception to the final disposal of the case after all rights of appeal have been exhausted. Three things must be brought to the reader's attention, which arise out of this method of proceeding.

The narrative treatment of both civil and criminal process will have to be interrupted from time to time to accommodate some features of our legal institutions and their working of which we should otherwise lose sight. These include such matters as the role of the Judicial Committee of the Privy Council, the influence of European Community law, and the European Convention on Human Rights.

Secondly, in order to avoid duplication of treatment some matters which are relevant to both civil and criminal process will appear only once. Thus, although, for instance, judicial review may be mentioned in connection with the criminal process it is also very important as part of the civil process.

The last point to note about the material in the next two chapters is that there are several themes which cut across the boundaries of the civil and criminal processes. These include the form of procedure, known as the adversarial procedure, used in English courts, which may be compared with forms of procedure adopted in civil law jurisdictions, and the whole question of appeals and the jurisdiction to review decisions. The latter topic, in particular, is sometimes selected for treatment as an integrated topic stretching across the whole spectrum of the legal process. Indeed, that is the treatment accorded to the whole question of appeals and review in Smith and Bailey's *The Modern English Legal System*.

In the succeeding two chapters, then, look out for references to themes that may emerge in different ways in different courses. Themes of this sort that may attract the teacher's and examiner's attention include:

(a)   The place of the common law in the context of the family of legal systems; with especial reference to other European national and supranational systems.

(b)   The integrity of the legal process, putting together the law of contempt, openness, freedom of information, checks on the abuse of legal process.

(c)   Modes of trial and procedure.

(d)   The management and administration of the courts.

All of these themes are connected with our legal institutions. The first of them, however, is also connected with the nature of our law itself and its sources. Whilst in general it is sufficient to give warning to students to be aware of these possible integrative and cross-boundary themes and to prepare to use material from a variety of sources in parts of the course handling those themes, it may be useful to deal in more detail with the first of these themes relating to the common law as a member of a family of legal systems. This theme appears as a topic in a number of courses and may produce examination questions but it is more likely to be the subject of a seminar or tutorial discussion. The influence of European Community law is receiving more emphasis in legal systems courses.

In most cases, a seminar discussion on a topic connected with the theme of 'the common law system' will occur towards the beginning of the course. Inevitably, therefore, the treatment will be elementary, but not superficial, designed to bring out the main distinguishing features of the common law system and to demonstrate its links with international law and other legal systems. If this, or a similar topic, appears in your seminar or tutorial programme towards the beginning of the course it will be, to an extent, an opportunity for you to get used to gathering information from a number of sources on a selective basis, as most of the standard textbooks do not deal with this matter as a discrete topic. Let us imagine then, that for your first or second tutorial in the English legal system course you are asked to demonstrate the following:

(a) The meaning of the term 'common law'.
(b) The distinguishing features of a 'common law' legal system.
(c) The role of international law in English law.
(d) The effect on English law of membership of the European Community.
(e) The significance of the European Convention on Human Rights.

On first receiving such a task, which you know will have to be disposed of within the confines of a tutorial hour, you may despair and wonder at once whether you have chosen to study the wrong subject. Each of the items set out is capable of extensive treatment and, novice though you may be, you suspect that the last three are almost subjects in their own right. What is the tutorial group leader up to? Is it simply a case of demonstrating to the students at the beginning of the course who is boss? Or, worse, is the tutor malevolently deriving pleasure from the discomfiture of the students?

Having decided to give the tutor the benefit of any doubts about his or her sadistic tendencies (after all you have only recently become acquainted), second thoughts about the task may help in reducing the task to manageable proportions. See if you can discover in the question set for discussion, taken in the context of the rest of your course in the subject so far, what it is that you are being asked to learn and why you are being asked to do it. If it is still not apparent at the end of the tutorial meeting, ask the tutor, in private if you suspect you are the only member of the group still in ignorance, what it was all about.

The answer to such a question in the present case might be on the following lines: 'In this tutorial you were expected to learn how to distinguish between different usages of the term 'common law', and to realise that other legal systems have different ways of organising their material and their legal procedures. That knowledge will provide you with a starting-point for comparison and criticism of our own legal system as not only this course progresses but also other subjects and courses in the degree curriculum. You were also meant to realise that in the modern world there is a growing degree of interdependence between legal systems and that this is both necessary and desirable in our world of instant communications and constant movement between countries of people, goods and capital. Lastly, by preparing for the tutorial you will have had to go to a variety of books and source materials, which is the common lot of the lawyer whenever he is preparing his work, whether in practice or as an academic study.'

It remains to say what should have been prepared to enable you to take part fully in a tutorial meeting requiring discussion of the five points set out above.

A first consideration is whether all of the points merit equal treatment. The natural inclination is to give less than equal treatment to those points coming last on the list. It may be, however, that the points appearing at the end of a list or towards the end are the most significant and only appear in that position because they arise naturally out of points coming higher up the list.

Secondly, preparation for this tutorial should be based firmly on the recognition that it is a tutorial about the very foundations of the English legal system and is not about either the details of Community law or human rights, although you should have sufficient material available on those subjects to show that you understand their significance in relation to the rest of English law and the English legal system. A brief perusal of the convention in the library will show with what sort of substantive rights the convention is concerned.

Most standard works on the English legal system will have something to say on the first two items on the list. When coming to the tutorial be prepared, when asked about the meaning of the term 'common law', to show your understanding of the various meanings the term has acquired by being able to compare and contrast it with other terms, and to give examples to reinforce your own understanding as well as to demonstrate it to the tutor (and other members of the tutorial group). If you say, for example, that common law may be distinguished from equity, you must at least be able to go on to say that in this context the common law refers to the rules of law and procedures to be found in the practice and decisions of the royal courts of justice that were established over a period of time following the Conquest, whereas equity is that body of law that came to be recognised first as the personal jurisdiction of the Chancellor and from the 15th century onwards as the law administered by the Court of Chancery. If this tutorial does occur at an early stage in the course, then you will score bonus points if you can go on to say that common law remedies are available 'as of right' but equitable remedies are discretion-ary, and that the relationship between law and equity was sometimes a bitter one involving conflicts of jurisdiction which had to be worked out over a long period of time. To go further in this tutorial on this point would be to encroach on topics for other tutorials of a more detailed description on the nature of equity and its history. There is plenty left to say on the other meanings of the term 'common law', such as the distinction between common law and statute law, a distinction often drawn in the context of criminal law, where there are often references to certain offences as common law offences and to others as statutory offences. There are, of course, four other separate items on the list.

When asked to explain the distinguishing features of a 'common law' system students are often tempted simply to say that it is an 'unwritten' system of law. As a matter of literal truth this is patently a falsehood as any visit to a law library will show. However, the phrase persists and some attempt must be made to discover what that convenient shorthand term, 'unwritten law', really means. It refers of course to the fact that a 'common law' system is not founded on a set of authoritative texts setting out the law, but is a system constructed originally out of the decisions in individual cases. Such a statement made in the tutorial may cause the tutor to ask what form those authoritative texts might take in systems of law described as being based on 'written' law. Other questions for which you might prepare will be designed to discover whether you know why members of another family of legal systems found in the world today are known as 'civil law' systems; and whether, since legislation is now the dominant source of law in the English legal system, any basic distinguishing features of common law and civil law systems still remain.

Passing on to the role of international law in the English legal system you will have to discover the meanings of sovereignty and jurisdiction and then look to books such as Starke's *Introduction to International Law* to find how far and on what terms English law and courts recognise and give expression to international law. You will discover that different States adopt different stances, depending upon whether they follow the dualist or monist view of international law. In view of the last two items on the list for consideration in this tutorial exercise, particular attention must be paid to the effect of treaties and the ways in which their provisions become part of States' laws. In particular you will discover that in the case of the United Kingdom, the treaty-making power belongs in the realm of the prerogative, and that the treaty is not effective as part of the internal law of the United Kingdom until it is incorporated by legislation of the United Kingdom Parliament.

The last two items may be considered now. In the first place they are similar, in that both concern treaties entered into by the United Kingdom. They are dissimilar in that the European Communities Treaties have been incorporated into United Kingdom law by the European Communities Act 1972 but there has been no act of incorporation of the European Convention on Human Rights. You can then go on to elaborate on the significance and consequences of each treaty, pointing out that the European Community has a developed legal order independent of the laws of the member States with

its own executive and judicial powers; that the treaties require member States
to accept and abide by the executive and judicial acts of the Community; that
Community law is to take precedence over the laws of member States and
that all of these features raise issues relating to the sovereignty of the United
Kingdom Parliament. With respect to the European Convention on Human
Rights you should point out that the United Kingdom has accepted the
obligations of the Convention to allow United Kingdom citizens recourse to
the European Commission of Human Rights and the European Court of
Human Rights. For example, the *Spycatcher* case was ruled upon finally by
the European Court of Human Rights at the end of November 1991 (*The Times*,
27 November 1991). (Note should be taken in passing of the separate
identities and functions of the Court of Justice of the European Communities
at Luxembourg, a Community organ, and the European Court of Human
Rights at Strasbourg, established under the Convention.) Access to the
Commission and Court of Human Rights depends upon exhausting all
national judicial remedies, and you should note also that the 'rights' accorded
under the Convention are highly specific and that it is not sufficient for an
aggrieved citizen simply to show that he has suffered injustice at the hands
of the State of which he is a citizen. Finally, you should be able to discover
that there are difficulties for both the United Kingdom citizen and government caused by there not being an enacted Bill of Rights and by the
Convention not being incorporated into United Kingdom law.

The influence of European Community law has reached the stage of a
surging incoming tide, to adapt the phrase used by Lord Denning MR in *H.
P. Bulmer Ltd* v *J. Bollinger SA* [1974] Ch 401. Aspects of Community law are
both integrated into various parts of our law syllabuses and studied
independently. In the context of a legal systems course there is often a study
of the major institutions of the Community. This change in attitude is
reflected in the new material contained in the recent editions of standard
textbooks, such as Ingman's *The English Legal Process*. The change is very
marked in the 3rd edition of Farrar and Dugdale's *Introduction to Legal Method*.
It is now essential to deal with the interpretation of Community law and the
supremacy of Community law as part of the legal system course.

It is not being suggested here that there will be a tutorial on this topic as
part of every course. What is being suggested is that towards the beginning
of a well-designed course there will be a tutorial designed to set out the
framework of the subject and its boundaries and also to erect signposts to
other parts of the course and indeed other subjects in the curriculum.

If you are reading this part-way through your English legal system course,
it would still be worthwhile for you to go over again the material in the first
tutorials of the course and see how they might even now assist you in 'getting
your bearings', before embarking upon a final consolidation and revision
before the examinations.

The next two chapters on the civil and criminal process assume that you will be working for an examination, which will inevitably include questions on the present-day system of courts and disputes settlement. If you are not following a course which imposes an examination but which requires you to acquire a working knowledge of the court system, the advice given to examinees will serve you equally well in acquiring knowledge of the court system; that is, 'working' knowledge that can be put to good use in the contexts in which it will be assumed. There is a table included after the next two chapters, setting out a list of topics common to both civil and criminal processes, which may serve as points of comparison and as a guide to possible alternative themes for examination questions and essays.

6 THE CRIMINAL PROCESS

In looking at the mass of material comprising the subject of the 'English criminal process' let us first take stock of what has already been learned and assimilated. The material which emerges from chapter 3 concerning the 'basic tools' for the job of the law student is a good starting-point. So far as that material is relevant to a study of the criminal process it may be summarised in the following way.

The courts with criminal jurisdiction as courts of trial are the magistrates' courts and the Crown Court, which is a part of the Supreme Court. The magistrates, or justices of the peace, preside in the magistrates' courts; trials in the Crown Court are before a professional judge and jury. The professional judges are High Court judges, circuit judges and recorders. Recorders are part-time judges. There may be an appeal from the magistrates' court to the Crown Court or to the Divisional Court of the Queen's Bench. (A further appeal on a point of law may be made from the Crown Court to the Divisional Court of the Queen's Bench.) From the Crown Court appeal lies to the Criminal Division of the Court of Appeal. The appellate committee of the House of Lords is the final court of appeal in criminal matters (excluding purely summary offences which cannot be appealed beyond the Crown Court). This structure can be set out in a simple diagram.

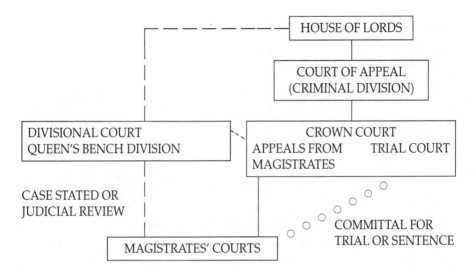

The principal concern in this review of a course on the criminal process will be to add detail to the above framework and to populate it with accuseds, convicted persons, court officials, lawyers, juries and judges, whilst, at the same time, highlighting and pointing out those features of the system that may give rise to examination questions which require some basic analytical skills.

The court system and its attendant procedures are highly suitable for this sort of exercise as the present system of criminal (and civil) courts is based on a relatively small number of statutes, which, on the whole, are logically organised and do not contain too many difficult problems of statutory interpretation. Students, therefore, are expected to become familiar with this basic statutory framework. A good way of doing so is through the use of a book of statutes. Of course, our courts of common law and equity did not always have their jurisdictions set out in statutory form. In looking at the contemporary court structure as a whole you should learn the significance of the Supreme Court Act 1981, s. 1. Note that it does not bring the court into existence, but says what it shall consist of for the future, namely, the Court of Appeal, the High Court of Justice and the Crown Court. This marks off those courts which are deemed to be superior courts from inferior courts. Knowing how to classify courts in those terms is useful in two respects in a study of criminal courts and their procedure. It enables you to recognise those courts whose acts are subject to judicial review and to say which courts have an inherent jurisdiction subject only to specific statutory restrictions. Thus the Crown Court has, by the Supreme Court Act 1981, s. 46, been given exclusive jurisdiction over trials on indictment, wherever the offence was committed, provided the offence is one within the jurisdiction of English courts. The distinction between superior and inferior courts is also relevant in deciding whether a court has an inherent power to punish for contempt. These basic facts about our courts must be understood before you can get on with the business of analysing the criminal process with an eye to success in the examinations.

Having said that our present court system is based on a relatively few statutes, they had better be set out at once, with an indication of their contribution to the overall scheme of things. The list follows the order of events in the course of criminal trials:

(a) Prosecution of Offences Act 1985 — the establishment of a national prosecution service — supervision of the 'discretion to prosecute'.

(b) Bail Act 1976 (as amended by the Criminal Justice and Public Order Act 1994) — release from custody, pending and during trial.

(c) Magistrates' Courts Act 1980 and Criminal Justice Act 1988 — classification of offences — getting the accused to court — jurisdiction over summary offences — selection of mode of trial in offences triable either way — committal proceedings/transfer for trial and committal for sentence — appeals to Crown Court — appeal by case stated — provision for judicial review.

(d) Criminal Justice Act 1967 — form of committal proceedings.

(e) Supreme Court Act 1981 — constitution and jurisdiction of the Supreme Court (Court of Appeal, Criminal Division — Divisional Court of Queen's Bench — Crown Court) — provision for rules of court and administration.

(f) Courts and Legal Services Act 1990 and Courts Act 1971 — the appointment and tenure of circuit judges and recorders — circuit arrangements.

(g) Criminal Justice and Public Order Act 1994 — inferences to be drawn from the accused's silence.

(h) Criminal Appeal Act 1968 and Criminal Appeal Act 1995 — grounds of appeal following conviction at the Crown Court — powers of the Court of Appeal (Criminal Division) — conditions for further appeal to the House of Lords.

(i) Appellate Jurisdiction Act 1876 — constitution and jurisdiction of the House of Lords as a final court of appeal in criminal matters.

(j) Criminal Justice Act 1991 and Criminal Justice Act 1993 — sentencing.

Although it is an essential part of understanding the criminal justice system to know the constitution of the different courts in terms of their judicial manpower, the 'professional' judiciary merits treatment as a separate topic in most courses and detailed treatment of the judiciary is reserved for the last chapter of this book as part of the 'law in action' approach to the subject, as our judges are more frequently put under the scrutiny of the media. The selection of the judiciary to appear in the last chapter of this book is not intended to indicate that, as an academic topic, their role in society is an unimportant one. Nor is their appearance in the final chapter a judgment on the importance of the judiciary as a potential examination subject in an English legal system course.

The immediate business in hand is to take each of the stages of the criminal process exemplified by the statutes set out above and analyse each of those stages in terms of its examination potential. It is safe to say that every legal system examination paper will include at least one if not two questions on some aspect of the criminal process. In considering a section of a syllabus such as is found in many courses under the general heading 'the criminal process' or 'the administration of criminal justice', consideration must be given to the basis of selection for examination topics. Over and above the general guidance given in chapter 2, the following points refer particularly to this section of the syllabus. First, remember the possibility of both 'broad' and 'narrow' questions on the same topic. For example, it is possible, although not likely, for there to be an examination question which simply requires a discussion of 'the provisions for appeal following conviction'. Such a question requires consideration of all the occasions on which a person may be convicted, at the magistrates' court and at the Crown Court. There is implied in the question the need to offer a comparison of the two on broad terms. A much 'narrower' question would be one limited to a discussion of the 'right to appeal and the grounds for allowing the appeal following conviction by the Crown Court'. In effect, such a question calls for a detailed commentary on the opening sections of the Criminal Appeal Act 1968 (as amended by the Criminal Appeal Act 1995). This is obviously important in view of the report of the Royal Commission on Criminal Justice, which was established following the cases of the 'Guildford Four' and the 'Birmingham Six'.

You will also discover that within this section of the syllabus there are certain 'set pieces' or small self-contained topics which by their very nature must occur in examination papers from time to time, for example, the question of the granting of bail.

Before such 'set pieces' can be regarded as 'bankers' in the examinations stakes, it must be realised that these topics are often either fashionable or topical. Watch out for the publication of government White Papers, the reports of royal commissions and media comment. Above all, develop the ability to gauge the importance being given to a topic *in the year you are studying the subject*. Indications to watch for include: the insertion of a new topic not included in the previously published syllabus; a topic taking up more than its allotted time on a lecture schedule; more than usual enthusiasm on the part of the teacher, and many other little signs you will learn to recognise. Some topics recur periodically in examination papers and some by their topicality and urgency demand to be given a place in an examination in a particular year. This is especially true of the 'fast-moving' and constantly changing subject of criminal justice. To check that statement look at the list of statutes in any textbook on the subject and see how many of them are entitled 'Criminal Justice Act' or 'Administration of Justice Act'. These topics require specially careful, detailed and accurate preparation. In these topics an overview will overlook vital points.

Two of the 'set piece' topics, contempt and legal aid, have been singled out for separate treatment. That is because these topics do not by any means appear in every syllabus and, even when they do, they receive variable treatment from year to year. They remain good examples of potential examination material in a number of courses.

Having come to the conclusion that the administration of criminal justice may produce one or two questions out of a typical paper of nine or ten questions, where and how will the examiner strike? In order to begin to read the mind of the examiner let us remind ourselves of the various stages in the criminal process.

This produces a list of possible topics for questions and work assignments. Not all of them merit a whole question to themselves on the examination paper and some of them can be combined in different ways to form part of yet more themes. Such themes may cross the artificial boundaries set by the arrangement of this or any other book. For example, a question may occur on the desirability of all civil cases beginning in the same court, as all criminal cases begin in the magistrates' court. Such a question obviously requires an answer which draws on material which in this book comes under the heading of the criminal process as well as material relating directly to civil jurisdiction and process. As will be seen, there are also substantial topics hidden away inside some of the topics now listed:

(a) The decision to prosecute — subtopic: the DPP.
(b) Getting the accused to court.
(c) Bail.
(d) Classification of offences.
(e) Choice of mode of trial for offences triable either way.
(f) Committal proceedings / transfer of proceedings.
(g) Summary trial — subtopics: the office and work of JPs — the magistrates' clerk.
(h) Trial on indictment — subtopic: the jury.
(i) Challenging the magistrates' decisions — appeal to Crown Court — case stated — judicial review.
(j) Appeals from the Crown Court to the Court of Appeal.
(k) Appeals to the House of Lords.

(l)   References by the Home Secretary and the Attorney-General.

THE DECISION TO PROSECUTE — THE DPP AND THE LAW OFFICERS

The initiation of criminal prosecutions in English law has been traditionally in the hands of private persons. A witness to this is the style under which criminal cases tried summarily are reported, where the prosecutor's personal name appears as one of the parties even where the police are the prosecutor; for example, the case of *Hobson* v *Gledhill* [1978] 1 WLR 215, which was a prosecution under the Guard Dogs Act 1975, and the appellant, Hobson, was the police officer who laid the information.

Even following the establishment of a national prosecution service by the Prosecution of Offences Act 1985, the potential for private prosecutions is preserved. Many public bodies with a law enforcement role will continue to bring prosecutions. These include the Customs and Excise and the Health and Safety Executive.

However, it must be acknowledged that the passing of the Prosecution of Offences Act 1985 marked a turning-point in English law. That Act established a national prosecution service which became fully operational throughout England and Wales in October 1986. By April 1987 the Press were reporting the 'teething' troubles of the new service, including alleged low morale amongst the professional staff of the service. Such a situation is meat and drink to the hungry examiner searching for new material. Examiners will be concerned to explore students' understanding of the reasons why the service was set up. An adequate answer to a question of this sort will have to deal with previous arrangements for bringing prosecutions and the subsequent conduct of prosecutions and the deficiencies in those arrangements. The findings of the Royal Commission on Criminal Procedure (Cmnd 8092, 1981) are the best authoritative statement but that Royal Commission's report was followed by a White Paper (*An Independent Prosecution Service for England and Wales,* Cmnd 9074) which did not follow all of the Royal Commission's proposals. Your textbooks, such as Smith and Bailey, *The Modern English Legal System,* 2nd ed., pp. 616–23, will provide the necessary basic information on the pre–1985 Act position. There is a good summary of the arguments put forward in a report by the private organisation of reforming lawyers called JUSTICE, as long ago as 1970, on p. 619 of Smith and Bailey, *The Modern English Legal System,* 2nd ed.

After a year or so of the operation of the CPS the nature of questions relating to the decision to prosecute, and the exercise of the discretion to prosecute, underwent a change. The emphasis changed to two main aspects of the topic. Questions are asked which are designed to test knowledge of the structure and working of the prosecution service as it is currently evolving, including the continued role of the DPP in controlling certain types of prosecution.

Secondly, there are questions requiring an evaluation of the service both in terms of its success in fulfilling the purposes for which it was established, and in terms of its success in avoiding new problems. In preparation for a possible question of the first type just mentioned, the commentary on the Act in *Current Law Statutes Annotated* will provide much useful material. In relation to evaluatory questions concerning the service, see the Annual Reports of the Crown Prosecution Service.

It was mentioned at the beginning of this section that, traditionally, private prosecutions were the normal method of prosecuting offenders. However, the question is now often asked whether the right to bring private prosecutions should be retained at all. Their retention under the 1985 Act was controversial, both as to the continuance of the practice at all, and as to the way in which private prosecutions may be brought. The continued existence of the practice is challenged on the grounds that it may provide opportunities for private vengeful prosecutions and that it may permit the holders of minority and perhaps extreme views to impose their views on society as a whole. However, the 1985 Act amended the Supreme Court Act 1981 to make it possible to have a person declared a vexatious litigant for the purpose of instituting criminal proceedings. An obvious area of concern in this connection is the law of obscenity and public morality. Even though private prosecutions are to continue, there is scope for further argument about the degree and manner of control which should be exercised over them.

Before leaving this section it is appropriate to give a reminder that a syllabus often includes as a topic 'the personnel of the law', and that material concerning the office of the Director of Public Prosecutions and the two law officers of the Crown, the Attorney-General and Solicitor-General, which is dealt with under the heading of 'personnel of the law', may be relevant and useful in preparing the topic of 'the prosecution of offences' as dealt with in this section.

Taking all in all, this section is likely to figure in future examinations on the English legal system in one or other of the ways outlined here on a regular basis.

GETTING THE ACCUSED TO COURT

This is a short topic in terms of the usual English legal system syllabus, and may be dealt with by a sentence or two in a lecture, the question of arrest more usually forming part of a constitutional law course or a specialised civil liberties course.

However, the student of the English legal system is expected to know, and to show that knowledge as appropriate, how an accused person is brought to court. So, the expected answer to the question, how is the accused brought to court, is not (to echo the American humorist, James Thurber) 'in the police van'. What is referred to here, of course, are the procedures whereby the accused is compelled to attend the court. There are three such procedures. Two of those, the issue of a summons and arrest on a warrant, are set out in detail in the Magistrates' Courts Act 1980, s. 1, and the Magistrates' Courts Rules 1981. The powers of the third procedure, arrest without warrant, are set out in the Police and Criminal Evidence Act 1984 and a large number of statutory powers of arrest given to constables by different statutes. From a practical point of view, although it will not give rise to a whole question in its own right, this topic in the English legal system syllabus is important in the following ways: as a possible item in a problem question dealing with the powers of the magistrates and their clerk; and its connection with the next section on bail. In the first place care must be taken to distinguish the occasions on which the magistrates' clerk may act in the issue of criminal process from the occasions on which the process must be issued by a magistrate in person, and it is also important to be able to say whether a proper case has been made out for the issue of a warrant rather than a summons. Secondly, this topic is one which leads into the next topic of bail, as the police have a duty to produce persons under arrest to a court as soon as is practicable or to release them on bail pending their appearance at court on a specified day.

Whenever a person is arrested and kept in custody it becomes relevant to ask when, if at all, he should be given his liberty before trial. Look out then for this small topic being a vital if small element in a question that might cover in essay or problem form the whole span of time from the decision to prosecute an offender until the offender is asked to plead at his trial. In other words, do not neglect this little area of law. Treat it as an integral part of the whole pre-trial stage of the criminal process.

BAIL

The next stage of the criminal process, at any rate in cases where there is going to be some time passing before the accused is brought to trial, is to decide whether the accused should be kept in custody during that time or released on bail. The law relating to bail and the considerations regarding the granting or withholding of bail in any particular case are just about sufficient to provide material for an examination question. Alternatively, questions of bail might appear as part of a problem question covering a stage or stages of the criminal process as it might work in the case of a person supposed to have committed certain offences. Essay questions might require an analysis of the law or be geared towards a 'law in action' approach requiring a discussion of the balance to be struck between the liberty of the accused, but not yet found guilty, person and the need to protect society from the commission of further crimes. In either case a sound knowledge of the basis of the law of bail is necessary, supplemented by some facts and figures about the current workings of the system of bail and one or two leading cases on the law of bail.

The law is to be found principally in the Bail Act 1976, the Magistrates' Courts Act 1980, the Supreme Court Act 1981, and the Bail (Amendment) Act 1993. Note also the important changes made by the Criminal Justice and Public Order Act 1994. A useful analysis of the topic might proceed on the following lines:

(a)   Preliminary. Make sure of definitions and terms, especially *surety* and *recognisance.*

(b)   General principles. The Bail Act 1976, s. 4, creates a *presumption* in favour of bail being granted. It is for the prosecution to show grounds for not granting bail, bearing in mind the distinction between the case where the defendant is accused of an imprisonable offence and one where the defendant is accused of a non-imprisonable offence. (In a problem question you may expect to be told if an offence is not one carrying a possible sentence of imprisonment.) Be sure also that you understand the significance of the way in which the burden of proof faced by the prosecution is expressed; that is, that the court must be 'satisfied that there are substantial grounds for believing' that one of the specified situations exists, and the effect that this burden of proof has on the likelihood of bail being granted, both generally and in particular cases.

(c)   Successive applications. There is a duty to produce the accused before the court at regular intervals pending trial and the question arises whether on each occasion there may be a fresh application for bail. Two matters need to be borne in mind: the different intervals at which an accused must be produced depending upon whether he consents to a longer remand than eight days *and* is legally represented and whether the magistrates must hear a further application.

(d)   Occasions for making applications for bail. Not only must you know that there are four types of bail application, but you must also know when there is a possibility of a grant of legal aid specifically for the issue of whether bail should be granted. An adequate treatment of the topic will also deal with whether there is a duty to consider the question of bail or whether there is a discretion to do so. The discretion to consider the question of bail, for example, given to the police when a person is arrested without warrant and will be brought before the court the following morning (within 24 hours), must be carefully distinguished from the process of deciding whether an application once made is successful or otherwise. The four occasions upon which application may be made are: to the police, following arrest without warrant; to the magistrates' court (the court is under an obligation to consider bail even if no application is made); to the Crown Court; and to the High Court. Note that the police, and not just the courts, may now attach conditions to bail and that in relation to certain offences the prosecution are given a right of appeal against a magistrates' decision to grant bail. This appeal is made to the Crown Court. Care should be taken in answering essay-type questions to distinguish the powers of the Crown Court from the greater but more rarely exercised powers of the High Court under the Criminal Justice Act 1967 (as amended by the Bail Act 1976). A further distinction between applications to the Crown Court and the High Court is that, in the latter case, legal aid, if granted, is civil legal aid.

(e)   Consequences of breach of bail. This final consideration of the law of bail concerns not only the accused, but also any surety who has guaranteed the appearance of the accused and his due surrender to custody. For the accused to fail to surrender to bail is a separate offence, for which the accused may be arrested.

Having considered the question of bail, we are now in a position to consider the types of offence of which a person may be accused and the consequences of classifying offences for the way in which the accused will be tried and also the type of sentence for which the accused will be liable in the event of conviction.

CLASSIFICATION OF OFFENCES

Criminal offences are classified for a number of purposes and in different ways at different stages of the criminal process. Our immediate concern is with the major classification of offences which was set out in the Criminal Law Act 1977 and now appears in a slightly different form in the Magistrates' Courts Act 1980 (see also sch. 1 of the Interpretation Act 1978). That is, for the purposes of mode of trial, offences are classified into three types: summary offences, indictable offences and offences triable either way. Knowing that fact and the consequence of an offence coming into one class or the other is an essential part of understanding the criminal process and relevant to dealing with questions on how different offences are handled, from the point of view of what is the court of trial, what is the maximum penalty and what opportunities there are for an appeal. In the case of offences triable either way, their classification as such immediately gives rise to two further points: how the court of trial and mode of trial are to be selected and the special rules about sentencing in the event of the magistrates deciding their powers of sentencing are inadequate in a particular case after they have convicted the accused following a summary trial. What has just been said assumes a clear understanding of the concepts of summary trial and trial on indictment.

Beyond knowing this classification of offences by the Magistrates' Courts Act 1980 and the consequences referred to above, it should also be appreciated that there is scope here for using a knowledge of the rationale behind the classification of offences in questions about the nature of the English criminal justice system in general. For example, it may be useful in answering questions about the comparative efficiency of using the magistrates' courts rather than the Crown Courts to be able to point out the effects of the classification of offences on the distribution of the workloads of the two courts of trial respectively. The present classification is based on the recommendations of the James Committee on *The Distribution of Criminal Business between the Crown Court and the Magistrates' Courts* (Cmnd 6323, 1975). The result was the transfer of many offences to the category of 'summary only'. Such transfers on a large scale raise the whole question of the comparative quality of work achieved by the Crown Court and the magistrates' courts and the extent to which justice for the individual is to be made to give way to the pressures of expediency and cost. Further transfers are contained in the Criminal Justice Act 1988. There is an assumption of a greater likelihood of justice being done in the Crown Court than in the magistrates' courts. Faced with an overwhelming volume of work, the quality of justice in the Crown Court can be maintained by transferring some of that work elsewhere. Here the good student may be expected to comment on and question the in-built assumptions. Are there really no alternatives? Could not the machinery of the Crown Court be improved or the capacity of the Crown Court be increased? What will be the effect on the workload of the magistrates' courts? The arguments are neatly illustrated by the special treatment accorded to offences of criminal damage and the proposals for making theft a summary, only offence where the value of the stolen property does not exceed £20.

The whole question of the classification of offences is one which has its counterpart in our system of civil justice. That issue can be expressed as a search for a set of criteria by which to distinguish serious from less serious cases on the assumption that in a system with limited and finite resources it is justifiable to provide two sets of decision-making procedures, one rather more elaborate and deliberative than the other one. These are matters of great concern where the issue for the individual is his liberty, reputation and future livelihood and you should be armed with the arguments for and against making as many cases as possible come into the 'less serious category'. As the James Committee pointed out, society must choose between two conflicting issues: the right of the citizen to be tried by judge and jury on any charge of theft, however small the amount involved, and on the other hand the right, especially important to anyone defending a serious charge, to be tried as soon as possible. Let Lord Edmund-Davies, speaking in the Lords debate on the Criminal Law Bill, have the last word before we go into court to see how an accused fares there when he is brought before the court. So long as ' . . . people lose a lifetime's reputation for probity by a single action of dishonesty of a material triviality . . . small thefts remain offences which are serious in the eyes of all honest men'.

THE MAGISTRATES' COURT

Choice of Mode of Trial for Offences Triable Either Way

It will be apparent from the immediately foregoing remarks that in some quarters there is an opinion that the magistrates' courts can be further burdened with work and that there may be other opinions suggesting that the quality of justice may be already somewhat strained in those courts. Magistrates' courts and their work as a whole could well form the basis of a question on the criminal courts. Let us, therefore, pause and consider how best to handle information about the magistrates and their courts before proceeding with a more detailed analysis of the criminal process.

There are many ways in which to study the magistrates' courts; there have been historical studies of the office of justice of the peace and the survival of local jurisdictions. In the author's home town, which is one of the three places mentioned in the beggar's litany ('From Hull, Hell and Halifax, good Lord, deliver us') the local magistrates had a jurisdiction, until 1651, whereby cloth thieves caught within the parish and in possession of the stolen cloth were summarily tried, found guilty and beheaded by a gibbet, which was the prototype for the French guillotine. One of the blades used in the gibbet is still preserved in the local museum. Similarly, there have been sociological studies of all aspects of the magistrates' courts, and also what may be termed utilitarian studies of the environment and facilities of the courts and the effect these have on those who have to attend them. There has also been a Scrutiny report on the management of magistrates' courts. It is, however, a prerequisite for attempting examination questions of a historical or sociological nature to have some legal material relating to the courts which can then be set in the appropriate historical or sociological framework.

The best help that can be given to all students doing an English legal system course which includes a study of the magistrates' courts is to set out a structured way of arranging the material which will be presented in lectures, seminars and texts referred to in those classes. Thereafter, an indication can be given of some likely ways in which essays can be set, whether in examinations or as part of some form of assessment.

The magistrates' court is a local court with roots deep in English history. The business of the magistrates' court was originally conducted according to the old meaning of the word court, which simply signified a place where official and public business was transacted. It was the nature of the office of justice of the peace that was all-important. The justices were the local representatives of the Crown for all government purposes and as such their acts were subject to review by the royal prerogative exercised by the common law judges in the name of the Crown. As a court of law, the justices conducted summary trials and also sat as courts of quarter session to try more serious offences which were not sent to the assizes. The justices of the peace were and remain lay men and women. From the 16th century they conducted preliminary inquiries into all indictable offences.

In the course of the 19th century, with the passing of such statutes as the Summary Jurisdiction Act 1848 and the separation of the justices from their local government functions in town and country, the magistrates' courts began to take on their modern form. Because of the justices' involvement through watch committees with the administration of the new police forces, the courts presided over by the justices came in some places to be so closely identified with the police that they became known to the public, quite wrongly and inappropriately, as police courts.

At the present day, then, the magistrates' courts can be said still, with a few exceptions where there are stipendiary magistrates, to be local courts presided over by lay justices of the peace with strong local connections and a local jurisdiction. Their principal work is a criminal jurisdiction over minor offences. They have a limited civil jurisdiction, principally in family law matters, and they retain some administrative functions especially in connection with licensing. They are subject to judicial review by the superior courts. Such a statement may serve as a brief general description of the work of the magistrates' courts.

The next stage in the analysis is to examine the courts with reference to their constituent elements as set out in the statutes establishing them and governing their operation. The constituent elements of the magistrates' courts would appear to be as follows:

(a)   Constitution. The Magistrates' Courts Act 1980, s. 121, establishes the constitution of the court by reference to the people sitting (normally two justices) and the place of sitting (in a petty-sessional court house). For the office of JP, see Justices of Peace Act 1979.

Note: In times past, one of the many objections to the conduct of the justices was that they purported to exercise their jurisdiction in a variety of places, including public houses and their own drawing-rooms.

(b)   Criminal jurisdiction and procedure. The issue of process, committal proceedings/transfer of proceedings, summary trial, selection of mode of trial in the case of offences triable either way.

(c)   Powers in respect of offenders. General restriction on powers of magistrates to impose imprisonment (limited to 6 months in any one charge or not more than 12 months in aggregate); maximum penalties and fines; power to commit to Crown Court for sentence; limits on compensation orders.

(d) Civil jurisdiction and procedure. Procedure by way of complaint, recovery of debts and domestic proceedings.

(e) Enforcement powers.

(f) Witnesses and evidence.

(g) Appeals. Appeals to Crown Court and by case stated to High Court. Challenge also by judicial review under Supreme Court Act 1981 and Rules of the Supreme Court, Ord. 53.

All of those elements, except where noted above, are set out in the Magistrates' Courts Act 1980 and the 'arrangement of sections' at the front of a copy of the Act will be found to be a useful aid in thinking about the work of these courts as a whole.

When it comes to an evaluation of the role and work of the magistrates' courts you should bear the following matters in mind. With a view to both increasing efficiency and avoidance of unnecessary hardship and inconvenience to accuseds and witnesses, a number of changes have been introduced in the past 30 years or so. These include the possibility of accepting *certain* guilty pleas in the absence of the accused and the increasing reliance at all stages of the criminal process on evidence in written form and a greater openness in the use of evidence generally; particularly where the prosecution is under a duty to disclose evidence it does not intend to rely on itself at the trial.

When a person stands before the magistrates charged with an offence triable either way, it is the first duty of the magistrates to determine the mode of trial. The procedure for doing so, which is set out in ss. 18 to 25 of the Magistrates' Courts Act 1980 (as amended by the Criminal Justice and Public Order Act 1994), is a favourite with examiners who are intent upon getting the student to show mastery of a relatively intricate procedure. This part of the criminal process will figure in both problem questions and essay questions, especially the latter if they are designed to enable the student to show an appreciation of the distinction between serious cases and non-serious cases and the difficulties attached to deciding that issue in individual instances of a crime such as theft, which, depending upon the circumstances, can be a trivial offence or one of the most serious.

From an analytical point of view the principal features to note about this procedure for selecting the appropriate mode of trial are the following (taken directly from the wording of the Act):

(a) The procedure applies where the accused is 18 years or more of age.

(b) The court must make the decision before any evidence in the case is given. *Note*: Distinguish evidence from representations about the circumstances of the alleged offence; see below.

(c) The decision must normally be reached in the presence of the accused.

(d)   The decision may be taken by a single justice, but in that case a single justice may not proceed to summary trial.

(e)   Before reaching a decision the court must hear representations from the prosecution and the accused as to whether the case appears more suitable for summary trial or for trial on indictment, after the charge is written down and read to the accused.

(f)   The matters to be considered are: the nature of the case; whether the circumstances make the offence a serious one; whether the powers of punishment of the magistrates would be adequate in the event of conviction after a summary trial; and any other circumstance relevant to the decision.

(g)   If the magistrates decide summary trial is more suitable then, before proceeding (which may be after an adjournment) with a summary trial, should the accused consent to such, the magistrates must explain the decision to the accused in *ordinary language* and warn him of the power to commit for sentence to the Crown Court if he is tried summarily.

Note: It is worthwhile pointing out in an answer to a question on this procedure, that the power to commit for sentence is exercisable after the magistrates have heard of the accused's character and antecedents following conviction. They will not have this information at the earlier stage when they consider mode of trial (see (f) above). The reason for this arises out of the application of the well-known principle that one is presumed innocent until proved guilty (see below on trial on indictment for rules of evidence designed to protect the accused from unfair prejudice before conviction).

(h)   The accused must then give his consent to be tried summarily and if he consents the magistrates proceed to the summary trial, otherwise they will continue to inquire into the case as examining justices and proceed with a view to transferring the proceedings to the Crown Court (see below).

(i)   If the court considers that the case is more suitable for trial on indictment the court shall tell the accused that that is the case and proceed as examining justices with a view to transferring the case for trial in the Crown Court.

Note: The accused has no further say in the matter if the choice is for trial on indictment. The reason is that trial on indictment before a judge and jury is regarded as the best form of protection of the accused's interests. Also, someone must make the final decision.

(j)   If the accused is represented by counsel, or a solicitor, the court may carry out the procedures for determining mode of trial in the absence of the accused. If and only if the accused's consent is given or signified the magistrates may, if they so decide, proceed to summary trial. Otherwise they must proceed as with a view to transfer for trial.

Note: In the event of proceeding to summary trial the warning set out in (g) above cannot be given. Presumably, the person representing the accused is expected to explain the position to the accused. The possibility of proceeding in the absence of the accused is especially useful in cases where the accused is other than a natural person, such as, for example, a limited company facing charges under the Health and Safety at Work etc. Act 1974.

(k)   The court has a power to switch from summary trial to proceedings of transfer for trial and vice versa.

Note: This power is exercisable only where *no* evidence has been given *for* the accused. The power is also subject, in the case of a switch to summary trial, to the requirements in (g) and (h) above being satisfied.

It is to be noted that nothing in the criminal justice system is beyond question. In July 1995, the Home Secretary issued a consultation paper concerning *Mode of Trial*. In this paper it was suggested, *inter alia*, that an accused should not have an absolute right to elect for jury trial and that certain offences, including 'minor theft', be reclassified in order to permit trial by magistrates only. Such suggestions show a redrawing of the balance between the rights of accused persons and the perceived need to make the trial system more efficient.

We shall now assume that the accused has been charged with an offence triable only on indictment, or has been told that the offence with which he is charged will be tried on indictment, or has elected to be tried on indictment. In any of those cases, the magistrates must proceed, as examining justices and conduct committal proceedings with a view to transferring the proceedings to the Crown Court for trial.

COMMITTAL PROCEEDINGS AND TRANSFER OF PROCEEDINGS

At the time of writing committal proceedings are still operative pending the introduction of the transfer of trial procedures. It is unclear when this change will take place and therefore both procedures are included.

At this stage of the process an accused is subject to committal proceedings, whereby magistrates ascertain whether or not the prosecution have established a case for the accused to answer. If the prosecution case is defective, e.g., there is no evidence to prove an ingredient of the offence alleged, then the accused may be discharged.

Over a number of years it was considered that the purpose of committal proceedings was not being fulfilled in reality, that is the proceedings failed to filter cases effectively. Also, in many cases the process of committal had become a formality, with the accused being committed for trial following a 'paper' committal rather than the 'old style' committal with a full hearing. A perceived advantage of the latter form of committal was that it provided the defence with an opportunity of hearing and testing the prosecution evidence, without having to reveal the case for the accused. However, the Royal Commission on Criminal Justice pointed out that 'old style' committals accounted for only 7 per cent of all committals.

This jurisdiction is abolished by the Criminal Justice and Public Order Act 1994, s. 44 and is to be replaced by transfer of trial proceedings. The new procedure of transfer of trial still allows the defence an opportunity to apply to have the case dismissed on the basis of the prosecution having insufficient evidence. Apart from this process the transfer of proceedings is automatic. The procedure requires the prosecution to serve on the magistrates' court and the accused a notice of his case. This consists of the charge or charges against the accused and a set of the documents containing the evidence (including oral evidence) on which the charge or charges is or are based.

As with all innovations, you need to be alert to how the new transfer of trial proceedings are working. Has the change made rectified the previous defects? Have new problems emerged? It can be readily seen that such a development may give rise to an examination question, or indeed be incorporated in a more general answer to a question about the effectiveness of recent reforms of the criminal justice system. Once again you need to be aware of the background to the change and any subsequent comment on the operation of it.

You should also know of the restrictions that exist on the reporting of committal proceedings and which will exist for transfer of trial proceedings, and the reasons for the introduction of these restrictions as part of the machinery of justice seeking to ensure a fair trial for the accused before an unbiased and impartial jury.

Before leaving the pre-trial stages note should be taken that in criminal cases there are now extensive requirements for the disclosure of evidence and other material by the prosecution. With the exception of alibi evidence (see Criminal Justice Act 1967, s. 11) and other minor defences in certain specific offences, the defence can reserve their case and make no disclosures at all. Whether to do so is always wise is another matter. There is also provision in some criminal proceedings for a pre-trial review as occurs in civil proceedings. Knowing the facts can provide good points of comparison between civil and criminal cases and procedures, also it can be pointed out that the apparent imbalance between prosecution and defence in criminal cases, compared with the balance of openness sought between plaintiff and defendant in civil proceedings, can be justified in order to protect the accused's otherwise vulnerable position. There are counter-arguments and proposals designed to prevent the 'springing' of defences at trial. So far, these arguments have prevailed only in the case of alibi evidence. However, note the related issue of the possibility of adverse inferences being drawn from an accused's failure to mention facts, relied on ultimately in his defence, when being questioned or charged. This represents an important shift in the balance between prosecution and defence in a criminal trial.

The final point to be made about the pre-trial stages is that on committing a person for trial on indictment/transferring trial proceedings the magistrates must comply with s. 7 of the Magistrates' Courts Act 1980 (in the latter case as amended by the Criminal Justice and Public Order Act 1994) and select an appropriate venue or place of trial. Matters to be considered are the nature of the offence, expeditious hearing of the case, and the convenience of the defence, the prosecution and the witnesses. The first of these matters is affected by the classification of offences tried on indictment by reference to the judges who may try particular classes of offence at the Crown Court. The student's concern with s. 7 of the Magistrates' Courts Act 1980 is the bearing it has on the question of the administration of the Crown Court in the circuit system and the principle that so far as possible there should be a flexible use of judicial manpower in accordance with the recommendations of the Beeching Commission (Cmnd 4153, 1969).

Special Arrangements for Fraud Cases

Long and complex fraud cases have created problems at several stages of the criminal process. In response to these problems the Roskill Committee on Fraud Trials was set up. Following its report, modifications in the arrangements for the trial of serious or complex fraud cases were made by the Criminal Justice Act 1987. Two particular points should be noted: the curtailment of committal proceedings and the formal arrangements for 'preparatory hearings', designed to identify the main issues and to expedite the hearing before the jury. These arrangements are set out in ss. 7 to 10 of the Criminal Justice Act 1987, supplemented by a set of rules (SI 1988 No. 1690). You should be prepared to consider the following matters:

(a)   why fraud trials were selected for this special treatment, and

(b)   the long-term effect of these arrangements on pre-trial proceedings generally.

SUMMARY TRIAL AND TRIAL ON INDICTMENT

Summary trial and trial on indictment may be taken together because they together constitute arrangements for the hearing of criminal cases, and it is possible to make some preliminary comments that apply to all criminal trials, whether summary or on indictment. In English law, only courts with a criminal jurisdiction have power to impose punishment on offenders. (To remind yourself of the significance of the term 'court' in the English legal system generally, refer back to chapter 3.)

Basic features, which will form the background of your study and examination preparation in the area of the criminal trial, include all of the following. The procedure at trial is adversarial and that is closely connected with the question of the burden of proof. The burden of proof rests on the prosecution, because of the 'golden thread' running through the English criminal justice system that a person is innocent until proven guilty. In a criminal trial proof of the accused's guilt must be established beyond reasonable doubt. Every student knows so much. As a good student you should know also about the exceptional cases, with examples, where the burden of proof is placed wholly or partly on the accused, as this will be useful in dealing with questions about the extent to which the criminal process closely reflects such principles as that which presumes innocence until guilt is proved. Also, develop an understanding of the significance of 'reasonable' doubt as opposed to 'no' doubt and the effect this has on the rate of convictions.

In both summary trial and trial on indictment a distinction is drawn between law and fact, though in the two forms of trial this distinction takes different forms in practice. Finally, in any sort of trial, the finding of guilt or innocence is a finding according to law, and that means not only the correct application of the rules of substantive law, but also the following of correct rules of procedure and evidence. It is well known that the best of cases on the merits can be lost through procedural errors or for lack of admissible and cogent evidence.

Turning now to summary trial, what can be expected of the examiner on this topic specifically? That is a difficult matter, because, as Smith and Bailey say in their book, *The Modern English Legal System,* not a great deal has been written on summary trial in the magistrates' court. However, there are at least two matters which deserve attention. The first of these arises out of the very large number of cases handled by the magistrates and the measures adopted to deal with such a large volume, particularly the procedure under s. 12 of the Magistrates' Courts Act 1980 whereby they may receive certain *guilty* pleas in the absence of the accused (note the extension of this process under s. 45 of the Criminal Justice and Public Order Act 1994). The volume of cases and frequency of sitting in a local jurisdiction may also have a considerable bearing on the impression sometimes given, that in contested cases with a not-guilty plea, the magistrates' are pro-police. The comparatively low chance of an acquittal in the magistrates' court may have as much to do with the number of accused who are not legally represented. A watch must be kept, therefore, for information coming through the media as well as legal periodicals, about the impact of such schemes as the duty solicitor schemes under the Legal Aid Acts 1974 and 1982, and the general availability of legal assistance at the police station as well as at trial. Indeed, this latter scheme has been the subject of some criticism. See the Royal Commission on Criminal Justice 1993.

The other matter worth detailed attention is the constitution of magistrates' courts and the role and status of the justices' clerk. Much can be said, from the viewpoint of the place of magistrates in society generally, about their mode of appointment and social background, and most textbooks, as well as specialist works, deal with this aspect in some detail. Different courses, it must be repeated, lay different emphasis on such matters as the effect of the social composition of a bench of magistrates on the rate of acquittals in their court and the type of sentence apparently most favoured by different benches. Statistics are often presented in the books, illustrating this theme, especially with reference to the treatment of first offenders. (Consider why, for example, it has been thought necessary to introduce such provisions as those which restrict generally the power of the court to send a person to prison for the first time.)

Every student must know how magistrates come to be appointed by the Lord Chancellor and the terms of their appointment. Special rules about magistrates sitting in youth courts are also essential knowledge. In the execution of their daily tasks in dealing with summary offences, the way in which magistrates deal with issues of fact and law differ markedly from the way in which these issues are handled by a judge sitting alone and by a judge sitting with a jury, and these differences can become useful points to make in answers to questions seeking an evaluation of different models of the adversarial trial. Sometimes, for example, a question may seek a comparative knowledge of the composition of the courts in different legal systems or even in different parts of our own legal system. What, for example, are the virtues of trial by judge alone compared with trial by judge and jury? When is it appropriate to have lay assessors, or what might be the occasion for introducing into English law the so-called composite tribunal found in some Continental systems?

It helps in answering these questions to know that magistrates decide both fact and law. In most cases the magistrates do not make explicit their findings of fact or the reasons for their decision. Compare this with the judgment in a county court case and the requirement that, if asked to do so, a tribunal must give reasons for its decisions. As to questions of law, you must understand the role of the justices' clerk in advising his magistrates and the care he must take to see that the decision on the law not only is, but is seen to be that of the magistrates. This is summarised in the *Practice Direction (Justices: Clerk to Court)* [1981] 1 WLR 1163 issued by the Lord Chief Justice with the concurrence of the President of the Family Division. The emphasis is now on the need to see that the magistrates receive proper advice. Those are the main points which usually arise in examinations with reference to the magistrates' court as a court of summary trial constituted in accordance with the Magistrates' Courts Act 1980.

In the case of trial on indictment, there are three areas of investigation which deserve particular attention. These are:

(a)   Outline procedure at trial and especially the verdict.

(b)   The jury.
(c)   Some rules of evidence.

The essential background to these three areas is, of course, the fact that the Crown Court is given exclusive jurisdiction over matters relating to trial on indictment, by the Supreme Court Act 1981, s. 46. The constitution of the Crown Court is set out in s. 8 of the same Act and the mode of trial and procedure, that is, trial by judge and jury, is preserved by s. 79 of the Act. Against that background it is useful to be able to deploy an outline knowledge of procedure in the context of questions relating to the efficiency and fairness of the system as a whole and the following particular points should be noted: the order of events, especially the significance of the defence having the last word, the features to look for in the judge's summing up, as this has a bearing on a high proportion of subsequent appeals, and the taking of the verdict and subsequent conviction, following a guilty verdict. More will be said about the jury's verdict shortly. At this stage it is important to note that the jury may be advised that it can convict of alternative offences to those charged in the indictment. This power is not available to the magistrates, although in both trial on indictment and summary trial the prosecution may agree to accept a plea to a lesser charge. This often comes about as a result of plea bargaining, which is a nice neat topic which can be relied upon to produce questions from time to time. If plea bargaining has figured in your course then it is worthwhile preparing some material on the subject. The ground rules of this practice are the starting-point. They can be found in the case of *R v Turner* [1970] 2 QB 321. In the recent Criminal Justice and Public Order Act 1994, s. 48, the practice of a sentence discount being given as a result of a gulity plea was put on a statutory footing.

The issue of plea bargaining, including the possibility of charge bargaining, is one of justice versus administrative convenience. Justice in this context means justice to both the victim — the accused should be charged and sentenced according to the gravity of the offence — and to the accused — pressure should not be exerted so that an accused pleads guilty to an offence he did not commit. Administrative convenience encompasses the saving of resources and time, a recurring theme when considering the criminal justice system.

Thought should be given to the merits and demerits of the practice as a matter of ethics. In this way, material prepared specifically with a view to answering a question on plea bargaining will be useful also in connection with other matters of an ethical nature such as the use of informers, or certain rules of evidence which render evidence against co-accuseds inadmissible, which, taken together, form part of a more wide-ranging enquiry into the ethical standards of the English criminal trial and the difference between justice and justice according to law.

The last point I would mention is to look carefully at the role of the judge in a trial on indictment and the ways in which he can influence the outcome of the trial, even though there is a jury who are supposedly the final arbiters of questions of fact.

The English jury has been called the bulwark of the liberties of the subject and is regarded by many as the 'jewel in the crown' of the English criminal trial process. On the other hand, the jury has its critics both as to its general usefulness and as to the details of its working. Add to that, that a lot has been written about the jury (the Contempt of Court Act 1981 makes it almost impossible to investigate the actual workings of juries in real cases) and you have a perfect recipe for examination questions. Once again, the starting-point for preparation of material on the jury must be a thorough knowledge of the basic law relating to juries, set out in the Juries Act 1974. To that must be added a critical awareness of current controversies relating to the working of the jury system and legislative changes, such as the removal of the right of peremptory challenge altogether.

Not so long ago it would have been safe to predict that a question on the jury would be connected with the theme that the English jury was 'middle class, male, middle minded and middle aged'. Reforms in the qualifications and eligibility for jury service in the 1970s may have reduced the importance of that theme, but contemporary conditions, not least with respect to efforts to combat sexual and racial discrimination, have produced new material for study. It is apparent though that a thorough understanding of the basic principles upon which jury trial is founded will provide the necessary insight in order to discuss contemporary problems.

For example, the principle that the jury is to be selected at random may be used to test the reasons for abolishing peremptory challenge and propositions seeking to justify the practice of jury vetting. This latter practice comes up for discussion from time to time as an examination topic and, therefore, the Attorney-General's guidelines on jury checks (1980) 72 Cr App R 14, and the cases of *R v Sheffield Crown Court (ex parte Brownlow)* [1980] QB 530 and *R v Mason* [1981] QB 881 will repay careful attention. (*The Brownlow case* also illustrates the position of the Crown Court as part of the Supreme Court. As such the Crown Court is not amenable to the process of judicial review.)

Another basic principle of trial by jury, that the accused is entitled to be tried by his peers or equals, is also at the root of some contemporary discussions about the composition of the jury. Consideration of this principle leads to a discussion of whether jurors should be subject to a literacy test and whether certain cases justify taking steps to ensure that there is a balanced representation of the sexes on a jury or that a jury is not racially biased in its composition. This principle is also the starting-point for a critical appraisal of the proposals of the Roskill Committee on fraud trials as they appeared in the Criminal Justice Act 1987.

Recent concern over the matters just referred to should not obscure the continuing concern with the fundamental question of whether juries do in fact return the 'right' verdicts. You should remember that, on occasions, justice has been seen to be done where, at the time of a trial of some notoriety, a jury has asserted its independence (as established in *Bushel's case* in 1670) and given a verdict which did not seem to be supported by the evidence given at the trial. Nevertheless, proper attention must be paid to the views of those who feel that the jury system contributes to their general feeling of unease, that far too many guilty people are in fact being acquitted. There are other contributory factors at work in the opinion of those who take this view, which will be mentioned below. However, before leaving the jury mention must be made of the introduction of majority verdicts in 1967. The taking of a majority verdict is subject to strict procedural rules and juries must still try to reach unanimous verdicts in the first place. Majority verdicts were introduced as a response to fears of interference with juries which could lead either to a wrong acquittal or to a mistrial; leading either to the case being dropped or the expense of a new trial.

The different views about the proper role of the jury in holding the balance between justice and mercy are well summarised as the narrow and broad approaches in Smith and Bailey's *The Modern English Legal System*. As those authors point out, it is for each one of you as student and citizen to make up your minds about what constitutes a 'right' verdict. It is for the present author to point out that before you disclose your choice to the examiner you must be prepared to show that your preference is based on principle and fact and is not merely a set of assertions based on prejudice. In tackling a question which challenges trial by jury as an appropriate mode of trial in cases of serious crime it may be advantageous to compare the history of trial by jury in civil cases. In civil cases in England, it is only in those special categories of case preserved by the Supreme Court Act 1981 that there is a qualified right to jury trial. Trial by judge alone is the norm. Why this should be so and how it has come about is an instructive comparison when considering the arguments for reducing the number of criminal cases to be tried by jury. The statement of principle in *Ward v James* [1966] 1 QB 273, although it has been questioned in subsequent cases, may be taken as setting out some criteria not only for the continuance of jury trial in civil cases but also as a set of criteria for defending trial by jury in criminal cases. These criteria refer to issues of credibility, honour, integrity and reputation of the parties (in civil cases). Surely, issues of this sort can be used as the basis of a defence of the use of the jury in criminal cases as well, where these issues may relate to the witnesses as well as to the accused. The last part of this consideration of the criminal process, namely, appeals and judicial review, is, so far as jury trials are concerned, a follow-on from the question of whether the jury has reached the 'right' verdict, or at least one that is not 'unsafe or unsatisfactory'. But before leaving the trial stage of the criminal process it is necessary to take account of certain aspects of the law of evidence, especially with reference to the protection afforded to the accused. The extent of the protection afforded by the law of evidence is the other main factor which gives rise to the feeling, referred to above, that perhaps the desire to see that no innocent person is convicted has been pursued to the extent that too many guilty persons are being acquitted.

Courses differ greatly in the amount of detail they require students to know and to be able to handle about the law of criminal evidence and procedure. In some courses, the English legal system component includes, logically, the law of evidence and procedure from the time of arrest up to the verdict, whether after a summary trial or trial on indictment. Whatever the stance adopted by individual courses, it is essential for an understanding of the criminal process as it works at the moment, to know sufficient about the law of evidence and procedure to be able to make an informed judgment about the contribution of the law of criminal evidence towards making the English criminal legal process what it is. Especially, this applies to a judgment, which you may be called upon to make, on whether there is an even-handed approach to maintaining a balance between the interests of society as a whole and the interest of accused persons. One might attempt to make a balance sheet by taking a number of the features of our criminal evidence and procedure and assigning them to one side or the other, where the dividing line is whether something works for or against the advantage or protection of the accused.

Beginning at the investigation stage of the proceedings, account must be taken of the Judges' Rules and their replacement by the Police and Criminal Evidence Act 1984. Arising out of the investigation stage there is the attitude taken by the law to confessions. The attitude is slightly ambiguous in that, even if it is shown that a confession is improperly obtained, nevertheless it may be admitted at the discretion of the court.

At the trial stage, the spotlight is on the position of the accused as a witness. It is well to remember the history of the law's attitude to allowing the accused to give evidence as this illustrates changing views on what constitutes reliable evidence. At the present day the accused is in a privileged position as a witness. He is not compellable but may choose to give evidence. However, should the accused decide not to give evidence then the court or jury may draw adverse inferences from such silence. There are special rules designed to exclude unreliable evidence in the case of evidence by spouses and co-accuseds. Often the effect of these rules is to give protection to the accused by excluding otherwise cogent and relevant evidence. Special care is taken nowadays before admitting evidence of identification. On the other hand the accused has to give notice of alibi evidence and in only a few cases is corroboration of the testimony of a single witness necessary for a conviction.

Only in certain cases is the character of the accused an issue to be tried. Otherwise the accused's previous record is not to be disclosed to the court before conviction, unless the accused puts his character in issue by attacks on the character of a prosecution witness. Finally, some more general aspects of evidence and procedure should be noted. The evidence given must be relevant and not offend against the rule against hearsay, which is strictly applied in criminal cases. The conduct of the case by prosecution and defence is also important, for the prosecution's duty is to put the evidence and the law before the court in a fair manner and not to strive to the utmost to obtain a conviction, whereas the accused is entitled to the best possible defence from his lawyer. These points will form the basis of an answer to most questions which will be encountered dealing with matters of evidence and procedure in criminal cases. It goes almost without saying that an accurate knowledge of the rules referred to above is essential before any discussion of the merits and demerits of the law of criminal evidence and procedure is possible.

However fair and just you find the procedural rules of criminal investigation and trial to be, it remains true that mistakes will be made on questions of both fact and law. The modern law recognises that this is so and provides elaborate machinery for the review of decisions of the magistrates' courts and certain decisions of the Crown Court, and for appeals in all cases. Therefore, before concluding this chapter it is necessary to look at the provision made for judicial review and appeals following criminal trials at all levels of the English legal system. Once again it will be convenient to deal with all items relating to review and appeals in the criminal process together and to open the discussion with a few words about review and appeals generally before dealing specifically with criminal appeals.

CHALLENGING MAGISTRATES' DECISIONS, APPEALS FROM THE CROWN COURT TO THE COURT OF APPEAL, APPEALS TO THE HOUSE OF LORDS, REFERENCES AND THE PREROGATIVE OF MERCY

The four items appearing as the heading to this section constitute the procedures provided in the English legal system for the review of and appeal against decisions taken by trial courts in the administration of criminal justice. Before proceeding to an analysis of those procedures it is necessary to ensure that you understand the basic distinction between the power to review and the consequences of a successful review, and an exercise of a right of appeal. Rights of appeal are all based on statutory grounds and are in substitution for the common law procedures based on writs of error which previously lay to courts of superior jurisdiction.

As the procedures for both review and appeal as they exist in the legal system as a whole, and in particular in the case of criminal jurisdictions, are complex, they provide an admirable opportunity for examiners to test students' skills of analysis, comparison and succinct description. Quite often this is achieved by setting problem questions in the context of opportunities for appeal following the trial stage. Those questions sometimes require the ability to follow the fortunes of a party who has lost his case at trial and sometimes they require a comparison of alternative routes of appeal, as, for example, a comparison of the rights of appeal following conviction of an offence triable either way, when the accused is tried either by the magistrates or in the Crown Court. That being so, it is an obvious first step in mastering the complexities of the appeal procedures to adopt a pattern of enquiry that will work in every case. As Smith and Bailey point out in their book, *The Modern English Legal System*, there are a number of factors which must be taken into account when considering *any* legal procedure for redressing a grievance:

(a) Who can institute an appeal (or seek review)?
(b) Can the appeal be brought as of right or only by the leave of a court?
(c) What are the permissible grounds for an appeal?
(d) What is the time-limit within which an appeal must be brought?
(e) To which court or tribunal does the appeal lie?
(f) What material may the appellate body consider?
(g) Who may appear as parties on the appeal?
(h) What are the powers of the appellate court?

Let us now begin to apply this set of key factors to the system of appeals in the administration of criminal justice in England and Wales. First, account has to be taken of the variables involved. These are:

(a) There are two courts of trial: the magistrates and the Crown Court.
(b) The 'mistakes' to be put right may be mistakes of fact or mistakes of law.
(c) The grievance may arise out of the fact of conviction or the sentence imposed.
(d) Either party, defence or prosecution may have a grievance.
(e) Is there a further right of appeal?

This list produces at least eight possibilities to consider in answering a question which ranges at large over the availability of appeals in criminal cases, not taking account of the possibility of reviews. Before attempting to apply these variables to Smith and Bailey's eight factors which must always be considered, it may be said that there is at least one general principle (which may prove to have exceptions) which will assist in coming to the right conclusion in the event of having to rely on common sense (that is a polite way of saying 'guesswork') rather than actual knowledge. That is the principle that an accused should not be put in 'double jeopardy'. Generally speaking then that should predispose you to decide against saying that the prosecution can appeal against an acquittal or that an appellate court can order a new trial. Do beware, however, that, useful as they are, principles are not universally applicable and they have their exceptions. For example, the Court of Appeal (Criminal Division) has the power to order a new trial under the Criminal Appeal Act 1968, s. 7. This power has been extended by the Criminal Justice Act 1988, s. 43. A further general point is that appeals on law are usually as of right. (Note, however, the changes made by the Criminal Appeal Act 1995, whereby, for example, an appeal from the Crown Court against conviction on any ground requires the leave of the Court of Appeal or a certificate from the trial judge.)

Having worked through your lecture notes and read your textbooks what more can be done to meet the examiner on equal terms in this matter of criminal appeals? Consider each of the factors in turn against the appropriate variable and then write down your comments. These will be, for instance, why you think there are differences between appeals against conviction following summary trial compared with conviction following trial on indictment; why one should be as of right and the other be as of right only on points of law but need leave if there is any question of fact. Again, why should there be three distinct procedures available following summary trial, appeal to the Crown Court, appeal by way of case stated to the Divisional Court, and judicial review? The answers to these questions lie in the fact that the magistrates' court is a court of inferior jurisdiction, together with the important practical matter of the differing volumes of work in the two courts of trial and the effect that has on their procedures and handling of cases generally.

Taking some of Smith and Bailey's factors and applying them to the variables involved in summary trials and trials on indictment respectively, leads to the following statements:

Who Can Institute an Appeal or Review?

In the case of summary trials, the Magistrates' Courts Act 1980, s. 108, permits any person convicted to appeal against sentence and/or conviction (if he pleaded not guilty). In the case of trials in the Crown Court, the Criminal Appeal Act 1968 permits a person convicted to appeal against conviction and also against sentence. Following an appeal to the Crown Court from a magistrates' court, there is a further right of appeal by way of case stated to the Divisional Court of the Queen's Bench Division. Either prosecution or defence may so appeal.

Any person who is aggrieved by a decision of magistrates can require the magistrates to state a case for the opinion of the High Court (Magistrates'

Courts Act 1980, s. 111). There is a further right of appeal direct to the House of Lords.

Either party to summary proceedings may in an appropriate case seek judicial review.

In relation to trials on indictment, an appeal against conviction or sentence may be made by the defendant to the Court of Appeal, Criminal Division.

Where there is a *further* right of appeal conferred, for example, from the Divisional Court to the House of Lords, or the Court of Appeal to the House of Lords, either party to the original appeal may exercise the further right of appeal.

Section 36 of the Criminal Justice Act 1988 permits the Attorney-General to refer cases of allegedly 'too lenient' sentences to the Court of Appeal.

Can the Appeal be Brought as of Right or Only by the Leave of a Court?

Following summary proceedings, appeals are as of right to the Crown Court and by way of case stated to the Divisional Court of the Queen's Bench Division, but an application for judicial review is subject to the normal rules of application, by way of seeking leave.

On the other hand, when there is an appeal following trial at the Crown Court, leave to appeal is always needed except in the case of an appeal on a point of law alone (see Criminal Appeal Act 1968, ss. 1 and 9), but note the changes made by s. 1 of the Criminal Appeal Act 1995.

Appeals to the House of Lords always require leave.

What are the Permissible Grounds of Appeal?

Appeals to the Crown Court from the magistrates are not dependent upon any specific ground being established, and the hearing at the Crown Court is a full rehearing of the case. Appeals by way of case stated are by their very nature limited to appeals on points of law. Judicial review is dependent upon showing one of the established grounds for judicial review exists, with reference to the exercise of their jurisdiction by the magistrates.

Following conviction in the Crown Court, the grounds of appeal are more circumscribed, in that the appeal must be on a point of law or a question of fact or against sentence. Furthermore, the Criminal Appeal Act 1968, s. 2, sets out an *exhaustive* list of the grounds for allowing an appeal against conviction, together with a proviso for dismissing an appeal if it would otherwise be allowed, in the event that the Court of Appeal thinks that no miscarriage of justice has actually occurred. This section has been extensively modified by s. 2 of the Criminal Appeal Act 1995, which opens up the possibility of a question requiring comparison of the two provisions.

Lack of space forbids detailed working out of the other factors and variables in a similar way. However, students who take the trouble to do so will find that, at the end of all eight factors, they have a comprehensive guide to tackling virtually any question of a descriptive and comparative nature that the examiner chooses to set. Whilst a look at a number of different institutions' examination papers shows a preference for that type of question in this area of study, you should also be prepared for questions requiring an evaluation of the appeal process as it currently exists and operates.

Obviously, there are going to be matters of topical interest from time to time, such as the controversy over miscarriages of justice. Over and above these topical questions there are several more enduring questions on which good students will always be able to produce at least the standard comment. A clue to the more long-standing issues in the appellate process may be found in a reconsideration of the objectives which appeal and review procedures seek to attain, the administration of justice generally and criminal justice in particular. These may be said to be:

(a)   To correct mistakes made in deciding questions of fact and law.
(b)   To achieve consistency in sentencing.
(c)   To settle doubtful questions of law.
(d)   To maintain a balance between the claims of the liberty of the individual and the claims of society.

When you look at questions of an evaluative nature about the system of criminal appeals against these objectives you can begin to see the reasons for some of the features of our criminal appeal system and can begin also to form a critical judgment of the system and some of its individual features. For example, the role of the House of Lords becomes understandable if it is seen as having a primary concern with settling doubtful questions of law, though this does not preclude criticism of the way it discharges its role. Again, the fourth objective sheds light on the reasons why in so many instances leave is required before an appeal may be brought. Related to the fourth objective is the historic fear of the bringing of frivolous appeals. In times past, these were discouraged by giving the appellate court the power to increase sentences and to disallow time spent in custody before the appeal as part of a sentence. To summarise: evaluation of criminal appeals depends upon a consideration of the present rules of the system and their history, in the context of the objectives of the appellate process in criminal cases.

The criminal appeals process remains topical in the light of defects identified in cases such as the Birmingham Six and the Guildford Four and the remedies proposed by the Royal Commission on Criminal Justice. It was recommended by the Royal Commission that the Home Secretary's power to refer cases to the Court of Appeal should be replaced by a process whereby alleged miscarriages of justice would be reviewed by a new body, the Criminal Cases Review Commission. This has now been enacted in the Criminal Appeal Act 1995, ss. 3 and 8–25 (at the time of writing the Act has not been brought into force). The establishment of such a body, its terms of reference, powers and how it might operate, are of great interest to students of the English legal system and, no doubt, will form the basis of examination questions.

Initially questions may be directed to a comparison between the old and new systems and the extent to which the weaknesses of the old system have been addressed by the 1995 Act. Ultimately, questions will arise as to how the Criminal Cases Review Commission is operating in practice.

The following points concerning the Criminal Cases Review Commission may be noted:

(a) The Commission is to consist of 11 members, of whom at least one third are to be legally qualified and at least two thirds must be persons who have knowledge or experience of any aspect of the criminal justice system. There is also the possibility of lay persons being appointed.

(b) A conviction or sentence imposed on an accused or on a defendant following trial on indictment or summary trial may be referred to the Court of Appeal. Such referrals are to be treated as if they were appeals under s. 1 of the Criminal Appeal Act 1968 (as amended) or s. 108 of the Magistrates' Courts Act 1980, respectively.

(c) It is not surprising that a reference from the Commission may be made only if an appeal has already failed, or leave to appeal has been refused.

(d) Generally the Commission will refer a case only if it considers, *inter alia*, that there is a real possibility that the conviction, verdict, finding or sentence would not be upheld were the reference to be made (see also s. 13(1)(b)). In exceptional circumstances the Commission may refer even if this criterion or those in (c) above have not been satisfied.

Of great potential significance is the insertion of s. 23A in the Criminal Appeal Act 1968, allowing the Court of Appeal on *an appeal against conviction* (obviously following trial on indictment) to direct the Commission to investigate and report on any matter appearing to the Court to be relevant to the determination of the cases. The important point is that this investigation relates to the initial appeal. The Court of Appeal need not rely solely upon the arguments and evidence presented by the parties, but may initiate a report and use it in determining the appeal. This represents a departure from the adversarial process and the introduction of, at least in part, an inquisitorial procedure.

It is now time to consider how to target your efforts in examination preparation for this part of the syllabus. As was suggested towards the beginning of this chapter, the criminal justice system and the criminal process form an important part of all legal systems courses dealing with legal institutions. The administration of criminal justice is a vast subject in itself, but in English legal system courses at first-year level it merits possibly two out of nine or ten questions on an examination paper. How then to prepare the material in a relevant way so as to be able to cope with those two questions, whatever they may be?

This chapter has concentrated on the analytical approach but has brought out also the possibilities for arranging the basic materials in a variety of ways. This will help in identifying probable questions and the requirements of answers to them without the need for recourse to the cruder methods of question spotting and that sort of selective learning and revision which, in the last analysis, is pure gambling. However, in the case of the criminal process there is further help available.

Most English people are aware of a number of aphorisms of an almost mythical nature which contain within themselves basic truths about the English system of criminal justice. The English system of criminal justice is still one of the things which many English people regard as one of the hallmarks by which they distinguish themselves from 'lesser breeds without the Law'. For the moment we are not concerned with whether these English people are justified in their thinking, in the face of open demands for a more inquisitorial system, but only with the help that students of the system may gain by reflecting on those well-known sayings. There are four such outstanding sayings:

(a)   Justice is blind.
(b)   Justice must not only be done, but be seen to be done.
(c)   A man is presumed innocent until proved guilty.
(d)   A man should not be put in jeopardy twice for the same offence.

These sayings can be useful in identifying probable questions (and their scope) on the criminal justice system in the following way:

(a)   Take each saying in turn, consider its connection with a feature or features of the system of criminal justice.

(b)   What changes have there been or what changes have been proposed to that feature of the criminal justice system?

(c)   If those changes have been implemented or if they were to be implemented, would they involve a departure from the principles implied in the saying?

(d)   Would the principles implied in the saying still be a valid part of the system of criminal justice?

(e)   If the principle is so eroded by the changes as to cease to be valid, what are the policy grounds upon which the change was brought about?

(f)   Is there some new principle discernible in the new law?

This list of questions can be expanded. For example, as a follow-on from question (f), there is the question of whether the actual results of the change are what was intended or not. Question (e) is the point at which you will have to offer your own subjective judgment, but at least the answers to the other questions will provide you with a grounding of fact upon which to base your opinion. Here is a list of some connections, to get you started. The topics you eventually choose will, of course, depend upon your perception of the way in which your own course has been taught and your perception of the emphasis within it. The connections noted below are just a few of those that you may wish to make relating to changes which have been proposed, which may be made or have been made so as to redress the balance of the scales of justice by adding to or taking from the weight in each of the scales representing the interests of the accused and the prosecution respectively.

Saying	*Connected with*
(a) Justice is blind	(i) Equality of treatment of all accused persons: effect of this on sentencing. (ii) In a jury trial: random selection of jurors, right of challenge: literacy of jurors.
(b) Justice must not only be done but be seen to be done	(i) Trials to be held in open court. (ii) Opportunity for appeals to rectify mistakes about conviction and sentencing. (iii) Appeals by prosecution. (iv) Discharge of burden of proof. (v) Discretion to prosecute: duties of prosecution in conduct of proceedings. (vi) Power of magistrates to commit for sentence.
(c) A man is presumed innocent until proved guilty	(i) Rules of evidence protecting accused's character and 'right of silence'. (ii) Incidence of burden of proof. (iii) Provisions for bail. (iv) Status of confessions.
(d) A man should not be put in jeopardy twice for same offence	(i) Power to order new trials on fresh evidence. (ii) Taking offences into consideration. (iii) Autrefois convict and acquit. (iv) Review of lenient sentences.

This short list of connections produces a number of questions of an evaluative nature. For example:

Arising out of (b)(ii) and (iii) and (c):

To what extent do the scales of justice need to be tipped in favour of the prosecution, in contemporary society?

Arising out of (c)(i):

'Too many guilty persons are being acquitted.' Consider the status of the accused in the law of evidence in the light of this statement.

Arising out of (d)(iv):

Discuss the alternatives available for achieving an 'adequate' level of sentences, with especial reference to the incidence of 'too lenient' sentences.

Before concluding this chapter with two questions, your attention is drawn to the section at the end of the chapter on the civil process indicating topics of common interest to both the criminal and civil process. At this stage, two such topics, which have not been mentioned in this chapter, need to be borne in mind; first, the way in which the Court of Appeal (Criminal Division) sets about its task of deciding appeals, by comparison with the Civil Division of that court, and secondly, the possibility in criminal cases of these being part of Community law which requires or results in a reference to the European Court of Justice. The latter will be considered in detail in the next chapter on the civil process.

EXAMINATION QUESTIONS

The first question, taken from the list of questions just enumerated, represents the evaluative and critical type of question that may be expected. The second question represents the analytical type of approach that may occur in the context of a problem question.

Question 1

To what extent do the scales of justice need to be tipped in favour of the prosecution, in contemporary society?

The assumption made in the question is that currently the law is too favourable to the accused. This is open to challenge by any robust answer.

The question is a 'large' one, ranging over the entire criminal justice system and this governs the amount and level of detail that can go into an answer: unless you can convince the examiner that there is one area which is decisive. It is much safer to 'play the field'.

Suggested Outline Answer

Open by asserting that the objective is to hold the balance between the interests of the individual's liberty and the claims of society to protection from crime.

Comment that there never was a 'golden age' when all would agree that equilibrium existed. It is a matter of subjective opinion.

It can be said, however, at any one time, that majority opinion thinks that the scales of justice are weighed down one way or the other. And, you can say what has been done which results in a perceptible shift in the balance, and whether that shift was against the weight of public opinion.

Thus, in that sense only, we can say, after looking at the recent history of the criminal justice system, whether opinion generally is looking for further shifts in the same or opposite direction.

In conclusion, a personal judgment may be made.

The review of recent history and future proposals may be chronological. However, it is probably better to adopt a thematic approach, taking the criminal process stage by stage. Adopting a thematic approach, consider each of the following and gauge the effect they have had on the balance of interests between accused and prosecution:

(a) *At the pre-trial stage:*

(i) The effect of the Police and Criminal Evidence Act 1984 on the rights of a suspect.

(ii) The effect of the Prosecution of Offences Act 1985 on the way in which the discretion to prosecute may come to be exercised.

(iii) The fact that the list of offences triable summarily only continues to grow, and the effect of this on bringing many more cases before the magistrates, with their less formal procedures.

(iv) The abolition of committal proceedings and introduction of transfer of proceedings.

(v) Pre-trial disclosure of evidence.

(b) *At the trial stage:*

(i) The fact that more evidence is given in written form and there is less reliance on oral testimony, tested in cross-examination.

(ii)   The current repute of the system of trial by jury and removal of the right to make peremptory challenges, changes with respect to fraud trials arising out of the belief that juries cannot handle long complex cases. Whose fault is that? The juries or the procedure which condemns them to endure lengthy trials with inadequate facilities?

(iii)   Challenges that have been made to the accused's right to silence and the ability of the court or jury to draw inferences from the fact that the accused has not given evidence or has failed to put forward his defence at the earliest available opportunity.

(iv)   The effect of the introduction of majority verdicts in the Criminal Justice Act 1967, and the increase in the proportion of guilty verdicts that this may have entailed.

(c)   *At the post-trial stage*

(i)   Restrictions on rights of appeal, and continued inadequacy of help in drafting grounds of appeal.

(ii)   Recent attitudes to sentencing. Especially the search for ways of putting right 'too lenient' sentences.

(iii)   Restrictive approach to admitting new evidence.

In conclusion, note how many of these actual changes and proposed changes have, on one pretext or another (generally an appeal to greater efficiency), curtailed or at best maintained the existing protection previously attained, after many hundreds of years struggle. Do you think (and say in conclusion what you, the student, think) that our contemporary society is so much under threat from the commission of crimes of all types, that we should seek, and endorse, a further tilting of the scales in favour of the prosecution by, for example, . . . and then give one or two examples of what you consider would be undesirable or further desirable shifts in favour of the prosecution, depending upon the point of view you adopt. (Some of you may want to revisit the gibbet law — see above.) The work of the Royal Commission on Criminal Justice provides a contemporary setting to this question.

Question 2

Your client, aged 22, has been convicted of theft (an offence triable either way) after pleading not guilty, at the New Keep magistrates' court, and fined £100. It was not his first offence. You believe that there was insufficient evidence on which to convict your client and that the magistrates misapplied recent case law. Explain the avenues of appeal available to your client and the powers of the courts which may deal with the various appeals that may be made.

This question deals with a small section of the criminal process and therefore requires some attention to detail. On the other hand, it is of a finite nature and you can tell more easily than with question 1 when you have produced a sufficiently complete answer.

Suggested Outline Answer

In this case, the client, who pleaded not guilty, has two avenues of appeal open to him:

(a)   Appeal on the merits to the Crown Court (Magistrates' Courts Act 1980, s. 108).
(b)   Appeal by way of case stated to the Divisional Court of the High Court (Magistrates' Courts Act 1980, s. 111).

In either case, legal aid will be available and notice of appeal must be given within 21 days. If notice of appeal by way of case stated is given, then the right to appeal to the Crown Court is lost (Magistrates' Courts Act 1980, s. 111(4)). A comparison of the two procedures in the context of the client's case reveals the following points:

(a)   Appeal on the merits to the Crown Court entails a complete rehearing before the Crown Court (sitting without a jury, but with magistrates). New evidence may be called by the prosecution.
Also, under Supreme Court Act 1981, s. 48, the Crown Court has an extensive range of powers, including the power to impose *any* sentence that could have been imposed by the magistrates' court. If the appeal were not successful, this could result in the imposition of a heavier penalty than the comparatively light one of a fine of £100.
(b)   Appeal by way of case stated under Magistrates' Courts Act 1980, s. 111, is governed by the Magistrates' Courts Rules 1981. The appellant must get the magistrates' court to formulate a case for determination by the High Court. The case must show clearly the points of law for determination. Insufficiency or otherwise of evidence is treated as a question of law. In this case then there will be two points for determination. The case would be heard by the Divisional Court of the Queen's Bench and would involve argument on the law only. The Divisional Court has wide powers under Summary Jurisdiction Act 1857, s. 7.
(c)   If it is decided to appeal to the Crown Court, there is no further appeal on the merits. However, if the Crown Court falls into error or follows the errors made by the magistrates, either party may require the Crown Court to state a case for the opinion of the High Court, under Supreme Court Act 1981, s. 28. This is possible because it is only in connection with trials on indictment

(and this would not be so) that the Supreme Court Act 1981, s. 28(2) excludes the jurisdiction of the High Court.

(d)   On balance, it seems that the client's interests would be best served in this case by asking the magistrates to state a case for the opinion of the High Court, for three reasons:

(i)   It will exclude the risk of the prosecution improving their case by introducing new evidence.

(ii)   It will minimise the risk of an increased penalty being imposed on the client.

(iii)   It will prevent the prosecution seeking to restore the rulings of the magistrates, if they are overturned by the Crown Court, by making a further application to the High Court by case stated.

Against this must be set the more remote possibility that, if successful in the Divisional Court, the client could face a further appeal by the prosecution to the House of Lords, under Administration of Justice Act 1960, s. 1. Such appeals are relatively rare and require a certificate from the Divisional Court that there is a point of law of general public importance and also leave from either the Divisional Court or the House of Lords.

FURTHER READING

Ingman, T., *The English Legal Process* (5th edn., Blackstone Press, 1994).
Smith, P.F. and Bailey, S.H., *The Modern English Legal System* by S.H. Bailey and M.J. Gunn (2nd edn., Sweet and Maxwell, 1991).
Zander, M., *Cases and Materials on the English Legal System* (6th edn., Butterworths, 1992).

7 THE CIVIL PROCESS

At the time when the Institute of Judicial Administration was established within the Faculty of Law at Birmingham University, Professor Borrie, as he then was, wrote that it was no use having an enlightened and fair law of consumer rights, family rights, civil liberties and so forth, if the State did not ensure that there were correspondingly fair and accessible institutions charged with the responsibility of seeing that these rights were recognised and enforced for the benefit of all those entitled to them.

Similarly, Professor Harry Street in his Hamlyn lectures on 'Justice in the Welfare State' called attention to the need to provide suitable institutions for dealing with large numbers of claims by citizens against authority, that are of immense importance to those concerned, yet trivial as individual instances when looked at from the point of view of the system as a whole. Professor Street drew the comparison between the desirability of having a 'Rolls-Royce' High Court system of justice and the need to accept a modest 'family saloon' system of adjudication when it is a case of that or 'nothing at all'. This chapter, then, is going to look at English institutions of civil justice in accordance with a critical approach to their structure and operation, to see how far they measure up to Professor Borrie's requirements, but bearing in mind Professor Street's readiness to travel by Ford Escort, when the Rolls-Royce was not available. The process must be presently considered against the background of Lord Mackay's exploration of forms of 'alternative dispute resolution' and the publication of Lord Woolf's interim report on *Access to Justice*.

However, before laying out the route for a journey through the institutions of civil justice (during which we shall meet some veteran and vintage 'vehicles' of justice, as well as some smart little 'runabouts'), it is necessary to take stock of progress up to this point. The criminal process is relatively more complex in its structures than the civil process, and lends itself more readily to analytical study of the structures themselves, thus providing examination material. So, the criminal process can be dealt with as a chronological series of events. In dealing with the civil process it will be more fruitful to adopt an approach based upon an inquiry into a number of issues of both lasting and immediate concern. (Of course, in the examinations immediately after the appearance of this book, I shall be proved wrong in this, by examiners setting questions concerned with analysing the progress of cases from the issue of proceedings until the enforcement of judgment after the disposal of all rights of appeal. If that is the case, and you are faced with the prospect of such a question, do not despair and begrudge the money spent on this book, for it will still be the case that the work and the thinking you will have done on this part of the syllabus will enable you to deal more than adequately with such questions.)

For, as the first stage of taking stock of progress to date, you must ensure that you have mastered the contents of chapter 3 (basic tools for the job). This will give you a framework within which to develop a closer understanding of English institutions of civil justice. Briefly, you will know what types of cases are dealt with by the different institutions and the method of dispute settlement adopted in a particular institution, and the possibilities for appeals. You will also know who decides the case at first instance.

Changes in the system and law reform both come about in response to problems and issues. So, the second part of the stocktaking exercise is to look again at chapter 4, in so far as it deals with the history of the courts. Look at the modern history of the courts not so much as a narrative, but as a key to understanding how the present court system came about in response to issues and problems of former years. It may also provide a key to evaluating present-day proposals for dealing with the problems and issues to be faced in the 1990s and the likely effects of proposed changes.

Having mastered the facts of the present structure of civil institutions and provided yourself with an understanding of how the structure developed into its present form, it is necessary to look at the underlying facts and 'conditions of life' within which any system for the settlement of disputes according to law must operate.

Marshalling your knowledge and information about English institutions for settling disputes according to the following scheme will assist in identifying and focusing attention on a number of issues which are meat and drink to those who set essays and examination questions and devise projects.

TYPES OF DISPUTE

One of the hardest things for professionals, and especially lawyers, to accept is that there are some occasions on which their professional expertise is not only not useful, but is actually harmful. Quite plainly, there are some types of dispute that are not the business of lawyers. Some of these are readily accepted as such by lawyers (e.g., disagreements between friends as to which is the best disco in town), others are controversial. These latter include domestic disputes between members of a family, certain aspects of industrial relations, disputes involving economic policy. When considering the appropriateness of assigning disputes for settlement to a particular institution or type of institution two factors must be borne in mind. First, appropriateness may be a question of social or political policy. Thus, there is disagreement of a political nature about whether a dispute between a trade union member and the member's trade union is a matter for the 'ordinary' courts or a specialised institution, possibly excluding all normal features of a recognisable legal process. The second factor relates to the inherent nature of the dispute itself: is the dispute, as we say, one that is justiciable? In other words, is it susceptible of solution by legal techniques? There were, for example, initial doubts about whether matters relating to restrictive trade practices were truly justiciable, before the establishment of the Restrictive Practices Court in 1956. These particular doubts have somewhat diminished by the experience of the jurisdiction and procedures of the European Court of Justice, but the point remains for consideration whenever there is a discussion about the need to provide a forum for the resolution of disputes that may arise in some new area of activity. As will be seen shortly, there is a similar decision to be made within the context of the legal system about the form to be adopted once it has been decided that a type of problem is a legal problem producing disputes to be settled by legal process.

In the case of English legal institutions dealing with civil matters, there is one other 'condition' to recognise, which gives our English civil jurisdiction its distinct flavour. That is that, in fact, there is a great difference between a dispute between citizens and disputes where one of the parties is the State or a public authority. The peculiarity of English law is that the State or the Crown is, on the whole, treated in theory as just another litigant in the courts, with the consequence that there are no separate legal institutions to which resort is to be had simply because one of the parties is the Crown, or the State. However, because of the nature of the *subject-matter* of their jurisdiction there are some institutions in which the Crown or some other public authority is virtually always one of the parties to a dispute brought before them.

FORMS OF DISPUTE RESOLUTION

Within the tradition of a legal system, there are at least the following forms of dispute resolution. They each have their own characteristics and strengths and weaknesses. All the forms listed below are of the rational type and may be claimed therefore as modern. They do not include irrational forms, with which the student may be familiar either from a study of legal history or from childhood memory of settling playground disputes by some process of drawing lots or 'dipping'. Irrational forms of dispute settlement, or at least what 20th-century people regard as irrational forms, included trial by ordeal and wager of law. A case may be made out for saying that modern litigation depends just as much on chance as did wager of law, perhaps more so.

However, here is the list:

(a) Litigation.
(b) Arbitration.
(c) Conciliation.
(d) Decision after consultation.
(e) Grievance procedures.

It is the element of procedural regularity that binds all these forms of dispute settlement together and gives them their quality of 'legality'. The degree of procedural formality varies very much from one of these forms to the other. In litigation, for example, the judge is largely bound by pre-existing procedural rules, having the full force of law, whilst the conciliator may choose his own method of proceeding and make it known to the disputants at the time of the conciliation. Of the five forms listed, lawyers like to think of litigation and arbitration as being 'mainstream' forms of settlement. That means only that they are the forms with which lawyers are traditionally familiar. Lawyers are, perforce, becoming more familiar with (e) above, as some new grievance procedures deal directly with grievances against lawyers themselves.

During the 1990s more has been seen of the forms of 'alternative dispute resolution' (ADR). These are alternatives to the established forms of dispute resolution, particularly litigation. They include mediation, conciliation, non-binding arbitration, the mini-trial, and adjudication. Note the terms 'conciliation' and 'mediation' are often used interchangeably. The underlying theme of many forms of ADR is to promote settlement of the dispute by the parties themselves. For example, mediation is designed to prevent the parties adopting adversarial positions and to promote communication between the parties. Ultimately, the mediator, who acts as a channel of communicaton between the parties and explores with them individually their respective cases, hopes to bring the parties together on common ground so as to allow them to settle their dispute. In the light of Lord Woolf's interim report, methods of promoting out of court settlement of disputes is likely to be a key issue in considering the civil justice system.

TYPES OF INSTITUTION

There is some correspondence between the forms of dispute resolution and the legal institutions in which that activity takes place, but the correspondence is not complete. For example, although litigation as a means of dispute settlement is conducted in courts, it is not invariably so, and the cases brought before certain tribunals such as industrial tribunals are undoubtedly instances of litigation. The types of institution which the legal system encompasses as places for the resolution of disputes in the first instance are these:

(a) Courts.
(b) Tribunals.
(c) Inquiries.
(d) Ombudsmen (if individuals may be described as institutions).
(e) Arbitral bodies.

It is difficult to draw up a complete table of correspondences between types of dispute settlement and institutions. The following table shows that the civil legal process in the English legal system is both complex in its structure and that it is wrong to characterise institutions by reference to a single type of activity. (This accounts for some of the difficulty in producing satisfactory definitions of legal institutions. See, for example, the difficulty arising in the case of *Attorney-General* v *British Broadcasting Corporation* [1981] AC 303 over whether an institution is or is not a court. See also the comments in Ingman, *The English Legal Process*, 5th ed., pp. 2 and 3.)

What is clear is that the name of an institution is not always the best indication of its character: a safer indicator of the character of an institution is the type of activity normally conducted in that institution.

Types of Dispute Settlement and Types of Institution

Settlement procedures	Institutions in which conducted
Litigation	Courts, tribunals
Arbitration	Courts, arbitral bodies
Conciliation	Rare in English law. Sometimes supervised by courts.
Decision after consultation	Inquiries
Grievance procedures	Ombudsman

CONCLUSIONS SO FAR

I believe that the following points can be drawn from what has been stated so far about the provision made for the settlement of disputes by the civil process of the English legal system:

(a)   There is a need to distinguish disputes that are justiciable from those that are not.

This point in itself is at the root of some examination questions which deal with the proper role of the courts, if any, in dealing with certain types of dispute. Some sorts of labour dispute are obviously included here. There is also the whole question of the legitimacy of the courts' role in checking and controlling the acts of the executive and democratically elected bodies, such as local authorities, as, for example, in the London Transport fares case of *Bromley London Borough Council* v *Greater London Council* [1983] 1 AC 768. Other areas at present within the jurisdiction of courts, such as claims for personal injury and some family disputes, could at some time in the future be taken out of the legal system altogether or the type of disputes procedure at present used could be changed.

(b)   There is a wide variety of procedures available for the settlement of disputes.

The fact that there are so many different procedures suggests that some types of dispute are more suitable for settlement by one means rather than another. Thus, the experience of sending workmen's compensation cases to county courts, between 1897 and 1948, persuaded Lord Beveridge in his report, which formed the basis of legislation introducing the post-war welfare State, that these disputes should be taken away from the courts and handled in a totally different way. The way chosen was for the initial decision to be made by an insurance officer with disputed decisions thereafter going to special tribunals, with the courts playing a very minor role as the ultimate arbiters in a few cases of complex points of law. I shall have something to say a little later about the reasons for Lord Beveridge's choice in this matter. That is but one example of many which could be cited, where dissatisfaction with an existing means of dispute settlement has brought about a change. This second conclusion is a starting-point for considering what appears to be another favourite sort of examination question, namely, one which raises the issue of whether or not the English legal system should develop by introducing further specialised courts, such as labour courts, and the proposal for a family court.

In connection with that proposal it is pertinent to note that some of the disputes procedures, e.g., conciliation, do not get much of an opportunity to show their worth in the present institutions of civil law and that it may be necessary to create entirely new institutions in order to make effective use of procedures such as conciliation. In considering the appropriateness of different types of dispute settlement note the use of ADR in connection with some disputes (such as commercial disputes in the area of contracting) which would normally go to an ordinary court. Matters to consider include the need for agreement to submit to the ADR process, whether the outcome is binding on the parties and whether it excludes further recourse to the courts, and the distinction between ADR and arbitration.

(c)   The name of an institution is not a clear indication of its institutional character.

You should be aware of two consequences which flow from this conclusion. The first one is concerned with the need to identify or define institutions at all. Why does it matter if an institution, whatever its name, is or is not treated in law as a court, or a tribunal or whatever? The answer, of course, is obvious. The law attaches privileges and immunities to certain institutions that it categorises in a certain way. Thus, only an institution which is accepted in law as a court has the inherent power to punish for contempt and only decision-makers sitting in courts as judges have immunity from liability in connection with their judicial activity.

In the second place, acceptance of my third conclusion will enable you to start constructing an answer to yet another type of question I have seen on more than one examination paper. The question takes a number of forms but, essentially, it asks you to compare the sorts of work and activity carried on in courts and tribunals respectively. The work of industrial tribunals and claims for unfair dismissal provide a useful case study in how close those tribunals have come to being courts in all but name.

THE ORDINARY COURTS

In this and the succeeding sections of this chapter I am going to assume, for the purposes of exposition and analysis, that the Supreme Court (excluding the Crown Court), together with the House of Lords and the county courts, form a group of legal institutions that may be referred to as the ordinary civil courts of the English legal system. That implies that these courts are the paradigm by which other legal institutions concerned with the settlement of civil disputes in the English legal system are to be measured and tested. Let me repeat, this characterisation is for the purposes of exposition only and is not intended to suggest that other institutions such as tribunals, ombudsmen and arbitrators, let alone such august bodies as the European Court of Human Rights and the Court of Justice of the European Communities, do not deserve to be studied and appraised on their own criteria and merits. Furthermore, in the course of your study of the English legal system you will encounter questions relating to the proper relationship in the system between these 'other' institutions and the 'ordinary' courts. That issue is inherent in questions dealing with the proper scope of judicial review and the need to provide rights of appeal from institutions such as tribunals, to the ordinary courts, as is the case with decisions about entitlement to supplementary benefit. There the question is, ought the courts to be excluded from meddling with the work of the DSS and, if so, why?

I am now going to select four areas of concern for you to use as the basis of your critical study of the ordinary courts as they exist today and as they operate today. Many of the issues I shall mention have been dealt with in the Lord Chancellor's review of civil jurisdiction and procedure. The topics are of permanent theoretical importance as well as being of immediate practical consequence, and are worth studying, therefore, whether or not any proposals which were made by the Lord Chancellor's committee have been implemented.

The four areas I have selected are these:

(a) The division of jurisdiction between the High Court and the county courts.

(b) The case for and against specialised courts.

(c) The working of the system of appeals.

(d) The remedies that may be granted and orders that may be made by the courts.

THE DIVISION OF JURISDICTION BETWEEN THE HIGH COURT AND THE COUNTY COURTS

Reference to chapter 6 on the criminal process will remind you that care is taken in fixing jurisdictional limits between higher and lower courts to separate serious from less serious cases. This is done on the assumption that it is proper to give more elaborate treatment to serious cases, however defined. In the criminal process the enormity of the crime and the risk to the liberty of the accused are major criteria in determining the type of trial the accused must undergo.

In the civil process the two courts of trial, as you know, are the High Court and the county courts. At one time whether an action for contract or tort proceeded in the High Court or county court was determined on the basis of the amount of the claim. This took no account of the difficulty of a case. Even cases with a small monetary value may give rise to novel and complex points of law. This was seen as not being the best use of resources (see the Civil Justice Review, Cm 394, 1988) and, in consequence, the Lord Chancellor was given power to reallocate business between the High Court and the county courts by s. 1 of the Courts and Legal Services Act 1990. This reallocation was effected by the High Court and County Courts Jurisdiction Order 1991 (SI 1991 No. 724); see T. Ingman, *The English Legal Process*, 5th ed., pp. 32–5.

The point to note is that if a county court has jurisdiction then, by art. 4 of the 1991 Order, proceedings may be *commenced* in either a county court or in the High Court. The 1991 Order abolished many restrictions on the jurisdiction of the county courts. For example, the county courts now generally have unlimited jurisdiction in relation to actions in contract and tort. The basic principle in art. 4 is qualified, however. Where the county courts have jurisdiction over an action, which includes a claim for damages for personal injuries and is for less than £50,000, then the proceedings must be commenced in a county court.

Where both the High Court and the county courts have jurisdiction, proceedings may be *tried* in either court subject to the following:

(a)   if the value of the action is less than £25,000 then it should be tried in a county court unless it ought to be transferred to the High Court under s. 42 of the County Court Act 1984 (having regard to the criteria set out below), or, if commenced in the High Court, unless that court considers that it ought to try the action;

(b)   if the value of the action is £50,000 or more then it should be tried by the High Court, unless the High Court considers (having regard to the criteria set out below) that the action should be transferred to a county court, or, where proceedings are commenced in a county court, unless that court does not consider (having regard to the criteria set out below) that the action should be transferred to the High Court.

Importantly, cases started in the High Court or county court may be transferred from one to the other court where appropriate under ss. 40–42 of the County Courts Act 1984. In deciding whether to transfer, regard is to be had to the following criteria:

(a)   the amount claimed;

(b)   the importance of the action, e.g., does it involve a point of law of general public interest;

(c)   the complexity of the facts, legal issues, remedies or procedures; and

(d)   whether the transfer is likely to result in a speedier trial (this ground is not sufficient in itself).

In this regard note also the *Practice Direction (County Court: Transfer of Actions)* [1991] 1 WLR 643.

The county courts also have an important jurisdiction in relation to small claims. An important point to consider is that if a whole class of case is predominantly disposed of by the small claims procedure in the county court with little or no opportunity for appeal, there is a danger that divergences may arise in the interpretation of the law in different parts of the country, and if at the same time these cases are unreported the law may become 'unknown'. Many consumer cases come within this category and the tendency noted above is reinforced by the periodic raising of the monetary limit of the small claims jurisdiction. In 1995 it was proposed to raise this limit from £1,000 to £3,000.

It is important to understand the rules for allocating business between the High Court and the county courts and the rationale behind the rules. This information would be vital if you were asked to consider a question of the following type:

> In relation to the following situations identify the court or courts involved, and explain the composition and jurisdiction of the court(s):
>
> (a) Bloggs wishes to sue Jones for breach of contract. He claims that as a result of the breach he has suffered damage estimated at £30,000. Upon seeking the advice of counsel, Jones discovers that his case raises a novel and difficult point of law.
> (b) Morse has appealed against a judgment of Lewis J, dismissing his action for negligence resulting in personal injury. He was claiming damages of £100,000. The appeal is heard by three Lords Justices of Appeal.
> (c) A defamation action brought by Clare is heard before Angel J.

The examiner, in asking the above questions, is seeking to discover primarily whether you possess an understanding of the civil courts. Whilst, in part, you are expected to describe the jurisdiction and composition of the courts, clearly the identification of the relevant courts and the reasons for your answers are most important. It is this part of your answer that demonstrates your understanding. The points you should note in each case are as follows:

(a) Both the High Court and the county courts have jurisdiction in relation to issues of contract — the High Court is a superior court and has unlimited civil jurisdiction and the county court is given jurisdiction over contract by the County Courts Act 1984, s. 15 (as amended). Proceedings in relation to an action for breach of contract may be commenced in the High Court or in a county court (High Court and County Courts Jurisdiction Order 1991 (SI 1991 No. 724), art 4).

The next question to consider is where the action will be tried. This depends upon the transfer provisions in ss. 40–42 of the County Courts Act 1984, and you would be expected to consider the transfer criteria, emphasising the value of the action and the novel and difficult point of law. On the facts of the problem it is not possible to say whether the High Court or a county court would definitely be the court where proceedings would be commenced or the action would be tried, but that does not prevent you from reasoning that one or other court might be more appropriate. Note that there are advantages in proceeding in the High Court, for example, speed and the possibility of summary judgment.

(b) As the action is one for personal injuries and is valued at £100,000, the most likely place to commence the action is the High Court. We can feel confident that this is correct as the action is heard by Lewis J, a puisne judge, who is likely to be sitting in the Queen's Bench Division of the High Court. Note, however, that a puisne judge may consent to sit in a county court (County Courts Act 1984, s. 5(3)). Additionally, an appeal from the High Court in such an action is normally heard by three Lords Justices of Appeal in the Court of Appeal (Civil Division) (Supreme Court Act 1981, s. 54(2)); if the appeal had come from a county court then two Lords Justices may hear the appeal (Supreme Court Act 1981, s. 54(4), and Court of Appeal (Civil Division) Order 1982, SI 1982 No. 543). Whilst the above is not conclusive, the circumstances would suggest that the action is tried in the High Court.

(c)   The county courts do not have jurisdiction over actions for the tort of defamation (County Courts Act 1984, s. 15(2)(c)). However, by s. 18 of the County Courts Act 1984, the parties may agree to a county court having such jurisdiction, or the High Court may transfer such proceedings to a county court under s. 40 of the County Courts Act 1984. As to this latter point, note the *Practice Direction (County Court: Transfer of Actions)* [1991] 1 WLR 643, which indicates that actions for defamation are not suitable for transfer to a county court. Again, note the judge involved is a puisne judge, which seems to show that the court is most likely to be the High Court.

The considerations which I have set out above lead on to the question which was raised by the Lord Chancellor's review of civil procedure and almost as a necessary consequence may continue to appear in some examination papers, namely, what would be the consequences of a unified civil jurisdiction, organised regionally, with all cases beginning in the equivalent of the present county court, with more important cases being transferred to the High Court, which might also be decentralised? There is already an example of this in the arrangements for the distribution of divorce and related business set out in the Matrimonial and Family Proceedings Act 1984, ss. 37 and 39. Arguments for and against a unified jurisdiction can be based on the various points made and considerations set out in this section. It is because the arrangements under the Courts and Legal Services Act 1990 stop short of creating a unified civil jurisdiction that this is still a subject for the evaluative style of examination question. I can offer two reasons which are possibly but not necessarily opposing reasons: a closer approximation to justice and increased cost-effectiveness. The resulting unified jurisdiction might look very different according to which of those two reasons was uppermost during the stages of implementing the proposal. An apparently minor provision or insignificant wording in the legislation could have far-reaching and unforeseen consequences. (See for example, page 55 on how the royal courts managed to interpret the provision 'not less than 40 shillings' to mean 'everything more than 40 shillings' so severely damaging the position of local courts.) You should consider Lord Woolf's recommendations concerning the structure of the trial courts.

THE CASE FOR AND AGAINST SPECIALISED COURTS

This is another basic theme for many examination questions. There is a history in the English legal system of courts with special functions and jurisdictions. The general historical movement, however, has been towards courts of a general jurisdiction, as in the present High Court, which is then split into divisions for administrative convenience. Originally, the common law courts of Exchequer and King's Bench were highly specialised courts, which extended their own jurisdictions at the expense of others by means of legal fictions. Likewise, the many local courts often had a special jurisdiction dealing with particular types of case. All of this can be rapidly checked out by referring to the detailed list of contents of vol. 1 of Holdsworth's *A History of English Law*. The jurisdiction of the Court of Chancery was also highly specialised but it also had a claim to a more wide-ranging generalised jurisdiction to put right the defects and shortcomings of the common law.

What has this historical tradition produced by way of specialisation within the 'ordinary' courts at the present time? If you consider the High Court, then you should look at the Supreme Court Act 1981, sch. 1, which sets out the distribution of business between the different divisions of the court, and ss. 20 and 21 of the same Act which provide for an Admiralty Court within the Queen's Bench Division. At the county court level, you will find by referring to the Green Book *(The County Court Practice)* that the county court not only has an ordinary jurisdiction governed by the County Courts Act 1984 but also a very wide-ranging number of special jurisdictions dealing under special rules with such diverse matters as insolvency, family law matters, landlord and tenant and race relations. There has at times been a tendency for Parliament to give jurisdiction over business arising out of new legislative schemes to the county courts as the general work-horses of the legal system.

From time to time there are attempts to promote some of these specialised functions of the ordinary courts. Sometimes this is even done as part of an 'export drive', as in the case of the Commercial List within the Queen's Bench Division. The use of this specialist function of the Queen's Bench Division was, for example, promoted in September 1987 when Sir John Donaldson MR asked for more specialist commercial judges to be appointed to take cases in this list. A large proportion of the litigants are non-British subjects and the court in this case is a useful export earner.

When the large number of tribunals, such as the industrial tribunals, are added to this list of specialist institutions in the field of dispute settlement, you will see that there is already a considerable degree of specialisation within the system. By a specialist court it must now be apparent that I mean one dealing with a limited number of types of factual situations and one more often than not having its own tailor-made rules of procedure and often also a composition that is unique to that specialist function.

If you want specific reasons justifying the establishment of specialist courts either within the structure of the ordinary courts or independently you should consider the following:

(a)   Is there a new area of work for the courts that cannot easily be accommodated within the existing framework?

(b)   In the case of newly established areas of work, is it thought expedient to adopt a type of dispute settlement (a form of arbitration, say, or conciliation) not found in the ordinary courts or which the ordinary courts might not easily assimilate?

(c)   Is there a need or is it desirable to have specialists sitting as part of the court involved in the decision-making, as in the case of Admiralty assessors?

We must not forget, of course, cases which are found to be non-justiciable (see above, page 114) or where there are good reasons for de-legalising altogether some sorts of dispute. For example, the Lord Chancellor has made firm proposals for a no-fault scheme for road accidents, where the claim is a modest one in terms of money.

Considerations which tell against the advisability of establishing a multiplicity of specialist courts include the following:

(a)   There are no neat categories of law within which typical factual situations can be confined. In unfair dismissal cases, for example, questions of taxation and insolvency may arise. It is sound policy to maintain that the law of taxation and insolvency is the same in whatever factual situation the same question of tax or insolvency law arises.

(b)   Inevitably with a multiplicity of specialist courts difficulties will arise over the classification of cases thus requiring the existence of a coordinating body with a jurisdiction to settle conflicts of classification, on the lines of the French Tribunal des Conflits which in French law determines whether a case is one for the civil courts or the administrative courts.

Before leaving this question of specialist courts I have to ask you to consider two more matters: what are the potential areas for future specialisation and what specialist 'courts' or other institutions already exist outside the ordinary courts?

Areas for Future Specialisation

Do not forget the active proposal for a family court. This court might also have some jurisdiction over property belonging to the family. You should think about the consequences of this for the state of land law generally. Other possible areas include labour law, unless you consider that the industrial tribunals are courts in all but name already. Note the transfer of jurisdiction over certain employment contract disputes from the county courts to the industrial tribunals.

There is also the whole question of the relationship between the individual and the State with the suggestion that is made from time to time for an administrative court, or at least an administrative division of the High Court. Such a move would have great potential for rationalising many of the disparate rules which are found in different legislative schemes and which could well be the same without any harm to any of the schemes involved. The establishment in 1980 of a panel of judges to hear cases on the 'Crown Office List' goes some way towards this objective. (See also below, page 136, on the distinction between public and private law.)

Already Existing Specialist Institutions

Apart from the many highly specialised tribunals there are several major institutions of which you should take note: these are all highly specialist bodies, with varying compositions. Some of them have an appellate function, hearing appeals from tribunals or, in the case of bodies such as the Revenue Commissioners, determining disputed decisions by officials. Note too, in passing, that some are constituted as courts of record, whilst others such as the Lands Tribunal are not. All of these points can be made in answers dealing with the divergency of forms of institution that exist in the legal system and the practical consequences of the differences between, say, the Revenue Commissioners and the Employment Appeal Tribunal.

The major institutions in this category include:

(a)   Employment Appeal Tribunal.
(b)   Restrictive Practices Court.
(c)   Inland Revenue Commissioners (Special and General).
(d)   VAT Tribunal.
(e)   Lands Tribunal.
(f)   Ecclesiastical courts.

Costs and Delay

These two sections, on the possibility of a reformed unified civil jurisdiction and the question of specialised courts, have one common underlying theme, which cannot be stressed too strongly as a potential ingredient of many examination questions. That is, the cost and delay involved in resolving disputes of all kinds in all ways, but especially the cost and delay involved in litigation. Cost and delay might well be a heading in notes you prepare for yourself, collated from a number of parts of the syllabus and from a variety of sources. Whilst standard works such as Smith and Bailey, *The Modern English Legal System* (2nd ed., pp. 472–92) and Ingman, *The English Legal Process,* comment on the cost and delay involved in litigation, you should seek out some representative figures as well from the published Civil Judicial Statistics and look out for articles in the periodical and daily press. With the publication of Lord Woolf's interim report in 1995 this is a particularly fertile time for such publications.

The Woolf Report

The Woolf Report is of immense significance for the civil justice process and you should be familiar with its main recommendations. In outline, it is recommended that control of the progress of cases should be taken from litigants and made the responsibility of the courts. The courts will manage cases by deciding what procedure is suitable, setting realistic timetables and ensuring that timetables and procedures are followed. Instead of separate rules of court for the High Court and county courts, there should be one set of rules and a single method of starting all claims. The procedures to be used should reflect the weight of the case in terms of the amount of the claim, its complexity and importance. Hence there is proposed a small claims jurisdiction, excluding personal injuries, up to £3,000 (possibly rising to £5,000); a fast track procedure, with a simplified procedure, fixed timetables and costs, for straightforward claims up to £10,000; and a multi-track procedure for cases above £10,000. Changes in procedure would be necessary, moving further away from the previous position of litigants 'keeping their cards close to their chest', with statements of case spelling out facts to be relied upon so that issues in dispute may be defined, and a new approach to disclosure of documents and the continuation of exchange of witness statements. The objective of promoting the settlement of cases is seen as part of case management. There are other proposals designed to aid the unrepresented litigant.

You should keep a note of how these recommendations are implemented, if at all, and be prepared to consider, in the fullness of time, whether they solve the problems identified by Lord Woolf. It is easy to see that the Woolf Report is the stuff of examination questions on the civil justice process and the more general topic of access to justice.

Before going on to the next section concerned with appeals, this seems to be an appropriate place in which to make general comment on handling the part of the syllabus to do with courts of trial. Most textbooks have a section dealing with these institutions in a descriptive way, often, as in Ingman's book, following the pattern of arrangement found in the Supreme Court Act 1981; that is, under the headings of constitution, jurisdiction, practice and procedure. Smith and Bailey follow this with a treatment of the process and procedure in the various courts earlier described. There are two sorts of question that may be asked about English civil courts. One of them requires a detailed knowledge and analysis of the constitution, jurisdiction, practice and procedure of the various courts, either individually or by way of comparison between two or more courts. For such questions, of which you may not be offered many, you may rely upon textbook expositions, supplemented by your notes. The other sort of question is an integrative one taking a theme, treatment of which demands detailed knowledge supplemented by an ability to analyse structures to discover:

(a)   their similarities and dissimilarities, and
(b)   the *effectiveness* of different structures in meeting stated objectives.

For example, why was the composition of the Restrictive Practices Court made to include 'persons with knowledge or experience of industry, commerce or public affairs' (Restrictive Practices Court Act 1976). Surely, the answer lies in the sort of issue that the court is called upon to decide, which is not always a straightforward justiciable issue. You ought to be able to go on to say how successfully this court has carried out its task in the light of the part played by the lay members in a number of representative decisions.

This second sort of question, then, requires that you have done some reading around in periodicals and have also sampled for yourself some of these decisions made in other ways. This means reading cases and in some instances trying to arrange to visit a variety of types of hearing. This is supported on some courses by requirements to attend, record and comment on hearings at different courts and tribunals. The sample you will be able to take during the course of a one-year course will be small, but get in the habit of finding things out for yourself as the basis of judgment. In carrying out your study always know why it is that you are looking for a particular piece of information.

In this chapter so far I have chosen to look at English civil legal institutions from three points of view:

(a)   Should there be a unified jurisdiction?
(b)   The place of specialist courts in our legal system.
(c)   The costs and delays in settling disputes.

Therefore, if I were preparing for an examination and thought that these were things I should know something about, I should record and learn the details of the courts and related institutions as set out in my textbook and then sample the work of each of them.

In the course of that sampling by reading, listening to and seeing cases I should be asking myself the following questions:

(a) Would this case have benefited from being dealt with in a unified jurisdiction?

(b) Is this a case which should be dealt with in a 'specialist' court or other institution?

(c) Is this case subject to delay or are the costs going to be outrageous?

Some cases, of course, are kept out of the courts when they should be heard in the interests of justice, by the daunting prospects of potential delay and costs, which a particular claimant has no means of paying, with or without legal aid.

So much the better for me, if I can search through the periodicals and scan the newspapers and find that someone has already done the work for me.

THE WORKING OF THE SYSTEM OF APPEALS

In coming to this stage of the civil process I must point out that the system of appeals is accorded different treatment in different syllabuses and textbooks. Basically, there are two approaches. To do as is being done in this book, and to deal with appeals as part of a legal process, or to deal with the questions of appeals and review of decisions as a separate topic. This latter way is the approach adopted in Smith and Bailey's book, which reserves its final chapter for a systematic treatment of appeals and judicial review. Dr Ingman also deals with appeals and the correction of the miscarriages of justice as a separate topic, combining civil and criminal appeals in a single chapter.

Whichever approach your course adopts, it is possible to make some valid observations on the appeals system in civil cases.

When beginning to prepare materials on appeals for an examination it will always be a necessary first step to ensure that you *know* properly the facts about the structure of the system as set out in chapter 3, on the basic tools for the job. Add to this a thorough grasp of the distinction between an appeal and judicial review referred to in chapter 4 and you are ready to begin a detailed preparatory study of appeals as part of the civil process.

In thinking about the role of appeals in our civil process, as part of an academic programme leading to an examination, I should identify two sorts of issues and, therefore, possible questions. These are: first, purely technical legal questions about the functioning of the appeals system and the differences, for example, between appeals from the High Court and appeals from the county court; secondly, there are broader questions on the purpose of having appeals at all and the efficiency of our particular system of appeals in achieving those purposes. An obvious question that almost asks itself in this context is: Why do we have two tiers of appellate courts? In looking at the technical side of appeals, there is no better starting-point than to take the eight points set out by Smith and Bailey, under the heading of 'Variable factors in appeal and review mechanisms', and relate each of those points to all the types of appeal included in your field of study, just as was done in the case of appeals in the criminal process (see page 101).

Civil appeals raise a number of particular points that you should be able to handle with confidence, as the working of the appeal system depends so much upon them. I would emphasise the following:

(a)   The ability to distinguish fact and law and questions of fact and law respectively.
(b)   The understanding of what is meant by an inference of fact.
(c)   The realisation that the success of an appeal from the appellant's point of view depends on the appellant discharging the burden of showing that the judgment appealed against should be reversed.

In considering appeals from the county court, the first three points of Smith and Bailey's list are the most important:

(a)   Who can institute an appeal? Note here that certain decisions of the county court are not appealable.
(b)   Can the appeal be brought as of right? Here the distinction between law and fact is not important. It is the amount of the damages or property in issue that determines this question, under the provisions of the County Courts Appeals Order 1991 (SI 1991 No 1877).
(c)   What are the permissible grounds for an appeal? Generally speaking it may be any question of law or fact.

When considering appeals from the High Court do not forget to take account of the 'leap-frog' procedure, although it may be little used. It may be necessary to apply a knowledge of this procedure, as set out in the Administration of Justice Act 1969, with appeals direct to the House of Lords, in answering a problem-type question seeking to explore your knowledge of the system in the context of a given set of facts. It may be a question in which you are asked to advise on the extent and likelihood of success of an appeal by a particular party. For example:

Advise X, who has obtained judgment in the High Court in an action for breach of statutory duty. The defendant Y has approached X with a view to a compromise, by paying 50% of the amount of the judgment in consideration of Y giving up a possible appeal. [In an actual question you would expect several other issues to be included as well.]

When it is clear, as in most cases, that the appeal will go to the Court of Appeal, bear in mind the restrictions on appeals from the High Court, which are set out in Supreme Court Act 1981, s. 18 (as amended by the Courts and Legal Services Act 1990). It is worthwhile saying in an essay, and where it is relevant, that there are restrictions and that they are to be found in s. 18. It is better of course to be able to give examples; such as the need for leave in most cases where the appeal is against an interlocutory order or judgment.

Finally, in the consideration of appeals in the Court of Appeal, try to work out the way in which that court decides appeals. This will mean looking at Ord. 59 of the Rules of the Supreme Court, particularly the general powers of the court as set out in r. 10 of that Order. A good way of understanding the working of the system of appeals is to attend and take part in moots, which are invariably set in the context of an appeal heard either in the Court of Appeal or House of Lords.

As to appeals to the House of Lords, the principal point to remember is the need for leave to appeal to that court and the manner of applying for leave, being careful to distinguish it from the procedure in criminal cases. The role of the House of Lords in relation to the development of the law is a separate matter and one also which may be discussed in the context of the doctrine of precedent.

Before looking at other broader issues, make sure that you know how the appellate courts approach the issue of appeals against damages awards, and appeals against judgments where the trial exceptionally has been with a jury (see the case of *Ward* v *James* [1966] 1 QB 273).

I have suggested above that there may be examinations in which there is a question which demands an ability to apply the rules of civil appeals in the context of a given set of facts. It is more likely that other broader issues will come into the questions that are asked. Every type of institution that processes transactions has a horror of being so overburdened that the system is overwhelmed and breaks down. Legal systems and institutions are no exception to this rule. Therefore provision is made to try to sift out 'unmeritorious appeals'. If a question comes up about the efficiency of the system, this issue of how to keep out appeals with no merit in them is an obvious point to include. To do this, you need to know not only some facts, but also how to relate them to the issue in question. For example, is the device of requiring leave an adequate means of sifting out appeals without merit? Take account too of the various measures introduced since Lord Donaldson became Master of the Rolls to reduce the backlog of cases awaiting hearing and to discourage hopeless appeals. These include the requirement to submit in advance of the hearing, skeleton arguments (see *Practice Direction (Court of Appeal: Presentation of Argument)* [1989] 1 WLR 281). How should one interpret the statistic that more than half the appeals set down are foregone conclusions? Perhaps there is something in the suggestion that sometimes an appeal is made simply as a delaying tactic. Measures have recently been taken to discourage this by subjecting the lawyers involved to threats of disciplinary action or loss of entitlement to their costs. These are the sorts of points to make in an essay on the broader issues of the working of the system of appeals. Incidentally, nothing seems to have been lost by way of justice by having many appeals heard by two judges instead of three. Yet again, the advice is to follow the legal and daily press, to pick up such items as the speech of Lord Donaldson MR to the International Bar Association in late September 1987.

The other question that is always worth thinking about is that concerning the justification for both a Court of Appeal and the House of Lords. Such rationalisations as are offered may be based on statements by the judges, worked up into articles by academics. What matters is that you know that there are explanations which are given. The most usual one is that the Court of Appeal is concerned to put right mistakes made at trial and to do justice between the parties to an action, whereas the House of Lords has a duty additionally to ensure the even and steady development of the law as a whole. Such thinking may be simply a rationalisation of the status quo and does not mean that a single tier of appellate courts could not ensure justice for the litigant and see to the well-being of the law as a whole. Be prepared to say so in an answer but only on the basis of some wider reading on the topic in such works as those by Paterson and by Blom-Cooper and Drewry on the House of Lords.

Finally, in connection with appeals, prepare a separate little section on appeals in administrative law matters. This is not merely a further reading up on the basis of judicial review. (You will have done that already.) What is at stake here is the ability of the 'ordinary' courts to check and control administrative decisions. There is no one set pattern, and the position is different in different areas of administration. If you are asked to comment on the role of the courts in this area do not be afraid to introduce arguments about policy into your work. Why, for example, should the administration wish to exclude the law from overseeing many of its decisions. It may be a dislike of 'legalism' which is a proper implied criticism of the ways of lawyers. On the other hand there may be a reluctance to acknowledge the claims of 'legality' on the acts of the administration. That is a situation, if it exists, that deserves greater efforts at check and scrutiny. There are also examples of how from time to time administrative schemes are changed for political and economic reasons and where the change takes the form of extending or restricting rights of appeal to the courts. Such a proposal to restrict rights of appeal in social security cases was made in 1986 and criticised by the Council on Tribunals. (This is noted in the *Current Law Year Book* for 1986 under the heading of 'Law reform'.) Your brief in handling questions like this in the context of an English legal system course covers both these policy considerations and being able to show an adequate knowledge of the wide variety of forms these appeals might take, ranging from a statutory right of appeal to the High Court (as in planning matters) to a right to have an administrative decision reviewed by a higher authority within a particular institutional structure, without any right of recourse to the courts. Other policy considerations include: the need to be able to implement an agreed policy without 'blocking' and 'wrecking' tactics, the avoidance of cost and delay and the avoidance of what are seen as objections based on mere legal technicality. Lawyers need a lot of convincing before they allow their own particular legal values of fairness, regularity and legality in general to be ignored and subverted.

REMEDIES AND ORDERS

By no means all English legal system courses contain a part concerned with remedies, or the orders available in law for redress of a grievance. Before going any further with this section reflect on the consequence of a matter giving rise to a grievance being outside the scope of the law because it is not justiciable (see page 115). Even when a grievance is one recognised by law, such as trespass, the law still recognises a limited right of self-help.

This section is concerned with the remedies by way of redress of a grievance which can only be obtained through the courts. But, as Dr Ingman pointed out in the preface to the first edition of *The English Legal Process*, 'The subject of remedies . . . is an integral and important part of the civil legal process'. Therefore, although many students' formal instruction in the law of remedies will take the form of an appendage to their study of contract, tort, equity and other substantive subjects, all students will benefit from at least a brief review of the subject of remedies as an entity by itself. If your main English legal system textbook does not deal with remedies as a separate topic (and both Ingman and Smith and Bailey do so) get hold of a copy of a specialist book on remedies, such as Lawson on *Remedies of English Law*, which will give you an overview of the types of remedy available.

In any event, this general conspectus of remedies will help you in understanding the remedial elements in subjects such as contract, tort and constitutional law. The need to know something about remedies in general may occur in connection with work in the form of case studies as well as straightforward examination questions. The common rubric to 'Advise X' may reasonably be interpreted to include advice on the appropriate remedy in the matter in hand, assuming that a cause of action exists and liability is made out.

The following outline would seem to be the minimum to make a study of damages worthwhile in the context of an English legal system course. Above that minimum you may build up more detailed knowledge, for example, in the law of damages or equitable remedies, as time allows. The outline is concerned only with judicial remedies. Additionally, some courses may include a requirement to know about methods of enforcement, and Smith and Bailey have a section on this aspect of remedies.

Before attempting to produce a classification of remedies, let me remind you that we are looking at the civil process and that as part of that process it is sometimes necessary or desirable for the courts to give a ruling on a preliminary issue. Such rulings are sought by either plaintiff or defendant to make plain a point of law, to assist in the conduct of the litigation, as by ordering a discovery of documents, or to protect the status quo until the outcome of the case; to guard against the possibility, for example, that property in dispute might disappear or be put beyond the reach of the court before judgment is given, let alone enforced.

These matters are dealt with as preliminary points of law, or by seeking an interlocutory order. In many cases, the litigation is settled or withdrawn as a result of these preliminary rulings and interlocutory orders.

As you might imagine from studying chapter 4, the remedies available in the English courts may be classified as common law remedies and equitable remedies. Look again then at the general relationship between law and equity before trying to understand the difference between common law damages and damages in lieu of an injunction. Find and read again the Supreme Court Act 1981, ss. 49 and 50. The first general point to make about common law and equitable remedies is that the former are available as of right whilst equitable remedies are discretionary.

In connection with damages as a common law remedy you should be able to explain the following matters and to be able to identify the appropriate occasions for the award of the different types of damages:

(a)   The general rule that damages are intended to compensate.

(b)   The distinction between liquidated and unliquidated damages (a necessity in understanding penalty clauses in the law of contract).

(c)   The meaning of and the distinction between general damages and special damages.

(d)   The meaning of nominal damages, distinguishing the contemptuous damages that were awarded in *Dering* v *Uris* [1964] 2 QB 669.

(e)   The meaning of exemplary damages and the types of case in which they may be awarded. See the case of *Cassell & Co. Ltd* v *Broome* [1972] AC 1027.

Apart from knowing the names of the equitable remedies and that they are discretionary, you should pay particular heed to the following in order to give suitable advice on remedies, when called upon to do so. First, learn the different types of injunction, paying attention to the difference between an injunction that is intended to be permanent in its effect and one that is not. The details of the different forms of injunction are set out in the main textbooks. Secondly, guard against the common fault of students, who forget or do not ever realise that specific performance is a purely contractual remedy. Finally, read carefully the passages in the textbooks that deal with 'declarations' as a remedy. At first you may find it hard to understand why anyone should be content with an order that merely states what the law is, without provision being made for the enforcement of the plaintiff's rights. Start by reading the terms of Ord. 15, r. 16, of the Rules of the Supreme Court. Next, remember that it is an equitable remedy. Finally, the court will not grant a declaration in a totally hypothetical case: there must be an actual dispute between the parties. It is no good in an answer, therefore, to use the declaration as an example of a test case used to settle doubtful points of law for the benefit of all other potential litigants. English courts will not give hypothetical rulings (see chapter 10 on case law and precedent).

Let us turn now to consider those remedies that are known as public law remedies. In his book, *An Introduction to Administrative Law*, Cane points out that, in private law matters, the first consideration of someone with a grievance is to find out whether he has a right that has been infringed. As my one-time tutor, Professor Bromley, used to say, 'First catch your tort'. In public law matters, on the other hand, Cane points out that the primary consideration is to determine whether or not there is a remedy. In this field of law it is still very true that English law is a law of remedies and not of rights.

In the context of most English legal system courses, it seems that public law remedies receive elementary treatment. They are not to be ignored for that reason or for the reason that they are often dealt with as a late item in the curriculum. One compelling reason for paying proper attention to them is that these remedies appear in the leading textbooks, which, in turn, are written by people who base them on their own teaching experience. That implies also an indication of those writers' expectations of students they themselves teach.

You may be called upon to do a number of things which require a knowledge of public law remedies. As always, the surest foundation for any of these tasks is to know what the public law remedies are and the degree of detail that is appropriate to your course. In the first instance, this means acquiring a basic knowledge of judicial review and the distinction between review and appeal. An elementary understanding of the meaning of *locus standi* in relation to public law is also essential.

Having next learned the principal characteristics of the prerogative remedies, *certiorari, mandamus* and prohibition, set them in the context of the procedure for application for judicial review. (Note that it is recommended that the titles of these remedies be changed to indicate their nature.) The fact that leave to apply is required under Rules of the Supreme Court, Ord. 53, and that ultimate granting or withholding of the remedy is discretionary are two facts which will always be necessary ingredients of any answer to a question on an English legal system paper that deals with the role and place of the courts as part of the governing process. The modern view is not that the courts provide a check on government's wish to govern, but that the courts are there to see that the processes of government are carried on in an orderly way in accordance with legality and without oppression of the individual.

There may sometimes be a question set in an examination paper or for an assessed piece of coursework that needs some detailed consideration of the availability of the appropriate remedy in a given situation. This raises two related issues. They are of contemporary significance because of the recent realisation by academics that the courts are beginning to distinguish public and private law concepts in connection with the activities of government and other administrative bodies. These issues are:

(a)   Is a private law remedy (damages, injunction etc.) available against some public body or other?

(b)   Where a public body is a proposed defendant, what is the relationship between public law and private law remedies?

Most of the textbooks refer to this. See, for example, Ingman, *The English Legal Process*, 5th ed., p. 343. This whole area is a minefield of uncertainty. Here are some guidelines to assist you in negotiating this area as a first-year student of the English legal system:

(a)   Under the application for review procedure the court can grant any of the prerogative remedies, along with a declaration or an injunction, either singly, in any combination or in the alternative. Where appropriate, damages may also be awarded.

(b)   The granting of the application is discretionary. It may be refused where there is a more appropriate remedy. Note that the existence of a right of appeal is not necessarily a bar to an application for review.

(c)   The court may refuse to grant an application for review because it considers that the matter is not justiciable. Is it susceptible of solution by legal techniques? See Types of Dispute, p. 114.

(d)   The courts no longer take the view that the application for review procedure must be used in all proceedings in which public law matters are challenged, subject to certain exceptions (*O'Reilly* v *Mackman* [1983] 2 AC 237), and now seem to be adopting a broad approach under which Ord. 53 would be insisted on only if private rights were not in issue (*Roy* v *Kensington and Chelsea FPC* [1992] 1 AC 624).

(e)   Problems continue over the definition of a 'public law matter'. Not every decision taken by a public body will fall within this definition (*R v BBC, ex parte Lavelle* [1983] 1 WLR 23).

(f)   The High Court will exercise its supervisory jurisdiction over bodies performing public law functions even where these bodies have not been established by statute or by perogative powers (*R v City Panel on Take-overs and Mergers, ex parte Datafin* [1987] QB 815). The test seems to be whether the State would take action were it not for the performance of functions by the body under review.

ALTERNATIVES TO THE ORDINARY COURTS

In the earlier sections of this chapter, I have mentioned both types of dispute and types of institution, and attempted to relate the two to one another. Now I want to look in more detail at those institutions which do not count as courts but which play a large part in providing the means for the settlement of disputes. Here is a list of some of those institutions:

(a)   Tribunals, both statutory and domestic.
(b)   Inquiries.
(c)   Arbitrations.
(d)   Ombudsmen, including the statutory commissioners, Parliamentary, Local Government and Health Service, the non-statutory ombudsmen for banking and insurance, and the legal services and conveyancing ombudsman.

Most English legal system courses will deal to some extent with all or some of these institutions. As such, you should be able to analyse each of them in terms of their constitution, jurisdiction, procedural characteristics and powers. Take, for example, the industrial tribunals. You should know under what statute they are established and their constitution in terms of the make-up of the tribunal (a chairman and wing-men), the types of case they hear, unfair dismissal claims etc., procedural characteristics in terms of attitudes to formal rules of evidence, rights of representation, and their powers to award compensation and to order reinstatement in employment backed up with enforcement procedures. We also know from previous study that if these institutions for the settlement of disputes are established by statute then they will in some measure be subject to the control of the ordinary courts, whether, as in the case of industrial tribunals, by statutory right of appeal on points of law or by the process of judicial review (see above). In other cases the decisions of non-statutory institutions may not be binding, as in the case of the insurance ombudsman, or the decision may be challenged by a private law action for breach of contract or a tort. This may happen when a member of an association is dissatisfied with the decision of a domestic tribunal of the association.

All of these matters are the proper subject of an analytical study of these institutions as institutions. On that ground alone they are proper material for inclusion in a legal system course, and you should be prepared to answer questions set in these terms. To that end, Smith and Bailey and Ingman both have relevant chapters.

However, these institutions are also of interest in our legal system courses because they are *alternatives*. Alternatives, that is, to settlement of disputes through the ordinary courts. Why should there be alternatives at all? Well, let us see!

I shall begin by reminding you of the basic nature of litigation in English courts. It is based on the adversarial system with issues between the parties being defined in the pleadings. (Look back at this stage to chapter 4 on the historical background to the English legal system.) At the High Court level the system is highly centralised and there are relatively fewer judges in the English legal system than in many others. There is a decentralised system of county courts with an ordinary procedure modelled on that of the High Court but with a statutory system of arbitration for 'small claims'.

What is wrong with such a system? In broad terms, there are complaints of excessive legality, delay (there was a medical negligence case heard 11 years after the alleged acts of negligence; *Whitehouse* v *Jordan* [1981] 1 WLR 246 is another example of protracted litigation), high costs (the theatrical impresario, Sir Peter Hall, withdrew a libel action against the *Sunday Times* because of escalating costs and, again on grounds of cost, in 1991 Orkney Council in Scotland had to consider withdrawing from a *public inquiry* into alleged child abuse, which shows that it is not only ordinary litigation that is very costly) and the fact that the adversarial system breeds conflict rather than encourages settlement. This last point applies particularly to family law matters.

A knowledge of the workings of the 'alternative' methods of dispute settlement and alternative institutions will help you to develop a critique of the ordinary courts as well as being a topic in its own right. In considering these alternative institutions as part of a critique of ordinary courts you might care to set them in the context of the following questions:

(a)   Do the ordinary courts as we know them suffer from some inherent defects which makes them unsuited to hear certain types of dispute?

(b)   What steps, if any, have been or may be taken to remedy those defects?

(c)   If no steps are taken or steps taken are inadequate, do the alternatives actually do a better job?

Here are some answers. There are, I am sure, other answers. Your task in preparing this part of the syllabus is to check the truth of the answers to those

questions by collecting examples from official statements, textbooks, periodicals and newspapers.

(a)   Enough has been said already in this section and previously to make
you aware of the defects in the ways in which the ordinary courts work. It is
regrettably all too easy to collect examples of delay, expense and undue
reliance on legal technicalities.

(b)   In answer to the second question, it can be pointed out that there have
been moves to create specialist sections within the High Court: for admiralty
cases, for commercial cases (in competition with arbitration), for Crown
Office list cases in administrative law matters. Some courts, such as the
Restrictive Practices Court, have laymen sitting on the bench as part of the
court, put there because of their expertise. There are suggestions for the
establishment of a family court, which would involve a modification of the
adversarial procedure existing at present. The small claims jurisdiction in the
county courts has been a success, in terms of its usage. As to steps that may
be taken, you need look no further than the recommendations contained in
Lord Woolf's report on *Access to Justice*.

(c)   There is no suggestion that any far-reaching fundamental reforms of
the ordinary courts will ever remove the need for other types of institution
for the redress of grievances and the settlement of disputes. The two will
continue to coexist. Students of the legal system have a legitimate interest in
discussing the proper scope of each and in discovering what lessons may be
learned for the improvement of *all* parts of the legal system by drawing on
the experience of each type of institution. For example, could the High
Court's pre-trial procedures benefit in any way by taking a look at the
investigative aspects of the work of the Parliamentary and other Commissioners, with a view to giving the courts a more active role in the gathering
of evidence and the marshalling of arguments, rather like the practice
adopted in some jurisdictions of having a '*juge rapporteur*'.

What is it about the alternative institutions themselves that make them
attractive as alternatives to the ordinary courts or as models for the reform of
the ordinary courts?

After all, the small claims procedure of the county courts was based on
previous non-statutory small claims arbitration schemes in London and
Manchester. Considering only tribunals, it can be said that: they are locally
based with a good geographical distribution; they have specialist members,
even though they may have a legally qualified chairman; their procedure is
less formal than in a court; they are not bound by precedent; lawyers do not
have a monopoly of rights of representation. In the right context and in the
right hands, these are all undoubted advantages in an institution where

disputes consist largely of disputed issues of fact. There is another side to this matter. In spite of the requirements of the Tribunals and Inquiries Act 1992 and the work of the Council on Tribunals there is a risk of some tribunals whose work is closely linked to a particular government department being seen as an adjunct of that department (compare the relationship between a magistrates' court and the local police). Also, extreme informality, where it exists, does not allow for the clear emergence of the matters in dispute that are relevant, in the way in which this happens in a skilfully pleaded action in the courts. On the whole, though, tribunals seem to steer a middle course which does not inhibit the emergence of points that are relevant and should be decided. Even the more relaxed modern rules of court procedure with generous provision for amendments of the case as pleaded, sometimes do prevent all relevant issues being raised and decided. (See, for example, the case of *Leaf* v *International Galleries* [1950] 2 KB 86 in which the plaintiff was told that the outcome of the case might have been different had he argued that there had been a breach of contract instead of relying on allegations of misrepresentation by the defendant.) It is wrong to suppose that tribunals hardly ever have to deal with complex points of law and for that reason alone it may be said that the unavailability of legal aid and advice is a clear disadvantage of the tribunal system. The lack of legal aid is a major contributory factor to the scarcity of lawyers with expertise in handling the type of case found in many tribunals. Finally, whilst delay is not a cause for concern in the vast majority of cases, it must be remembered that none of these alternatives to the courts can make final decisions without there being some risk of the decision being challenged in an application for judicial review or by way of a statutory appeal.

Before leaving these alternatives to action in the ordinary courts I must remind you of certain other possibilities for the alternative handling of grievances. The two most important possibilities are further development of the power of criminal courts to award compensation to the victims of convicted offenders, and a development of a true class action. This latter would avoid some of the difficulties encountered in dealing with a multiplicity of claims arising out of the same cause. Four notable incidents should tell you what sort of situation would benefit from the availability of the American-style class action: the thalidomide cases, the Bradford Football Club fire disaster, the Zeebrugge ferry disaster, and the Hillsborough disaster.

Another recent development in the civil process is the way in which the rules of procedure have changed so as to make parties to litigation 'put their cards on the table'. These changes followed the enactment of the Courts and Legal Services Act 1990, providing, for example, for the exchange of witness statements in civil cases. This development is designed to promote settlement by the parties.

CONNECTIONS

The Interlude on Legal Institutions (chapter 5) dealt with the position of the English legal system as a member of the family of legal systems in the world today. In order to round off this review of the English civil legal process you will have to take account of the fact that there are several institutions which are not part of the English legal system but which influence the law as it is administered in England and Wales (and also the rest of the United Kingdom). There are three principal institutions of this kind, one situated within the jurisdiction and two European institutions. The first is the Judicial Committee of the Privy Council, of which the decisions are highly persuasive but not binding on English courts.

You will recall that the European Convention on Human Rights is not part of English law, but the UK government has bound itself by treaty to allow its citizens direct access to the European Commission of Human Rights and the European Court of Human Rights. Decisions of that court are not binding on the UK government.

More significant, perhaps, as an object of study in a legal systems course is the Court of Justice of the European Communities (CJEC). This institution often comes up in examinations and a knowledge of the court is necessary in a number of ways to the student of the English legal system.

Stated briefly, the sort of points that may be made in essays by drawing on such knowledge are as follows:

(a)   The work of the CJEC as an organ of the European Union is a good example of an organic connection between two legal systems. The CJEC, by the Treaty of Rome, has to uphold and interpret the law of the Community; and by the European Communities Act 1972 that law is made part of the law of the United Kingdom.

(b)   Article 177 of the Treaty of Rome provides for references to the CJEC by courts of all member States on points of Community law, providing an example of how the courts of different legal systems may be linked together.

(c)   The constitution and working practices of the CJEC provide a useful comparative institutional study. You should note in particular, for potential use in such comparative studies:

(i)   The collegiate nature of the court, which gives a single judgment, without recording dissenting judgments.

(ii)   The role of the advocates general, who rank as members of the court.

(iii)   The terms of appointment and tenure of judges and advocates general.

(iv)   The fact that there is no strict doctrine of precedent.

(v)   The extent of reliance on written procedures and the limited use of oral argument before the court.

It is now time to look at two possible questions of the sort that frequently occur in coursework and examinations.

EXAMINATION QUESTIONS

I have selected two questions for commentary which will illustrate the different types of possible approach to testing the effectiveness of your learning and study of the civil justice process in England and Wales.

The first is a typical problem-type question such as you will encounter in the substantive subjects in the curriculum. The other one is of a more critical nature. Remember that tutors and examiners must bear in mind that this is essentially a first-year subject, assessed and examined within nine months of you beginning your studies. Before looking at the first question in detail check what is said in chapter 2 about answering questions in the context of a legal system course.

Question 1

Your client Y is seeking your advice on the points mentioned below in the following situation. He tells you that his neighbour X has threatened to apply for a High Court injunction to stop him, Y, from holding flower-arranging symposia in a tent in his garden. It seems that X is afraid that pests from the flowers brought to the flower-arranging events will infest valuable plants in his own garden, within 50 feet of the site of the proposed tent.

Assuming that there is a serious risk of this happening, advise Y fully of his position in the High Court action and of the possibility of an appeal if an injunction is granted.

Points to Cover in an Answer (in note form here)

(a)   Without dealing with any issues of the law of tort, set out alternatives on the basis of questions to the client:

(i)   Has anything been done towards arranging an event, e.g., erection of a tent?
(ii)   Is it intended to hold a series of events?
(iii)   Has litigation begun?

(b)   Explain to client that circumstances such as (i) and/or (ii) will affect the type of injunction X will be seeking; *'quia timet'*, perpetual, interlocutory. Explain especially the length of time for which each of these will restrict Y's intended use of his garden.

(c)   If it is an interlocutory injunction that is sought, explain that X may be asked to undertake to pay damages to your client in the event of X losing a subsequent action, and set out the criteria for the award of interlocutory injunctions in *American Cyanamid Co. v Ethicon Ltd* [1975] AC 396.

(d)   If a final injunction is being sought, whether or not a perpetual one (that may depend on whether there is to be one or a series of events — see (a)(ii) above) advise Y of the power of the court to award damages in substitution under Supreme Court Act 1981, s. 50, and the effect of such damages, if awarded, on the future use of your client's garden. (See *Miller v Jackson* [1977] QB 966 on the use of a field as a cricket ground.)

(e)   In the case of need to appeal:

(i)   If an interlocutory injunction has been awarded, leave to appeal is required under Supreme Court Act 1981, s. 18(1A).

(ii)   Explain the powers of the Court of Appeal; under Rules of the Supreme Court, Ord. 59: to draw inferences, to discharge the injunction, to vary or modify the terms (e.g., allowing the activity subject to conditions, moving the site of the tent), to substitute an award of damages.

(f)   In conclusion mention the *possibility* of a further appeal to the House of Lords.

The answer breaks down into six parts. Four of those parts, (b) to (e), contain the major points of any answer. It is thus comparatively easy to mark the question out of 20 marks, either impressionistically or according to a set scheme, such as 2, 4, 4, 4, 4, 2.

Question 2

Discuss the extent to which the distinction between courts and tribunals has become blurred in the English legal system.

Commentary on Question 2

Perusal of examination papers from several universities and polytechnics suggests that this is a favourite theme for questions. As this question requires discussion, assume that in some ways there has been a blurring of the distinction but that it remains sharp and clear-cut in other ways. Start by discussing the difficulty of defining what is a court. Refer to the criteria set out in the case of *Attorney-General* v *British Broadcasting Corporation* [1981] AC 303. The difference between a judicial issue and an administrative decision is a useful but not infallible basis of the distinction between the work of courts and the work of tribunals.

Compare, if necessary *seriatim*, the ways in which courts and tribunals respectively are constituted, their rules of procedure, attitudes to the law of evidence, rights of representation, powers to enforce their orders, including power to punish for contempt. Mention that some undoubted courts, e.g., magistrates', have had to have their position *vis-à-vis* contempt regulated by statute. By all means use industrial tribunals as an example of tribunals approximating to courts but raise the issue of how typical those tribunals are of tribunals as a whole. Conclude by saying that not only have tribunals become in some respects more like courts, but that courts have also adopted some features of tribunals, e.g., in the small claims jurisdiction of the county court. Ultimately, an institution, whether called by the name tribunal or court, is admitted to the ranks of the courts if it is accepted as such by the existing courts.

THEMES COMMON TO BOTH THE CRIMINAL AND CIVIL PROCESS

The last two chapters have kept the criminal and civil processes quite separate. There are, however, several themes which may occur in programmes of assessment, whether by examination or otherwise, which require you to consider both the criminal and civil process. The following list includes the most frequently met topics which require this knowledge. In many cases the rules of the criminal and civil processes are different in details which can be compared.

At the Trial Stage

(a)   The preliminary stages of a case: should all cases begin in the same court?

(b)   The use of speedy forms of trial for minor uncontested cases. Pleading guilty by post; the procedure for undefended divorces; undefended debt actions.

(c)   The criteria used for distinguishing serious from non-serious cases; and the procedure used for selecting cases for more elaborate formal types of trial.

(d)   A consideration of whether the courts should develop an investigative role at the preliminary stages.

(e)   The use of lay people on the bench — both entirely lay courts, as with the magistrates, and mixed courts, as where JPs sit with a circuit judge, compared with the use of lay members on certain civil courts.

At the Appeal Stage

(a) Sifting out non-meritorious appeals. The use of the device of requiring 'leave to appeal'. Other devices compared: powers for the variation of sentences; disallowance of costs.

(b) Expediting appeals in urgent cases.

(c) Powers of appellate courts:

   (i)   to decide a case on new grounds
   (ii)   to substitute convictions for other offences
   (iii) to hear new evidence
   (iv)   to order new trials.

(d) Appellate courts and the public interest: references by the Home Secretary and Attorney-General in criminal cases; attitudes to 'test' cases in civil cases; possible litigation at public expense to settle the law.

(e) Finality of appeals: exclusion in minor cases of right to appeal.

(f) Provision for further appeals from the Court of Appeal to the House of Lords.

(g) Clarity of the law in appeal cases. Should the courts give only one judgment, with the right to dissent preserved?

FURTHER READING

Ingman, T., *The English Legal Process* (5th edn., Blackstone Press, 1994).

Smith, P.F. and Bailey, S.H., *The Modern English Legal System* by S.H. Bailey and M.J. Gunn (2nd edn., Sweet and Maxwell, 1991).

Zander, M. *Cases and Materials on the English Legal System* (6th edn., Butterworths, 1992).

8 TWO SET PIECES — CONTEMPT AND LEGAL AID

Every subject has its set pieces or self-contained topics. If such topics are properly mastered and the teaching which you receive in a subject deals with a topic in such a way, then there is a good chance that you will have one question at least on an examination paper about which you can be quietly and justifiably confident. The two quite distinct parts of this chapter deal with two topics which appear in a sufficient number of legal system courses to justify including them in this book. Before spending a lot of time on the material in this chapter make sure that your course is going to deal 'this year' with either or both 'contempt of court' and 'legal aid'. In the 1990s, both contempt of court and legal aid have been lively issues which look as if they will continue to be of topical interest for some time to come. Legal Aid may be part of a wider treatment of 'access to justice'.

CONTEMPT OF COURT

If the law of contempt is thought of as a form of protection of the integrity of the legal process it has obvious connections with civil liberties issues. As such, it may be part also of your constitutional law syllabus, or perhaps a special subject on civil liberties. Certainly, as cases round the world connected with Peter Wright's memoirs, *Spycatcher*, testify, the law of contempt is very important for the freedom of the press. It may be that you decide to work up the topic of contempt of court in the hope of being able to write an essay or answer an examination question of a general sort about the effect of the law of contempt on some aspect of civil liberties.

Nevertheless, in this part of the chapter I intend to assume that first of all you need to be able to handle the law in a competent and flexible way: flexible in that you must be able to apply your specialised knowledge of the topic in at least two ways. These are to be able to answer problem questions about the law as it is and to be able to apply that knowledge as the basis of criticism of the law and the effects that it has. A good knowledge of the law and cases will enable you to comment with greater authority on the effect that the law of contempt has on the ability of the Press to comment freely on matters of public interest. Unless a question of that sort was limited by its terms of reference to the law of contempt, I believe that a proper answer would require treatment of the law of libel and confidentiality also. That requirement would rule out such a wide-ranging question based on the law of contempt from most English legal system schemes of assessment. Subject integration has not progressed so far yet in most courses. So I assume you will want to concentrate on learning the essentials of the law of contempt in the expectation that essays and problem questions will probe the areas of uncertainty in the law as well as requiring straightforward application of the law.

Some of the facts of the cases on contempt are memorable in themselves, so I shall begin in a lighthearted way by characterising the law by reference to several cases, some well known and some not so well known.

(a)   Contempt has its funny side. See the case of the laughing gas that nearly was (*Balogh* v *St Albans Crown Court* [1975] QB 73).

(b)   Contempt may be violent, both in its occurrence and its punishment. Walker and Walker recall the 1631 case in which the prisoner 'Ject un Brickbat a le dit Justice que narrowly mist, & pur ceo immediately fuit Indictment drawn per Noy envers le prisoner, & son dexter manus ampute & fix al Gibbet sur que mesme immediatement hange in presence de Court'.

(c)   Contempt may be born out of stubbornness bordering on stupidity. There was the case of the insurance broker who spent 18 months in prison for contempt because on the very day he gave an undertaking to the court not to repeat a libel, he did repeat the libel within hours of leaving the court.

(d)   Contempt may be explicable if not pardonable, as with the prisoner who had just received a heavy sentence and was heard to call the judge an 'old bugger' as he was being taken down to the cells. He was brought back immediately and sentenced to an additional term of imprisonment for the contempt.

Of those four cases, the first two and the last are examples of contempt in the face of the court. The third is an example of procedural or civil contempt. They are all easy and obvious examples. The legal interest in them and cases like them such as *Morris* v *Crown Office* [1970] 2 QB 114 lies in whether the behaviour is sufficiently serious to amount to a contempt and, if so, how severe a penalty should be imposed. (See Ingman, *The English Legal Process*, 5th ed., p. 146, for some doubts about the powers of magistrates.)

The more difficult areas of concern raised by the existence and enforcement of the law of contempt are these: the scope that is left for legitimate criticism of the courts (that means very largely the judges acting in their judicial capacity and not as individuals); the extent to which matters which are the subject of court proceedings should receive publicity; the peremptory power of punishment and related opportunities of appeal. To this should be added doubts about the effects of the Contempt of Court Act 1981. In shepherding the Bill through the House of Lords, Lord Hailsham of St Marylebone LC referred to it as his 'little ewe lamb', and the Bill was hailed officially as a liberal measure. In certain respects, however, the 1981 Act is by no means a liberal measure.

An analysis of the current state of the law of contempt will show that the difficult areas mentioned above continue to provide the salient points to be found in examination questions of the problem type, which test your ability to analyse the existing law and to apply it to situations involving some doubt about how an actual case would be decided in the courts. As such, the law of contempt provides a traditional vehicle for the development and testing of your legal skills.

In addition, those difficult areas which I have identified provide the material for a discussion of the way in which the law of contempt influences the sort of legal system we have and the way in which that legal system relates to society. In looking at some aspects of contempt law, such as the degree of criticism of the 'law' permitted by the rules of contempt as applied by the judges, you might consider whether or not there is some evidence that the law is isolated from the society it is meant to serve. Again, a knowledge of the law of contempt can be useful in tackling essays on the general theme of the public's 'right to know'. This is especially true where there is a suspicion that government may use the law of contempt (or the threat of it), as in the *Spycatcher* cases, to stifle criticism of the government's handling of affairs or to prevent embarrassment of the government.

For these reasons, there follows an outline analysis of contempt law which seeks to point out some of the common pitfalls and mistakes that students may make. This part of the chapter will conclude by reference to the treatment of contempt in different textbooks and a sample question. The textbook references will help you to fix in your own minds a good idea of the way in which this topic is approached in your own course. The question is one which raises most of the principal areas of difficulty mentioned above, and can therefore be answered as a 'straight' problem question or used as a vehicle for wider discussion of the issues raised by the law of contempt.

CONTEMPT: POINTS TO NOTE

For the purposes of exposition and learning it is wise for you to maintain the distinction between criminal contempt and civil contempt, although the Phillimore Committee (Cmnd 5794, 1974) recommended that these terms should be no longer used.

You must become familiar with the types of contempt which are classed as criminal. These may be classified as:

(a) *Behaviour and comment which interferes with the proper administration of justice in the courts.*
These contempts may be subdivided into:

(i) The interruption of court proceedings (see above).

(ii) Criticism that is more than 'moderate' in tone. Compare the cases of *R* v *Editor of the New Statesman* (1928) 44 TLR 301 with *R* v *Commissioner of Police of the Metropolis (ex parte Blackburn) (No. 2)* [1968] 2 QB 150. Does it matter who is the critic and in what form the criticism is voiced? Is matter that would be a contempt in the *Sun* equally a contempt when suitably rephrased in the *Modern Law Review*?

(iii) Preventing access to the courts. There was the case many years ago of a solicitor in Leeds who was disciplined by the court for bringing the office of his opponent in a case to a standstill by getting his own staff to make more than 60 telephone calls to the opponent's office in one hour.

(iv) Some witnesses, especially journalists, may face a dilemma in giving their evidence. The courts are loath to extend the types of confidential relationships involving privilege against disclosure. It is contempt therefore for journalists (see *Attorney-General* v *Mulholland* [1963] 2 QB 477) to refuse to answer questions in court on the ground that to do so would be a breach of confidence. Usually it is a source of information that is being protected. Do not forget that the Contempt of Court Act 1981, s. 10, provides that it is no longer contempt to refuse to disclose a source of information unless it is in the interest of national security to do so, or in the interests of justice or for the prevention of disorder or crime.

(v) As a result of the decision in *Re Lonrho plc* [1990] 2 AC 154, judges are officially more robust in their ability to withstand prejudicial material: in this case, copies of the *Observer* newspaper containing material designed to influence proceedings.

(vi) The large area of contempt law that has produced difficulties in the past and provides the core of reforms in the 1981 Act was the *sub judice* rule. This is replaced in those cases to which the Act applies by the concept of proceedings being 'active' (but see *Attorney-General* v *News Group Newspapers Ltd* [1989] QB 110 for a case where the Sun newspaper was fined although no proceedings were pending or imminent). When you are dealing with this part of the law which is concerned with interference with actual proceedings or at least potential proceedings you must take note of the following points:

(1)   The statutory strict liability rule set out in s. 1 of the 1981 Act only applies to 'publications'.

(2)   Also, it only applies to those publications which create a 'substantial' risk that the course of justice will be 'seriously' impeded. Take particular note of how the section may be interpreted, as to what constitutes a 'substantial' risk.

(3)   Schedule 1 to the Act provides a definition of when proceedings are deemed to be 'active' and when they cease to be 'active'. Note here that there are separate definitions for civil and criminal proceedings. Do not confuse them. On the whole the new rules make life a little easier for editors compared with the old *sub judice* rule when it was sometimes impossible to discover that a matter had become *sub judice* and therefore that there should be no further comment upon it.

(4)   Take note of the defence of innocent publication under s. 3 of the Act. The easing of the editor's position under (3) above is reinforced by this provision.

However, this defence now applies *only* to cases under the 1981 Act because of the provisions of s. 6. The Act does nothing to restrict liability which arises out of conduct *intended* to impede the course of justice.

(5)   Section 5 of the Act introduces a defence based on the protection of public discussion of a matter of general interest. If a publication which would otherwise come within the strict liability rule forms part of a continuing discussion of a general nature and the publication is in good faith there will be no contempt. The section and its difficulties have been discussed by the House of Lords in the case of *Attorney-General* v *English* [1983] 1 AC 116. The alleged general discussion here was on the sanctity of human life. The publication occurred in the context of the trial of Dr Arthur for the murder of handicapped babies, by withholding treatment from them. Useful comments appear in Lord Diplock's judgment. They are well summarised by Dr Ingman in the 5th edition of *The English Legal Process* at pp. 137–9. If contempt is one of your selected topics this is an essential case to read and check your own reading of the case against Dr Ingman's summary.

(6)   Section 4(2) of the Contempt of Court Act 1981 gives a court a discretion to order postponement of the publication of a report of a case. This power has been exercised with some regularity. There is now a right of appeal under s. 159 of the Criminal Justice Act 1988. The workings of this section were explained by the Court of Appeal in *Re Crook* (1989) *The Times*, 13 November 1989, in which the court also offered guidance on the exclusion of the public generally from legal proceedings.

(b)   *Civil contempt.*
This is also known as procedural contempt. The principal matter for you to learn here is the way in which proven instances of civil contempt are handled. The order which has been ignored may be enforced, if necessary by sequestration of the defendant's assets. Thus, a civil contempt may be disobedience of an order of a civil court and also disobedience of the order of a criminal court. Criminal courts have their own sanctions for disobedience. Additionally, civil contempt is in itself a crime and punishable as such. This is explained in the next section.

Form of Contempt Proceedings

Both criminal and civil contempts are criminal offences. Criminal contempt is a non-arrestable offence punishable by imprisonment and or a fine.
    Civil contempt as a crime is also punishable under the inherent jurisdiction of the court by imprisonment and or a fine. There is also the possibility of the sequestration of assets.
    If you are going to answer problem questions or comment on the law of contempt, accuracy in using these terms and knowledge of the consequences of each is essential.

Punishment for Contempt of Court

The peremptory and uncertain nature of the punishment for contempt was always the most notorious feature of this part of the law. It was only mitigated by the ability of the contemnor to purge the contempt by an apology and where appropriate by giving an undertaking to obey the order of the court. Regularity and an end to unlimited periods of imprisonment result from the Contempt of Court Act 1981, s. 14. You should be able to distinguish the power to punish for contempt according to the following list:

(a)   Powers of superior courts of record.
(b)   Powers of inferior courts.
(c)   Powers of magistrates' courts to punish for contempts in the face of the court (Contempt of Court Act 1981, s. 12).
(d)   Powers of Divisional Court to punish for contempt not within the statutory powers of inferior courts.

    The power to punish contempts committed in the face of the court is still extremely summary and lacking in impartiality. The power is to be exercised sparingly and alternative methods used whenever possible.

The Jury and Contempt

You should be prepared to include the material referred to in this paragraph as part of work connected with the institution of jury trial as a whole. The connection between the jury and the law of contempt is as follows:

(a) It is contempt to interfere or to attempt to interfere with the deliberations of the jury or to try to obtain information about the deliberations of the jury. Section 8 of the 1981 Act extended this to a degree where it is doubtful whether legitimate research may be conducted into the workings of the jury system if there is the threat that the Attorney-General may institute proceedings. (We know that on other matters such as sentencing there is some official hostility to academic research programmes.)

(b) Misbehaviour on the part of a member of a jury or a person called for jury service may be treated as contempt or punished as a summary offence under the Juries Act 1974. For example, a woman summoned for jury service went on holiday and asked a relative to telephone the court to say she could not serve on the jury panel because she was going away. Subsequently, she was fined £100.

Appeals in Cases of Contempt of Court

It is only since 1960 that there have been rights of appeal in cases of criminal contempt. Your business in this connection is to learn, as with all appeal structures:

(a)   The court to which appeal lies in any particular case.
(b)   The powers of the court hearing the appeal.

Generally s. 13 of the Administration of Justice Act 1960 gives the appellate court power to reverse or vary the decision of the court below.

TEXTBOOKS

The standard textbooks on the English legal system adopt a variety of attitudes to this topic. Draw your own conclusions about its importance in your own syllabus by considering which books are recommended to you as well as the teaching you receive in lectures and seminars.

(a)   Ingman, *The English Legal Process.* A short chapter devoted to an analysis of the law of contempt, on which the foregoing section in this chapter is based.

(b) Jackson, *The Machinery of Justice in England.* Scattered references to contempt indicating a treatment that integrates the law of contempt into other aspects of the legal process.

(c) Smith and Bailey, *The Modern English Legal System.* A single reference to contempt of court appears in the index.

(d) Walker and Walker, *The English Legal System.* A two-page section devoted to contempt containing a brief analysis with historical references.

(e) Zander, *Cases and Materials on the English Legal System.* A section entitled 'Publicity and contempt'. The emphasis is clearly on one of the issues raised by the working of the law of contempt. The effect of the law of contempt on freedom of publication is linked to restrictions on the publication of accounts of committal proceedings in the magistrates' courts. The public's right to be informed is shown balanced against the need to ensure a fair trial for an accused person. Fairness of that sort also applies in civil matters which can equally well be prejudiced by published comment.

You should now be aware of the sort of task that some of you may be set in your study of the law of contempt. Let us tackle a question together and see how the same set of facts can give rise to quite different types of question.

EXAMINATION QUESTIONS

The Facts

A drug manufacturing firm, Addicto Co. Ltd, have, for the past 12 years, marketed a drug as a mild tranquilliser with no addictive qualities. It has been widely prescribed to sufferers of nervous disorders. After six years in use, the drug was found to have addictive qualities and several users have actions pending against Addicto Co. Ltd. In recent weeks it has been rumoured that criminal proceedings may be instituted against Addicto as it would appear that its manufacturing techniques contravene statutory regulations on the production of such drugs.

After careful inquiries, the editor of the *Daily Slur,* a national newspaper, authorised the printing of a front page headline 'Drug Co. in Manufacturing Scandal' and a report containing the following information. That Addicto is faced with several actions for negligence by users and it would now appear that the company will be prosecuted. The editorial column picks up this theme and suggests in the light of the possible criminal proceedings that Addicto should now settle with all affected users who are undoubtedly victims of the company's negligence.

In the week following this report criminal proceedings are started against Addicto Co. Ltd.

On the evening of the commencement of the trial of Addicto the DBB TV Co. in a current affairs programme highlighted the problems of the drug industry. It was suggested that Addicto is not alone in carrying out practices which seem to contravene the statutory regulations.

Question 1

Advise (a) the *Daily Slur;* and (b) The DBB TV Co. as to their respective liability in the law of contempt.

Question 2

Comment on the issues raised by the above facts for the editors of newspapers and the producers of television current affairs programmes.

Commentary

General The two questions stand independently of one another. In question 1, the use of the word 'respective' in the rubric indicates that there is no need to relate parts (a) and (b) to one another. Your answer will be more clear and easier to follow if you do not attempt to cross-refer and compare the position of the *Daily Slur* with that of the DBB TV Co. By *looking* at the question and following up that look with a close reading it seems that there is less to say about the DBB TV Co. than there is about the *Daily Slur* and your answer will show this.

On the other hand, in question 2, the way in which the question is worded invites you to apply the lessons to be learned from the situation of both the *Daily Slur* and the DBB TV Co., generally, for the benefit of those working in the media. Note the difference between the specific requirement in question 1, to give advice, and the more generalised requirement to comment in question 2, which enables you to consider value judgments about the state of the law.

Remember: words and phrases used in problem questions are intended to be significant.

Question 1(a) The *Daily Slur.* (Commentary in note form; not a whole answer.)

(a) Whether or not the *Daily Slur* is in contempt of court depends upon the nature of a publication and the circumstances in which the publication occurred. The first point to establish is whether the publication is one which comes within the strict liability rule as laid down by ss. 1 and 2 of the Contempt of Court Act 1981. At the time of the publication are there any *particular legal proceedings* (sch. 1), civil or criminal? The facts given suggest, but do not conclusively reveal, that there are civil proceedings.

(b)   Assume that there are civil proceedings and proceed to the next stage.

(c)   Does the strict liability rule apply in respect of this publication? At this point discuss whether the publication 'creates a substantial risk' of 'seriously impeding or prejudicing' the course of justice *in those proceedings*. Refer to cases such as *Attorney-General* v *News Group Newspapers Ltd* [1987] QB 1. If no firm conclusion can be drawn on this point, assume there is such a risk, after stating that if there were no such risk the publication would not amount to a contempt under the Act.

(d)   If there is such a risk, there is still the question of whether the civil proceedings are 'active'. Refer to the provisions of s. 2 of and sch. 1 to the Act. Insufficient information to decide about the civil proceedings; e.g., nothing is said about arrangements having been made to set down the cases for trial. As to the criminal proceedings referred to in the third paragraph, the language used ('are started') suggests that you may safely conclude that the criminal proceedings were not active *at the time* of publication. This is because of the test laid down in sch. 1 dealing specifically with arrest, issue of summons etc.

(e)   If in spite of all the foregoing a court found against the newspaper on all the points it would be necessary to consider whether there was a defence of innocent publication under s. 3(1) of the Act. This point would almost certainly go in favour of the newspaper.

(f)   Note how all the aspects of the strict liability rule have been considered although more than one of them probably would not apply to the case of the *Daily Slur*.

(g)   Even if the *Daily Slur* was not in contempt under the strict liability rule, there is a residual form of contempt at common law. The Act specifically preserves liability for intentionally seeking to prejudice the outcome of proceedings. It is argued by some that there is a residual form of contempt where, possibly as in the case of the *Daily Slur*, it can be said that there is an attempt to persuade persons not to rely on their legal rights, or otherwise put pressure on litigants. This lets in a discussion on whether the conduct of the newspaper in *Attorney-General* v *Times Newspapers Ltd* [1974] AC 273 (the thalidomide case) would amount to contempt under the 1981 Act. If so, a case would be made out that the article in the *Daily Slur* amounted to such a contempt.

(h)   If the proposition in the previous paragraph is correct and was applied to the *Daily Slur*, the effect of s. 3(4) of the 1981 Act (repealing Administration of Justice Act 1960, s. 11) would be that the care taken by the editor to make 'careful inquiries' would not offer a defence. Liability would then depend on the old *sub judice* rule if proceedings were imminent.

(i)   You may conclude your answer by deciding whether any contempt would be treated as a serious one and suggest an appropriate penalty; probably a substantial fine.

Question 1(b)   The DBB TV Co. (Commentary in note form; not a whole answer.)

(a)   In answering question 1(a) you will have shown already whether you know a considerable amount about the details of the Contempt of Court Act 1981 and its effects on the pre-existing law. Therefore, although question 1(b) stands independently, you can assume:

(i)   That there will not be a repeat of the same points in 1(b).
(ii)   That, because of the length of the answer required to question 1(a), there will be fewer points in question 1(b).
(iii)   That it will not be necessary to repeat any argument about points already covered in 1(a) where it is necessary to refer to them, provided they are *the same* points.

(b)   The broadcast by the DBB TV Co. comes within the definition of a publication in s. 2(1) of the 1981 Act. Say so!
(c)   At the time of this broadcast the criminal proceedings against Addicto were undoubtedly active on the facts given, within the terms of s. 2 and sch. 1. Refer back to question 1(a) for the meaning of active criminal proceedings.
(d)   You must then point out that everything depends upon whether the defence created by s. 5 of the Act, relating to existing discussions in good faith of public affairs is applicable. Discuss the questions in the case of DBB TV Co. of:

(i)   whether the broadcast was part of a discussion of public affairs or of general public interest,
(ii)   whether the risk of impediment or prejudice to the proceedings against Addicto was 'merely incidental' to the discussion,
(iii)   whether the broadcast was in good faith.

This discussion is to be set against the background of the comments on the section to be found in the case of *Attorney-General v English* [1983] 1 AC 116.
(e)   Conclude your answer by commenting on the likely penalty that would be imposed in the event of liability.

Question 2   (Commentary in note form; not a whole answer.)

(a)   The answer to this question should be substantially different from the answer to question 1. It should not, however, be journalistic but should be a legal commentary on the state of the law as it affects newspaper editors and programme producers. The question is limited in its scope to the issues raised *by the facts given*. An answer containing mere generalities about the difficulties of staying on the right side of the law will not be acceptable. Because the requirement is to 'comment' rather than 'discuss', you should be prepared to point out specific ways in which the law is defective or might be improved.

(b) After an introductory sentence or two you should state that the issues raised by these facts relate mainly to the effects of the Contempt of Court Act 1981 on the law of contempt with particular reference to the freedom of the press, and other media, to comment on and criticise the workings of the courts, both generally and in particular cases.

(c) Prepare the ground further by reference to the unsatisfactory state of the law before the 1981 Act, and the reasons for the enactment of that Act, namely, the combined effect of the Phillimore Committee's report (Cmnd 5794, 1974) and the judgment of the European Court of Human Rights in the thalidomide case. Probably the most important defect in the law at the time was the degree of uncertainty attaching to it.

(d) Turn next to the specific issues raised by the facts given. In each case, use the case history as given to illustrate the problem to which you refer. For example, the first issue is clearly whether or not it is safe to rely on compliance with the terms of the Act to keep out of trouble. In the light of the restrictive nature of the protection granted under the Act and the possible existence of common law contempt in situations like the thalidomide case; you may point out the dilemma in which an editor may find himself where a party such as Addicto is concerned. To point out that Addicto 'should now settle with all affected users' may be doing no more than pointing out the *moral* duty of Addicto to the public at large. At the same time it may be construed as a contempt because it is putting pressure on a party to litigation to make that party forgo the right to defend the actions.

(e) If indeed the behaviour takes the editor outside the protection of the Act, the defence in s. 5 is not available.

(f) If the Act were to apply, the defence in s. 5 is relevant. Point out the differences between what was published in the thalidomide case and *Attorney-General* v *English* to highlight the difficulty of keeping particular comment incidental to the general discussion. If it is proved that the party mentioned, Addicto, was not alone in carrying on practices contravening statutory regulations (see the final sentence of the history of facts), is this going to be a factor in determining whether the mention of Addicto was 'incidental'? In other words, is an actual case available for use as a convenient example in making a general point?

(g) The facts given here about the stage reached by the various proceedings involves the issue of how an editor is to discover when comment must cease. Given that the facts in the case history are necessarily incomplete there is still an issue of how certain an editor can be that it is safe to publish even after 'careful inquiries'.

(h)   The combination of the more readily discoverable 'active' state of proceedings, as defined in the Act, compared with their 'imminence' under the old *sub judice* rule and the statutory defence of 'innocent publication' in s. 3 of the Act, probably means that on the score of certainty about his position *vis-à-vis* the law of contempt, an editor is now in a more favourable position than previously.

(i)   It may be otherwise if the Act does not apply.

(j)   Because the question is limited to the issues raised by the facts given, there is no *need* to deal with the position of distributors (s. 3(2) of the Act) and reports of proceedings which are published contemporaneously with the proceedings, or the power of the court to order postponement of publication. If you have time, *having dealt with the other issues*, these matters may be mentioned for the sake of completeness.

(k)   Conclude your answer by suggesting what it is that editors want from a law of contempt, compared with the demands of the public interest in the integrity of the legal process and express an opinion (making it clear that it is your opinion, if such it be; otherwise acknowledging its source) about whether the law of contempt as we have it now strikes a proper balance between the two.

LEGAL AID AND ADVICE

The heading to this part of this chapter should read, 'Financial provision for unmet needs', because the subject of legal aid and advice is part of the much wider question of the cost to the community of a first-class legal system at a price that the community is able and willing to afford. My definition of 'first class' would include the proposition that in such a legal system no person's grievance of a legal nature went without redress for financial reasons alone.

Now, perusal of the standard textbooks and the syllabuses of a range of courses in the field of 'legal systems' suggests that legal aid is a topic given some importance. That impression is reinforced by seeing questions on legal aid on many examination papers. A second look at these documents reveals the first point of value to someone whose course includes 'legal aid and advice'. That is, the ability to know what sort of question may be asked. My advice is based on looking at the sources mentioned above. You must supplement it by knowledge of the way in which your course is presented. The second look at the syllabus in several courses and the textbooks reveals that the approach and therefore related questions may be either *pragmatic* or an exercise in considering the *law in action*. The first approach depends very much on you having a good knowledge of the existing schemes for legal aid and advice and being able to apply that knowledge in a problem situation. Very often the questions include references to legal aid in the context of a problem where you are asked to advise a party about all the aspects of bringing or defending an action and defending a prosecution as an accused person. Such questions lay most emphasis on those parts of the scheme concerned with the procedure for obtaining legal aid and advice. There is usually no doubt that legal aid is available for the type of action that is mentioned in the problem.

The second, law in action, approach is more concerned with the adequacy of the schemes in relation to their coverage of legal matters and their percentage coverage of the population. In this sort of question it is often necessary to discuss alternatives to the present system. As the Legal Aid Act 1988 contains the major reforms of the structure of legal aid indicated in a White paper published in March 1987 (Cm 118), even courses with a heavy bias towards the pragmatic and analytical are likely to pay attention to this set of proposals and to discuss their impact on the present schemes.

For both approaches a working knowledge of the current schemes is the first essential. However, before embarking on a consideration of how to learn about the present schemes so as to be able to answer any question you may confront, it may be useful for you to know what approach is taken by the textbook recommended for your use. Three books are chosen by way of illustration. Much material in the *footnotes* of all the books is implied comment on the schemes:

(a)   Ingman, *The English Legal Process*. Legal aid and advice appears as a topic in at least three chapters. The emphasis is on integrating the treatment of legal aid and advice with the legal process in both civil and criminal cases. There is a separate reference to the availability of legal aid before tribunals.

(b)   Smith and Bailey, *The Modern English Legal System*. There is a separate chapter (chapter 9) on information and advice services which clearly sets the scene for a discussion of financial and other assistance for the redress of grievances in a wide context. This is followed by sections in chapter 11 and chapter 13 on obtaining legal aid in civil and criminal cases respectively. The limits on the scope of the civil legal aid scheme are stated factually in chapter 11, together with a special section devoted to a critique of the scheme which is limited to the material in chapter 9. Clearly, followers of Smith and Bailey can expect and be prepared for both types of question.

(c)   Zander, *Cases and Materials on the English Legal System*. In this work, legal aid is placed firmly in the 'law in action' category. The material on the legal aid and advice schemes is presented in the context of a chapter which discusses first the 'cost of British justice' and whether or not it is affordable. It also includes selected materials on alternatives to the present scheme.

PRIMARY SOURCES

These are the statutes and regulations on which the present schemes are based. In addition to being able to find your way around the statutes and relate them to one another you should consult the White Paper (Cm 118), which is also noted below. It is convenient to deal with the schemes for civil and criminal legal aid separately.

Civil Legal Aid and Advice

    (a)   Legal Aid Act 1988.
    (b)   Civil Legal Aid (General) Regulations 1989 (SI 1989 No. 339).

Criminal Legal Aid and Representation

    (a)   Legal Aid Act 1988.
    (b)   Legal Aid in Criminal and Care Proceedings (General) Regulations 1989 (SI 1989 No. 344).
    (c)   The White Paper (Cm 118).

General Comment

At this stage it should be noted that the Lord Chancellor's Department has been responsible for administering both civil and criminal legal aid since 1980. The Legal Aid Board is responsible for the day-to-day administration of the civil legal aid scheme and the Board is also to administer the statutory duty solicitor scheme.

At the outset be careful to distinguish:

    (a)   A legal aid *certificate:* granted by the Legal Aid Board to bring or defend a civil action.

    (b)   A legal aid *order:* made by the court to meet the costs of defending a criminal prosecution.

CIVIL LEGAL AID AND ADVICE

Let us assume that there is a straightforward question or part of a question that takes the following form:

A wishes to bring an action, for damages for injuries sustained in a road accident, against B who is insured.
What information do you need in order to advise whether A is eligible for legal aid?

Explain the procedure for applying for legal aid and advise A about liability for the costs of the defendant in the event of A losing the action.

In answering a question like this you should deal with the following points in some detail. The reason for putting two of the paragraphs in square brackets is given at the end of the answer.

[The costs of the initial interview at which A raises the issue of meeting the costs of the action might be dealt with under the green form scheme. The advice in this connection may be oral or written so long as the cost of the advice is within the financial limits of the scheme. Whether or not A would have to make a contribution at this stage will be assessed by the solicitor, using the key card and the green form. (These are reproduced in Smith and Bailey, *The Modern English Legal System.*) There is no test of the merits of the case.]

During the initial interview covered by the green form scheme, A will need to be told the following facts about his potential application for legal aid.

First, deal with the question of whether the case comes within the scope of the scheme as set out in s. 14 of the Legal Aid Act 1988 and sch. 2 to that Act. This is the sort of action that is clearly within the scope of the scheme. Although you should know the principal exceptions, such as actions for defamation and undefended proceedings for divorce, there is no need for you to set out these exceptions in answering this question. Do state, however, that the legal aid, if granted, will cover the cost of representation by both solicitor and counsel and will be available also in the event of any necessary appeal.

Your answer should continue by referring to the two tests which A will have to satisfy in order to qualify for legal aid. Explain that he must satisfy the local legal aid authorities that there are reasonable grounds for bringing or defending the action (Legal Aid Act 1988, s. 15(2)). Mention also the possibility of an appeal against an initial refusal.

On the question of the means test and related issues it is vital that you should cover the following points:

(a)   That the disposable income and capital limits may mean either that A has no contribution to make, has to make a contribution or is ineligible for legal aid.

(b)   The method by which the contribution, if any, is to be paid to the Legal Aid Fund.

(c)   The extent of the liability for own costs of a legally aided litigant is limited to the amount of the litigant's contribution. Note also the statutory charge.

(d)   The fact that the litigant is legally aided does not affect the normal solicitor-client relationship. The client's financial obligations, if any, are to the Legal Aid Fund. This has been reinforced by s. 59 of the Courts and Legal Services Act 1990.

The last part of your answer must deal with the position following judgment in the case. If A is successful, A's costs will be paid to the solicitor acting for A by the Legal Aid Fund. The Fund will seek to recover these costs from the unsuccessful defendant in accordance with the indemnity rule. However, should there be a shortfall in the amount the Fund receives by way of A's contribution and the costs paid by the defendant, the client must be made aware of the statutory charge. That is the right of the Legal Aid Fund to make good this shortfall out of any damages received or property preserved (Legal Aid Act 1988, s. 16(6)). That is why the damages are paid by the defendant to the Legal Aid Fund and not direct to the plaintiff.

On the other hand, if A is unsuccessful, A will want to know how the indemnity rule on costs will affect the position. If A is legally aided and making no contribution then A has no liability. However, if A is making a contribution towards his own costs then he may have to make a payment equal to his contribution. This is a result of the practice followed in applying the Legal Aid Act 1974, s. 8(1) (see now s. 17 of the Legal Aid Act 1988), which required the losing assisted person to pay towards the costs of the other party such an amount as is reasonable having regard to the means of the parties and their conduct in connection with the dispute. Conclude your answer by reminding A that his conduct may affect the continuance of the legal aid and also any amount A may have to pay ultimately to the defendant B in respect of B's costs.

[If the winning defendant B is not an assisted person, as he will be almost certainly because of compulsory third-party motor insurance, then B may recover some or all of his costs from the Legal Aid Fund. This will be dependent on B showing that he would otherwise suffer 'severe financial hardship' as explained in *Hanning* v *Maitland (No. 2)* [1970] 1 QB 580 and that he satisfies the other requirement of the Legal Aid Act 1988, s. 18.]

The two passages in square brackets are only included for the sake of making the exposition of the civil legal aid scheme more complete. The question as set out at the beginning of this section does not require these points to be made in an answer. Depending upon the precise wording of a question these points may have to be included in answers to some questions. A really wicked examiner might, for example, reverse the question to read:

Advise B's motor insurers about their potential liability for costs if they defend the following action. An action is being brought by A against B for damages for pain and suffering, arising out of a motor accident. The insurers have heard that A has applied recently for legal aid and has been granted a certificate with a very small contribution.

CRIMINAL LEGAL AID AND ADVICE

Your work in connection with advice and assistance in criminal cases should be concentrated on two objectives: acquiring a sound working knowledge of the system and noting the differences between the criminal and civil legal aid schemes. Those differences can be explained and compared in the course of many essays on legal aid of the 'law in action' variety. Also, knowing the differences between the two schemes will mean that you will avoid making simple mistakes of fact and terminology when answering questions in any context, be it in a seminar discussion or the examination room. Before offering a brief review of the criminal advice and assistance scheme, I shall set out a note of the principal differences between civil and criminal legal aid:

(a)   The applicant for criminal legal aid or advice has no choice about whether he will appear in court and become involved in the legal process. Therefore the criteria for granting legal aid are different. In most instances its grant in criminal cases is discretionary based on the requirements of justice.

(b)   In criminal cases, legal aid, when granted, is granted by means of a legal aid order: in civil cases the grant is by a legal aid certificate.

(c)   Because of the need for expedition in criminal cases, the legal aid order is granted by the court and not by the Legal Aid Board. Also, the means test is administered by court officials. In the case of applications to the magistrates' court that means the clerk to the justices.

(d)   The system of reviewing decisions refusing the grant of legal aid. In civil cases, a refusal may be appealed to the Area Committee, in criminal cases a refusal may be reviewed (not, note, an appeal) by the Area Committee. The review may be by way of a fresh application.

(e)   In each case, the system in force for the making of contribution orders and their enforcement is different. Contributions may be remitted where a defendant is acquitted or has an appeal against conviction allowed.

(f)   In civil cases involving legal aid, solicitors and counsel are prevented from taking any additional payment from clients. In criminal cases, 'topping up' is not disallowed although it is frowned upon by the professions.

The next stage is to organise your knowledge of the criminal legal aid scheme so as to be able to deal with a variety of questions. As with civil legal aid I intend to demonstrate this within the framework of a possible, although in this case not a very typical, question.

The suggested question is not typical simply because it is deliberately worded in a very wide form so as to justify a wide-ranging review of all parts of the scheme. It also takes account of the fact that in criminal matters there is a need for advice and assistance in the very first stages of the criminal process immediately after the arrest of a suspect and while the suspect is at the police station, both before and after being charged. At this very important and early stage of the proceedings, the provision of advice and assistance is part of the much wider issue of the need for protection of the suspect in general and from the abuse of police powers in particular. Material which is relevant to the early stages of the criminal process in connection with legal aid will, therefore, also be useful in dealing with questions which deal specifically with the protection of the suspect's position whilst in police custody. This link with another topic, which in some cases will be part of a constitutional law syllabus is reflected in the arrangement of the material in some of the textbooks, notably Zander's *Cases and Materials on the English Legal System*. Even if a question is limited to the legal advice and assistance aspects of a criminal case, there is a good point to make about the early availability of the advice and assistance of a solicitor, namely, that access at this stage to a solicitor's services is in itself some safeguard of the suspect's position and reinforces, for example, the rules to be followed by the police under the Police and Criminal Evidence Act 1984.

Question

What opportunities exist for a person suspected or accused of a crime to obtain legal aid, advice and assistance?

Comments on the Question and Points to Cover in Answer to the Question

Comments

The use of the word 'suspected' as well as the word 'accused' is intended to direct attention to the situation that arises from the time that a person is taken into police custody, whether arrested or not. Limiting the question to an 'accused' person strictly speaking would exclude consideration of legal aid for an appeal in the event of the accused being convicted of the offence in question. [For the sake of completeness mention will be made in this section of the availability of legal aid in the case of appeals.]

The phrase 'advice and assistance' is a reminder that in this context we are dealing with more than just financial support to meet the costs of defending a prosecution. That is the subject-matter of a legal aid order.

It is convenient in answering a question of this sort to structure an answer by following the different stages of the criminal process, because the conditions attached to the availability of advice and assistance vary at each stage.

Points in answer

At the police station   The judges made it plain that a suspect was entitled to contact a solicitor of his or her choice. Since 1986 there has been a statutory scheme under the Legal Aid Act 1982, as amended by the Police and Criminal Evidence Act 1984. This is a duty solicitor scheme. There is no merits or means test and solicitors are remunerated by the Legal Aid Fund. Responsibility passed to the Legal Aid Board, under the Duty Solicitor Arrangements 1989 (now 1994).

At the magistrates' courts   It is essential at this stage to distinguish first of all the different schemes under which advice and assistance may be available. Accused persons who have selected solicitors of their own choice may already be receiving assistance under the green form scheme. Alternatively application may be made to the court for legal aid.

In addition there are the statutory duty solicitor schemes in criminal cases in the magistrates' courts. Make a careful note of how the schemes operate together, so that, for instance, the duty solicitor scheme in the magistrates' court is not available to someone who already has legal aid or who is being assisted under the green form scheme. Under the duty solicitor scheme advice and representation are provided to the defendant free of charge. Duty solicitors are remunerated out of the Legal Aid Fund.

Whether an offence is summary only or triable on indictment also determines the scope and availability of legal aid.

In particular you must note the very restricted opportunities for fresh applications in the case of a refusal of legal aid in the case of summary offences. No application for a review may be made to the Area Committee.

You will of course know that the grant of legal aid is at the discretion of the court. You must know, however, that the major problem arises in connection with the exercise of that discretion in relation to *summary* proceedings. In this regard you should learn and be able to apply to given situations the 'Widgery criteria'. These are noted and set out in full in the standard textbooks, such as Ingman, *The English Legal Process,* and Smith and Bailey, *The Modern English Legal System.* They are now set out in s. 22 of the Legal Aid Act 1988.

In answering this question you should also deal with the scope of any legal aid order that is made. For example, that representation by counsel in the magistrates' courts is very limited. Normally, the order covers preparation and representation by solicitor and counsel.

The other point to cover with regard to applications to the magistrates' court is the type of proceedings for which the legal aid is granted.

In answer to this question you should state also what the accused has to do with regard to meeting the requirements of the means test. The question as put is more concerned with establishing the duty of the accused to furnish the court with a statement of his means than with stating that it is the function of the court to assess the accused's means, to decide whether the accused has to make any contribution. You should, however, find room in your answer to advise the accused that his contribution will be assessed, in relation to disposable income as a weekly contribution, to be paid during the period in force of the legal aid order, and in relation to disposable capital as a lump sum to be paid immediately (if readily available). Contribution orders may be varied.

At this stage you will have covered the possibilities indicated in the terms of the question. In preparing your material on criminal legal aid you must be prepared for questions which require you to deal in detail with further applications after an initial refusal and the availability of legal aid for appeals following conviction. In this case it is noteworthy that the original legal aid order under the Legal Aid Act 1988, s. 19, may now cover advice and assistance on appeal (if convicted).

LEGAL AID AND ADVICE IN ACTION

Unmet Legal Needs

It seems sensible to deal with the evaluative aspects of the legal aid schemes alongside a review of the unmet legal needs of the population as a whole. Under the heading of unmet legal needs it has become usual to deal with those agencies other than the legal profession which have perceived either a special need and done something about providing advice and assistance in that specific area of need or which have attempted to meet perceived and hitherto unmet legal needs in a more general way.

Textbooks tend to separate their treatment of the topics of unmet legal needs and an evaluation of legal aid schemes. Examiners cannot be relied upon to draw such neat dividing lines. The rest of this chapter will give you some guidelines for a more integrated approach under a general heading such as 'the availability of legal services in the community'. This is a topic which generates heat and controversy, so a word of warning is introduced at this point.

Resist the temptation to produce 'campaigning tracts' or 'journalistic pieces' in answers or more extended pieces of work. Criticism is more telling if it is based on knowledge and reasoned predictions of what will happen if X, Y or Z measures are adopted, rather than subjective impressions.

The problem is one of limited resources to meet indefinite needs. There is then the related problem of how to distribute the resources devoted to meeting all legal needs. Distribution is to be considered on three levels:

(a) Distribution between types of need or types of legal work.

(b) Geographical distribution of the resources. This relates to the location of professional offices and alternative agencies in the places where there is a community need.

(c) Distribution of the financial resources devoted to meeting legal needs between different population groups within the community as a whole.

The traditional wisdom amongst private practitioners used to be that certain types of profitable work, such as conveyancing, subsidised the less profitable work such as litigation, which often had a social service element in it. That is no longer so, especially in view of the statutory objective set out in the Courts and Legal Services Act 1990, which is concerned with 'new ways of providing legal services'. That part of the 1990 Act then goes on to provide not only for alternative provisions of conveyancing and probate services but also for the possibility of alternative providers of litigation services. Such measures can only diminish the scope for and the willingness of solicitors to subsidise one branch of practice out of the profits of another.

Having stated the problem, I am going to suggest that you add, to the material you will already have accumulated in learning about the schemes as they are, comment under the following headings:

(a)   Alternative provision for legal needs.
(b)   Evaluation of existing schemes to highlight deficiencies.
(c)   Proposals for change (or reform).

Alternative Provision for Legal Needs

'Alternative' in this context means three things:

(a)   Alternatives to the use of lawyers in private practice to meet the legal needs of the community.
(b)   Alternative methods of financing traditional forms of legal practice.
(c)   More radical alternatives of de-legalising some of the problems and the services provided to help in solving them, or at least simplifying the law.

As to (a), a study of your textbooks will quickly reveal the wide range of agencies at work, including law centres and Citizens Advice Bureaux. Do not forget some of the more specialised agencies providing advice and assistance in such fields as housing and child law. In (b), the established means of financing private practice are the payment of fees by the clients and the various schemes of legal aid, advice and assistance. The introduction of the Conditional Fee Agreements Order 1995 (SI 1995 No. 1674) allows lawyers and clients to agree that in the event of a case being lost no fees will be payable, but in the event of success that the lawyer will be able to charge an increased fee. At the time of writing this scheme extends only to personal injury and insolvency cases, and cases before the European Court of Human Rights. In the light of experience the scheme may be extended to other areas of legal work. Another issue to consider is the provision of insurance to meet the costs of litigation. The market for insurance against the costs of litigation is an existing and growing one. Such cover is available to householders as an extension of household policies. Most of these schemes are geared to providing advice and assistance in connection with potentially contentious matters, whilst many services offered by solicitors to private clients relate to non-contentious matters. Those of limited and modest means would often benefit from such services. A recent example of insurance against the costs of losing a personal injuries case is the Law Society's Accident Line Protect scheme. This was introduced in 1995 and is available where a conditional fee agreement is concluded.

Under (c), one could mention the possibility of removing compensation for accidents from the realms of tort liability. When considering simplification of the law you should remember that this applies to substance (e.g., simplifying the grounds for divorce in the Divorce Reform Act 1969) as well as to procedures. Care must be taken to evaluate what is lost as well as what is gained by the process of simplification. In this connection it would be a good idea to look again at the beginning of chapter 6 on what constitutes an ideal system for resolving civil law disputes.

Evaluation of Existing Schemes

In questions requiring an evaluation of the existing schemes for aid advice and assistance, the emphasis is usually placed on highlighting the ways in which the various schemes are inadequate from the point of view of the applicant. Whilst it is appropriate to produce work in answer to questions which contains such an emphasis, you should also bear in mind that there are at least two other viewpoints: that of lawyers who receive their remuneration from the Legal Aid Fund and that of the taxpayer who provides the funds in the first place. Once a decision has been made to provide a specific amount of funding, the taxpayer has a legitimate interest in seeing that value is received for the money disbursed. The White Paper discussed in the next section was very emphatic on this point.

Proposals for Change (or Reform)

It is agreed that it is a mark of civilised society that it has an efficient system of legal aid so that those of only modest means are not denied the benefit of their legal rights. What is not agreed is the method of balancing the claims of the taxpayer against the claims of justice. There is disagreement also on the extent to which even those of modest means should contribute towards the cost of their legal action.

These are matters upon which you and everyone else are entitled to have opinions as matters of general principle. Those opinions you will make known through your work. However, those whose task it is to judge your work in an academic sense in connection with your English legal system course will be concerned to see whether your expressions of opinion are both reasoned and reasonable within a given framework. In a general way, for example, it would not be reasonable to support a system of contributions set at such a level that only a very small minority would or could take up offers of legal aid on the terms allowed by the scheme. In concluding this chapter I am going to remind you of five things:

(a)   The proposals on legal aid in the Report of the Royal Commission on Legal Services (Cmnd 7648).
(b)   The government response to those proposals.
(c)   The Scrutiny report and the White Paper (Cm 118, 1987).
(d)   The Legal Aid Act 1988 and its effects.
(e)   The Green Paper, *Legal Aid — Targeting Need*.

The first three of these things form part of the necessary background to the new arrangements under the Legal Aid Act 1988 and further proposals thereafter.

The Royal Commission proposals
The detailed proposals were based on the following three principles:

(a)   Financial assistance out of public funds should be available for every individual who, without it, would suffer an undue financial burden in properly pursuing or defending his legal rights.
(b)   All those who receive legal services are entitled to expect the same standard of legal service irrespective of their personal circumstances.
(c)   The client, whether supported out of public funds or fee paying, should always have a free choice among available lawyers and should not be required to retain an assigned lawyer (see the Courts and Legal Services Act 1990).

Each of those statements of principle only needs the word 'discuss' added at the end to make them into examination questions.

The government response to the Royal Commission proposals
The response came in 1983 and Smith and Bailey in *The Modern English Legal System* (at pp. 460–4 in the 2nd edition) selected six typical items from the response. They are:

(a)   The case for the creation of a council for legal services is rejected.
(b)   The role of generalist agencies (e.g., Citizens Advice Bureaux) is endorsed, but with no additional funding.
(c)   The recommendation on citizens' law centres is still under consideration.

(d)   Eligibility limits for legal aid are to be retained, and the contributions currently payable are not unreasonable.

(e)   The 'free half hour' of advice will not be introduced.

(f)   Extension to the scheme for assistance by way of representation will be made when necessary.

The Scrutiny report and the White Paper (Cm 118, 1987)

The Scrutiny report was an efficiency audit of the legal aid schemes currently in force of the same kind as other such efficiency audits conducted for the government since 1979.

The Scrutiny report was to make proposals on the following aspects of the legal aid schemes: the arrangements for giving legal advice, the redesign of contribution procedures, and the curbing and elimination of unnecessary procedures.

The White Paper, *Legal Aid in England and Wales: A New Framework,* was published in March 1987. After a brief description of the present schemes, the White Paper set out the government's proposals, some of which would need legislation, in answer to the Scrutiny report. It was intended to consolidate the Legal Aid Acts 1974 and 1982 and related legislation; this legislation would also amend the existing schemes and bring about improvements. There would be a saving to the taxpayer of £10 million.

The principal proposals were:

(a)   Administration. A balance must be struck between the needs of the taxpayer and the applicant. There would be a Legal Aid Board, answerable to the Lord Chancellor, which would take over the functions of the Law Society.

(b)   Legal advice — the green form scheme. A better service could be provided at lower cost. The skills of the advice agencies would be used. The new Board would inquire into how this could be achieved. When some matters, e.g., advice on welfare benefits, were handed over to the advice agencies, those matters would then be excluded from the green form scheme. Advice on wills and conveyancing should not *normally* be paid for out of public funds. In the case of tribunals the Lord Chancellor was conducting an inquiry into the effectiveness of representation. There would be no general extension of the availability of legal aid in connection with tribunals. (Note, the issue of extending legal aid to representation before certain tribunals was under consideration at the time of writing, Summer 1995.) The arrangements for emergency advice would not be changed.

(c)   Applications — contributions — fees. In connection with criminal legal aid the government was reviewing its guidelines on the application of the 'Widgery criteria'. Speedier decisions would be reached by allowing court staff to refuse as well as grant legal aid.

When an application is made for legal aid, the opponents of the applicant would be able to make representations *before* the application was determined. The official view is that at present 70% of households qualify for legal aid. There is no intention to extend the proportion. An inquiry would be held to see whether the new Board should carry out assessments now done by the DSS. The incentives for applicants to consider the cost to the taxpayer and themselves of their applications, would be strengthened. Contributions would be put on a monthly basis payable *throughout* the duration of the case, instead of being limited to 12 months.

(d)   Remuneration. The government intended to set rates for all legal aid work, to provide 'fair' remuneration 'for work actually and reasonably done'. The use of standard fees (already introduced in criminal cases) would be extended. If this was achieved court staff in civil cases would be able to take over the assessment of bills from district judges. A right of appeal to the taxing master would be retained. There would be a permanent scheme for payments on account. The government intended to abolish the 10% deduction from High Court bills.

(e)   Procedures. All other existing procedures would be reviewed. There would be no extension of the rights of audience in the Crown Court. In order to ensure proper use of specialist skills there *may have to be* an enforced use of specialist panels of solicitors. (The President of the Law Society had something to say in this context about the dangers inherent in a nationalised legal service, in his presidential address in October 1987. See the third principle of the Royal Commission.) The future role of the Lord Chancellor's Legal Aid Advisory Committee was to be reviewed.

(f)   The Legal Aid Act 1988 and its effects. The Legal Aid Act 1988, based on the White Paper and the Scrutiny report, established the Legal Aid Board and transferred the administration of the scheme to the Board from the Law Society. Immediate academic interest centres around the following matters: the connection between the restructuring of legal services in the Courts and Legal Services Act 1990 and the methods of financing those services through legal aid and advice; the possibility of a franchising scheme under which only specialist firms of lawyers, or individual members of specialist panels, would be able to tender for legal aid work generally or classes of legal aid work, such as personal injury work; the future of the Green Form scheme and finally, a proposal by the Lord Chancellor that applicants for legal aid should be required to exhaust their own resources first, before becoming eligible for legal aid. The continued withdrawal of firms from the legal aid scheme and concern about the levels of remuneration for legally aided work are, without the matters referred to immediately above, sufficient in themselves to tempt examiners to set the question 'Comment on the extent to which the legal aid scheme has become a safety net for those would-be litigants who have no resources of their own or have exhausted them'.

The Green Paper, Legal Aid — Targeting Need

During the 1990s the number of people qualifying for legal aid, advice and assistance has been reduced, primarily because income and capital levels determining eligibility have been effectively lowered. Even those eligible are subject to greatly increased contribution payments. The Green Paper *Legal Aid — Targeting Need* heralds further changes to the system. The proposals consist largely of methods of controlling the amount of money available for legal services. Rather than paying according to demand, the Lord Chancellor has proposed fixing an annual monetary sum for legal aid work. Legal aid work is to be done by suppliers of legal services awarded a block contract, for example only solicitors awarded a contract to do, say, criminal work could offer such under the legal aid scheme. Suppliers of legal services who are franchised in this way would become fund holders with responsibility for administering a budget and deciding issues of allocation. The principle behind this last proposal has already been seen in operation in the health service. Such proposals raise issues concerning access to legal advice in terms of geography, not all solicitors will be awarded block contracts, and also the question of how legal aid is to be allocated. Again you need to be aware of the facts and the arguments for and against such changes. For a critique of the legal aid Green Paper, see M. Zander (1995) 145 NLJ 1098.

Be vigilant in relation to changes to the courts structure. For example, in response to the publication of Lord Woolf's interim report on *Access to Justice*, the Lord Chancellor proposed increasing the jurisdiction of small claims (excluding personal injuries) in the county courts from £1,000 to £3,000. The effect of this would be to cut legal aid eligibility as legal aid is not usually available for small claims.

Let me end this chapter by quoting the last sentence of chapter 9 in Smith and Bailey, *The Modern English Legal System*, 2nd ed., 'The argument is often heard that problems are not necessarily solved by throwing money at them; how are they solved if you don't?'

FURTHER READING

Ingman, T., *The English Legal Process* (5th edn., Blackstone Press, 1994).
Zander, M. *Cases and Materials on the English Legal System* (6th edn., Butterworths, 1992).

9 A NOTE ON LEGAL METHOD AND SKILLS

Many present day first-year courses in the general field of the English legal system are either limited to a study of legal method or devote a substantial proportion of the time available to legal method. The phrase 'legal method' often appears in the title of the course. What does this connote?

Most of these legal method courses are a study of case law and legislation as sources of law. In the case of legislation it is becoming usual to include the 'making' of legislation as well as its interpretation. Again, in some of your courses, after introductory sessions dealing with such matters as are contained in chapter 3, further legal method teaching is integrated into the teaching of substantive subjects such as tort, contract and criminal law. If your course is one of those, the material in the next two chapters will have to be directly applied to your work in those other subjects. The next two chapters are directly addressed to those of you who have to deal with case law and legislation as separate topics within an English legal system course, in the first year of a law degree. In particular, the chapter on case law stops short of the sort of analysis of judicial reasoning which is usually found as part of a study of legal theory.

Although a legal system course may be made up of a study of institutions and legal method in approximately equal parts, the 'legal method' sections of textbooks covering the whole syllabus are usually shorter than the sections dealing with institutions and procedures. There is probably less to know in a factual sense, at this level, about legal method but a great deal of effort needs to be put into understanding the workings of legislation and case law as the foundations of all your legal studies.

Nevertheless, if your course spends substantially a whole term on the legal method elements of the course it would be worth your while to acquire one or more of the specialist books that have been produced for such courses. These include:

General:	Farrar and Dugdale — *Introduction to Legal Method*.
	Holland and Webb — *Learning Legal Rules*.
	Lee and Fox — *Learning Legal Skills*.
	Twining and Miers — *How To Do Things with Rules*.
	Zander — *The Law-Making Process*.
Precedent:	Cross and Harris — *Precedent in English Law*.
Legislation:	Cross — *Statutory Interpretation*.
	Miers and Page — *Legislation*.
Reference:	Bennion — *Statute Law*.
	Maxwell — *Maxwell on the Interpretation of Statutes*.
Periodical:	*Statute Law Review*.

There is a growing awareness of the need for students to develop the skills needed by a lawyer at an early stage of legal education. Study groups have been established and books written about skills, such as *Learning Legal Rules* by J.A. Holland and J.S. Webb and *Learning Legal Skills* by S. Lee and M. Fox. The legal method part of an English legal system course is an area in which some of those skills can be introduced and activities designed to develop them. The introduction of drafting into the study of legislation is an obvious example. There are other examples. As an introduction to advocacy you may be expected to demonstrate that you can use authorities effectively in your arguments, based upon your understanding of the doctrine of precedent. Expect some part of the assessment of your course to be based on a test of competence in the appropriate skills, as much as on a test of knowledge. *Learning Legal Skills* by Lee and Fox provides a critical appraisal of the ways in which lawyers use their skills, in the context of contemporary but sometimes opposing points of view. Reading such a book will enable you to look at your work in legal method and skills development as a whole, especially when you are reviewing your personal development and progress.

There is one final point of general importance to the legal method parts of the syllabus. Insofar as legal method is a study of the sources of law and of law making in all its forms, you should be aware of moves in some courses to integrate the teaching and assessment of case law and legislation. For example, in 1986 the University of East Anglia set the following question in its English legal system paper: 'How are new rules added to English Law? What are the advantages and disadvantages of the various methods?' Plainly such a question needs an answer combining your knowledge of both case law and legislation concentrating perhaps on the advantages and disadvantages of one of them, say case law, and comparing and contrasting the factors discussed, with the way in which those factors apply in the case of other methods of law making. For example, compare precedent and legislation with respect to the question of retroactivity and the degree of certainty each brings to the development of the law.

10 CASE LAW AND PRECEDENT

'English law is a system of law based on case law and precedent.' Not too much probing of the first-year student's mind will elicit some such response to the question 'Name or describe one of the distinguishing characteristics of a common law system of law'. The textbooks refer to case law and precedent as one of the major sources of law in the English legal system. Reference to chapter 3 and the note immediately preceding this chapter will show that the doctrine of precedent is one of the principal agencies of our law-making process. Indeed, the treatment of the study of sources of law today is twofold. On the one hand, there is a study of the law-making process and the separate contributions to that process of the sources such as case law and legislation. That is the approach of books such as Zander's *The Law-Making Process*. On the other there is a study of the detailed working out of the methods of each source of law.

The business of this chapter is to look at both these aspects of the doctrine of precedent under four main headings:

(a) The doctrine of *stare decisis*.
(b) The meaning of *ratio decidendi* and *obiter dictum*.
(c) Judicial contributions to law making.
(d) The advantages and disadvantages of a doctrine of precedent.

There will be a short final section on the necessary contribution of law reporting in its various forms (including a computerised database) to the viability of a system based on precedent.

These are the headings under which most examination questions on this topic can be classified. In this topic, however, I shall not be concerned with examination questions alone. Because this is a fundamental part of English law, and reading cases for the law they contain is a basic skill of common law practitioners and commentators, it has become usual to set quite sophisticated exercises in the analysis of cases. Sometimes these exercises are course requirements not counting towards final assessment in the subject. In other courses, the exercises may count as one piece of assessed work. If a course is assessed by examination alone, similar exercises may appear in examination papers, as a question carrying more marks than others in the same paper. Often, these questions are compulsory. The key to answering such questions and doing exercises of this sort lies in having a structured approach to your reading of cases. It is a good idea for the structure you adopt to form the framework of the notes you make on cases which you read for your legal method work. Soon you will be applying this approach to cases you read for substantive law subjects such as contract and tort, with the result that you will amaze your contract and tort seminar tutors by the depth of your understanding in the law of contract or tort or whatever the subject may be. An exercise of this sort, partly based on one given at Bristol University, is included at the end of this chapter by kind permission of Mr A. M. Dugdale. It is also true to say that examiners are still relying on certain well-tried questions on all four aspects of the doctrine of precedent set out above. The perennial attraction of these questions is that they represent unchanging issues, but that the answers to them change as attitudes change, especially judicial attitudes. I shall summarise and conclude each section by referring to one or more questions found recently on examination papers somewhere in England.

Before studying the following sections in detail you should revise the material referred to in chapter 3 on the topic of precedent, that is, the outline of the hierarchy of the courts as the basis of the study of *stare decisis,* and Cross and Harris's definition of the *ratio decidendi* as the starting-point for your study of legal method.

STARE DECISIS

A system of binding precedent depends on three things. The ability to select and extract rules of law from decisions in cases. The availability of reliable records of those decisions in the form of law reports or some other form of permanent record. And where there is more than one court in a legal system, a settled hierarchy of courts.

It is that hierarchy of courts which gives rise to the doctrine of *stare decisis.* This doctrine sets forth the circumstances in which one court not only has to decide like cases alike, but has to follow the decision of another court above it in the hierarchy, even though that may result in a like case being decided in an unlike manner. It is not sufficient for a hierarchy of courts to be established by a statute such as the Supreme Court Act 1981, laying down avenues of appeal from one court to another until a case reaches the highest court in the land. For the system to work at all, the judges who have to make it work must accept the system and believe in it, although they may disagree with one another from time to time on points of detail and even of principle. That is the essence of judicial comity. It was in the interests of preserving judicial comity that Lord Hailsham of St Marylebone LC issued a 'magisterial' (per Professor Zander) rebuke to Lord Denning MR in the case of *Cassell & Co. Ltd v Broome* [1972] AC 1027 at p. 1054. In more picturesque language, Lord Denning was advised to sit down and stop rocking the boat of precedent.

Having become thoroughly familiar with the outline organisation of the doctrine of *stare decisis* and the hierarchy of the courts, you will need to know where to concentrate your attention. I believe that there are *three* features of the doctrine that merit special attention. They are selected because they are the features which have given rise to most difficulty in practice. We shall see at the end of the section that the questions asked are of two kinds. Both kinds of question may be asked of all three features. These are questions demanding a detailed exposition of the current position of particular courts and questions which require you to make a judgment about the extent to which a particular court should be bound by the doctrine *of stare decisis*. This latter type of question may deal with either or both of the following points. How far *should* court X (or all courts) be bound by its (their) own decisions? Or, to what extent *should* court X be bound by the decisions of court Y (the court above it in the hierarchy)?

Note that the word 'should' is the key word in these questions. It indicates quite plainly that there are clearly known rules about court X, but that there is a body of opinion that believes those rules could or should be changed. As we go through this section we shall discover that there is usually one established opinion or viewpoint and another minority opinion. We shall also discover that, historically, the minority sometimes becomes the majority opinion.

The three features of the doctrine, which I have selected for your special (but not exclusive) attention are:

(a)   The position of the House of Lords.
(b)   The position of the Court of Appeal.
(c)   The position of the trial courts when faced by conflicting decisions of the House of Lords and the Court of Appeal.

A particular feature of the doctrine that must not be overlooked in concentrating on the three features set out above, is the position of the Judicial

Committee of the Privy Council; especially its influence on the development of English law as in the rule relating to the remoteness of damage in tort, following the decision in *Overseas Tankship (UK) Ltd* v *Morts Dock & Engineering Co., The Wagon Mound* [1961] AC 388.

The Position of the House of Lords

There is a point to make about a court of last resort, such as the House of Lords, that is so obvious that it is not often made in the textbooks. If the law of a system develops through the decisions in cases, then the attitude of the court of last resort to its own previous decisions becomes all-important. Too rigid an attitude at that level can stifle the development of the law, especially when the legislature is either unwilling or too busy to take on the job of law reform and general development in the law to meet changing needs.

In the context of the late 19th century no such dangers were perceived and the opposite case was put by the Earl of Halsbury LC in *London Street Tramways Co. Ltd* v *London County Council* [1898] AC 375 at p. 380. Read that passage; it is set out in Professor Zander's book, *The Law-Making Process*. You may find arguments in favour of the new approach set out in the *Practice Statement* [1966] 1 WLR 1234. The precedent practice adopted by the House of Lords in the *London Street Tramways* case caused difficulties in certain branches of the law between 1898 and c. 1960. As a result of the inability to have points already decided by the House of Lords re-argued, Parliament had to intervene with legislation. Two examples must suffice here:

(a)   The limits of attempts to mitigate the effects of the doctrine of common employment were reached in the case of *Radcliffe* v *Ribble Motor Services Ltd* [1939] AC 215.

(b)   In the law of occupiers' liability, the distinctions between invitees, licensees and those coming on to premises under a contract were becoming unworkable by the 1950s (see *Jacobs* v *London County Council* [1950] AC 360).

The Practice Statement marked a new beginning. You should know it thoroughly, including especially the last two paragraphs. These set out the exceptions and state in terms that the statement will not affect the use of precedent 'elsewhere than in this House'. This latter might have been taken as a clear warning to the Court of Appeal, or some might have taken it as a challenge. It is important to note the retrospective nature of overruling. If an opinion of the House of Lords is overruled, it is as if it never was the law. Overruling thus has serious implications if such law has been relied upon. For example, if a solicitor advising a client on the creation of a contract relies on a House of Lords' opinion and then in a later case the House of Lords overrules that opinion the advice, although accurate, when given, will need to be recast. Any dispute relating to the contract will be determined on the basis of the later ruling. Hence the House of Lords' caution in relation to contract, etc. The importance of the *Practice Statement* is clearly indicated by the fact that textbooks, and not just cases and materials books, print it in full. Having absorbed the statement into your consciousness your next task is to discover the use to which it has been put in the past 25 years or so. Begin by collecting examples where there has been an undoubted case of a previous House of Lords decision being overruled. Textbooks contain numerous examples. Use your textbook as a guide to selecting those cases such as *Jones v Secretary of State for Social Services* [1972] AC 944 in which there is a discussion of the principles upon which the House decides whether to overrule one of its previous decisions. Quite independently of help you may derive from a look at Paterson's book, *The Law Lords,* and the same author's article, 'Lord Reid's unnoticed legacy', (1981) 1 Oxford J Legal Stud 375, you should be able to set out a number of points that can usefully be made in essays on the operation of the *Practice Statement.* Here are some of them in the form of questions you may ask yourself:

(a)   Has there been a major change in economic and social circumstances since the previous case?

(b)   Does it matter that the point in the case is purely one of statutory interpretation?

(c)   Is it more important to maintain certainty and consistency in the law on a particular matter than to correct previous errors?

(d)   Is there a difference when the case is a criminal one involving the liberty of the subject? (See *R v Howe* [1987] AC 417 overruling *Director of Public Prosecutions for Northern Ireland v Lynch* [1975] AC 653.) If there is a recent statute of importance, should initial errors of construction, based on first impressions, be put right at the earliest opportunity? (See the Criminal Attempts Act 1981 and the cases of *Anderton v Ryan* [1985] AC 560 and *R v Shivpuri* [1987] AC 1, in which Lord Bridge of Harwich said 'If a serious error embodied in a decision of this House has distorted the law, the sooner it is corrected the better'.)

(e)   If there is a case which is contrary to established principle, overruling it may restore certainty to the law. (See *Murphy v Brentwood District Council* [1991] 1 AC 398, overruling *Anns v Merton London Borough Council* [1978] AC 728.)

The Position of the Court of Appeal

In studying the position of the Court of Appeal in connection with the doctrine of *stare decisis* it is necessary to deal separately with the Civil Division and the Criminal Division as each division has its own traditions in this matter, the Criminal Division being the comparatively recent successor to the Court of Criminal Appeal. However, there are some general points for you to note about the position of the Court of Appeal compared with the House of Lords:

(a)   Although you must once again become familiar with the arguments for and against a court being bound by its own decisions you must bear in mind one essential difference in the position of the Court of Appeal compared with the House of Lords. Except in a small number of special cases it is *not* the court of final resort for litigants. That reduces the force of any argument based on the need to put right mistakes already made. The law relating to documents mistakenly signed in the cases of *Carlisle & Cumberland Banking Co.* v *Bragg* [1911] 1 KB 489 and *Gallie* v *Lee* [1969] 2 Ch 17 (sub nom. *Saunders* v *Anglia Building Society* [1971] AC 1004 in the House of Lords) amply demonstrates that proposition. It is a weak argument to say that the Court of Appeal must act because the House of Lords may not have the opportunity to do so because of the normal accidents of litigation or the unwillingness of litigants to spend even more money on going to the House of Lords. (See also chapter 6 on the relative roles of the two courts as part of the civil process.) This point is well put in judicial language by the judges in the House of Lords in *Davis* v *Johnson* [1979] AC 264, especially in the speeches by Lord Diplock at pp. 326-8 and Lord Salmon at p. 334. Consideration of this case at both Court of Appeal and House of Lords level gives you a clear insight into the arguments for and against the Court of Appeal (Civil Division) being bound by its own previous decisions.

(b)   In addition to the question of being bound by its own decisions, there is the need to deal with the extent to which the Court of Appeal accepts without demur that it is bound by decisions of the House of Lords. In a number of cases in the 1970s, culminating in *Miliangos* v *George Frank (Textiles) Ltd* [1976] AC 443, some Court of Appeal judges questioned whether they were always bound by decisions of the House of Lords. Note, however, as a point for use in essays, that the Court of Appeal never directly attacks the superior position of the House of Lords. There is always a plausible reason given for not following a House of Lords decision. These include:

(i)   The reason for the rule laid down by the House no longer exists (*Schorsch Meier GmbH* v *Hennin* [1975] QB 416).

(ii)   The decision of the House of Lords was given *per incuriam* (*Broome* v *Cassell & Co. Ltd* [1971] 2 QB 354).

In addition to these two reasons, which have been rejected by the House of Lords in no uncertain terms, remember that there are other traditional techniques to avoid being bound, based on distinguishing, which the House of Lords finds acceptable if not pushed to extremes. The extracts printed in Professor Zander's book are especially helpful, if you think that you may have to answer a question on this topic. They are helpful because they enable the reader to see in close juxtaposition the opposing views and reasoning of the House of Lords and the Court of Appeal, even though the justification by Lord Denning MR for the stance the Court of Appeal adopted in the *Schorsch Meier GmbH* v *Hennin* and *Miliangos* cases was written with hindsight in his book, *The Discipline of Law*. It is also helpful to have the issues posed in the form of questions, as set by Professor Zander for his readers. For example, is a court ever justified in knowingly breaking the rules of precedent in order to precipitate an appeal so as to get a more authoritative ruling on the matter? (Zander, *The Law-Making Process*, p. 205.) Perhaps, you may suggest, the answer to the problem lies in the more frequent use and extension of the 'leap-frog' procedure contained in the Administration of Justice Act 1969.

Civil Division of the Court of Appeal
For a moment we are on firm ground. There is a case to grasp hold of and clear principles laid down. In *Young* v *Bristol Aeroplane Co. Ltd* [1944] KB 718 there was a full court of six judges and Lord Greene MR laid down 'the clear conclusion that this court is bound to follow previous decisions of its own as well as those of courts of coordinate jurisdiction'. That bit is easy to remember. He then went on to cite the *only* exceptions to the rule, three in number:

(a)   A choice is allowed between the court's own conflicting decisions.
(b)   The court is bound to refuse to follow one of its own decisions which cannot stand with a decision of the House of Lords.
(c)   A decision *of its own* is not binding if that decision was given *per incuriam*.

So far so good. That is straightforward and easy to apply. The interest of examiners in this case lies in its subsequent history following the House of Lords *Practice Statement* of 1966. The history of *Young's* case raises the following issues, and I suggest that you should make your notes on precedent in the Civil Division of the Court of Appeal in the following form:

Young v *Bristol Aeroplane Co. Ltd* [1944] KB 718

(a)   The rule laid down: set out the passage from Lord Greene's judgment.
(b)   The exceptions to the rule. Note that Lord Greene said these were the *only* exceptions. Set out the exceptions.

(c)   The House of Lords *Practice Statement* and subsequent changes in attitude in the Court of Appeal. List the cases, with their principal points as they relate to the doctrine of precedent, and the reason given for not following an earlier decision, e.g., *Gallie* v *Lee* — rule acknowledged to be wrong, unjust from soon after it was laid down in *Bragg's* case.

(d)   Issues of principle raised by *Young's* case:

(i)   Can further exceptions to the rule be created? Apparently so, e.g., not being bound by interlocutory decisions of the court (see *Boys* v *Chaplin* [1968] 2 QB 1, but note the doubts expressed about this exception in *Langley* v *North West Water Authority* [1991] 3 All ER 610).

(ii)   If the exceptions become numerous, will they undermine the very rule itself? Lord Denning MR said in *Davis* v *Johnson* [1979] AC 264, '. . . the list of exceptions . . . is now getting so large that they are in process of eating up the rule itself: and we would do well simply to follow the same practice as the House of Lords'. Some of the exceptions claimed by Lord Denning in that same passage, are not true exceptions to *Young's* case. They are examples of practice in the Criminal Division (that division inherited a different tradition) and other exceptions mentioned were challenged by the House of Lords.

(iii)   How, as a matter of technique, could the Court of Appeal free itself of its self-imposed fetters? Is it open to the court to make a collegiate statement as did the House of Lords? Perhaps this is unlikely in any case.

(iv)   The case raises the basic issue of the nature of precedent. Are the rules of precedent rules of practice or rules of law? Rules of practice may be changed by agreement, unlike rules of law. On this point there is academic disagreement.

Notes structured in this way will provide you with ready-made essay plans. All you need to do is to select the relevant and appropriate component parts for an essay. The components can be rearranged as necessary to suit the angle of approach of any likely question on *Young's* case. Of course, notes such as these should be based on your reading of the cases and other literature.

Criminal Division of the Court of Appeal
Although precedent is not followed so strictly in the Criminal Division as in the Civil Division, following *R* v *Spencer* [1985] QB 771, there seems to be no difference in principle between the status of the doctrine of *stare decisis* in the two divisions. Nevertheless the Criminal Division is not bound to follow its own decision if the law was misapplied or misunderstood in it.

The Position of Trial Courts when Faced with Conflicting Decisions of the Court of Appeal and the House of Lords

My third special point on the doctrine of *stare decisis* is an issue which is incidental to the conflict between the Court of Appeal and the House of Lords. In the *Miliangos* case [1975] QB 487, Bristow J had to decide whether to follow the House of Lords decision in *Re United Railways of Havana and Regla Warehouses Ltd* [1961] AC 1007 or the Court of Appeal's decision in *Schorsch Meier GmbH* v *Hennin* [1975] QB 416. Bristow J chose to follow the House of Lords and was criticised later for doing so, by the House of Lords. The reason given by Lord Simon of Glaisdale was that for a court not to follow its own immediately superior court was contrary to law and was to invite chaos. If it later turned out that the intermediate court had been wrong, there was always the possibility of an appeal to the superior court. This may be logical, but at what expense to litigants are the mistakes of the court to be corrected?

   Before closing this section, I must repeat that you must not neglect other aspects of the doctrine of *stare decisis*. These are only the most obvious points. Their selection is justified by the number of assignments and examination questions set around these points. In conclusion, here are two recent questions. If you learn to handle your knowledge in a flexible way, neither question should hold any terrors for you.

Questions

   How far does precedent operate in the Court of Appeal?

   Should the Court of Appeal be free to adopt the same practice as the House of Lords in relation to its own previous decisions?

Comment
The first question requires a detailed analysis of the rule in *Young's* case and the extent to which it has been modified since the *Practice Statement* of the House of Lords in 1966.

   The second question requires a preliminary statement of the current position in each court followed by a rehearsal of the arguments for and against the proposition. The arguments put forward in the Court of Appeal and in the House of Lords in *Davis* v *Johnson* should form the backbone of your answer. Remember that just because the Court of Appeal is in an inferior position in the hierarchy it need not for that reason alone have the worst of the argument.

RATIO DECIDENDI *AND* OBITER DICTUM

There are two separable but linked activities which you will be asked to undertake as part of a study of legal method. They are the search for possible use of a formula to find the *ratio* and the assessment of the weight to be given to a precedent.

The first-mentioned activity turns out to be a sort of quest for the Holy Grail. The second is an art to be acquired by practice under the guidance of skilled teachers. This art should be practised throughout your course of study, and should not be viewed merely as part of the English legal system syllabus. Mastery of this technique, and its application to substantive subjects, will yield rich rewards, both in understanding and, ultimately, through marks in examinations.

Finding the Ratio

Professor Cross's definition of the *ratio decidendi* of a decision was set out in chapter 3. The time has come to qualify your understanding of the term and the related term, *obiter dictum.* The first thing to realise is the distinction between the *ratio decidendi* and the meaning of *res judicata.* This distinction tells you on whom the decision is binding. As a matter that is *res judicata* the decision is binding only on the parties to the action, whereas the principle of law, the *ratio decidendi,* becomes a binding precedent in accordance with the doctrine of *stare decisis.*

The most elaborate plan of campaign in the hunt for the *ratio,* is probably found in the Cross and Harris book, *Precedent in English Law.* There are two stages of the campaign to discover binding precedents:

(a)   What is the *ratio* of a particular judgment?
(b)   When there is more than one judgment, what is the *ratio* of the case?

Let us take them in order.

The ratio *of a judgment*

This is the stage at which attempts are made to apply a formula to the judge's decision and reasoning to discover the propositions of law contained in the judgment that may rank as binding precedents. The most influential test is that propounded by Professor Goodhart in his *Essays in Jurisprudence and the Common Law.* It is known as the 'material facts' test and it is set out in full in chapter 7 of *Introduction to Legal Method* by Farrar and Dugdale. Try to apply this test to some of the cases cited to you in your substantive subjects, such as contract, and see whether by applying Goodhart's test strictly you arrive at the same conclusion as your tutor and textbook about what the *ratio* of particular cases may be. Try it out, for example, on the case of *Leaf* v *International Galleries* [1950] 2 KB 86.

Having injected the possibility of uncertainty into the search, let us recover ourselves by taking heed of the words of Cross and Harris: 'It is *always essential* and sometimes sufficient in order to arrive at the *ratio decidendi* of a case to consider the facts treated as material by the court and the decision based on those facts, it is sometimes necessary to do a great deal more.' We shall come in due course to that 'great deal more'. First, you must accept that there is a need to learn how to determine what facts are material. The key to that is in the phrase 'It is always essential'. This is implied as a first step. Are there any guidelines to making this essential first step? I think that there are some that you may follow:

(a)   The material facts that count as such are the facts which a judge in *a subsequent* case thinks were the material facts in the case under discussion.

(b)   A judgment may contain more than one *ratio decidendi*, see, for example, the well-known case of *Carlill* v *Carbolic Smoke Ball Co.* [1893] 1 QB 256. The case is authority for propositions of law relating to the making of an offer, the manner of acceptance, intention to create legal relations and the definition of a wager. The important point here is that counsel raised a number of legal issues, each of which required an answer. In looking for the *ratio* or *rationes* of a case it is essential to identify what it is that the court is being asked to decide.

(c)   The foregoing situation differs from that in which a judge bases his decision on a single point on two different reasons. In such cases, there are conflicting views about the status of each of the reasons relied upon. The best view seems to be that expressed in *Jacobs* v *London County Council* [1950] AC 361, namely, that there is no justification for regarding any one of the reasons as *obiter dictum*. The same holds true in many cases of accidents at work, in which an employer may be found liable for both having an unsafe system of work and failing to provide proper supervision.

I propose to deal now with the problem of finding the *ratio* of a case where there is more than one judgment.

The ratio of a case
Essentially, the problem is one of deciding what binding precedents the case as a whole creates, when different reasons are given for the same decision. Cross and Harris deal with this problem in great detail. Farrar and Dugdale devote a section of a chapter to it. Professor Zander deals with the problem obliquely in looking at how precedent works, and Dr Ingman gives it as his opinion that in these cases the *ratio of* the case is 'whatever is agreed on by the majority'. My own advice would be to qualify slightly Dr Ingman's opinion

by making it read 'whatever proposition of law is agreed on by the majority'. My qualification is to enable account to be taken of dissenting judgments where the dissenting judge agrees about the law with one or more of the other judges in the case thus creating a majority opinion, but disagrees on the facts.

With so much disagreement about a scientific approach to finding the *ratio decidendi* by applying a formula, it is time to see whether the craftsmen of the law can by their art show us how to decide what weight should be given to a precedent. If successful in this enterprise we shall be able to do two things that may be required in an examination, that is, to comment on a case as in a case analysis, or the writing of a case note, and to apply a precedent properly in the development of an argument in the course of answering problem questions. These are both aspects of the lawyers' skills that you will use constantly in all your subjects and are in addition to the immediate task of learning about precedent *per se* and the way in which it works.

The Weight to be Given to a Precedent

The need for the lawyer's craft or skill in this matter arises out of the impossibility of reducing the decision-making process of courts of law to a single formula. Professor Goodhart's third rule in his test for the *ratio* is that the principle is not necessarily found by a consideration of all the ascertainable facts of the case and the judge's decision. However, in assigning weight to a precedent it seems that the judge must give consideration to many more facts than simply those deemed to be material. Often, as we shall see, these are not facts *in* the case, but facts relating to the context in which the case was decided. The opposite extreme is that adopted by Karl Llewellyn in *The Bramble Bush,* and quoted by Professor Zander: 'Everything, everything, everything, big or small, a judge may say in an opinion, is to be read with primary reference to the particular dispute, the particular question before him.'

There are two guidelines that you may rely upon in trying to exercise the lawyer's skill in handling cases:

(a)   There is general agreement that it is necessary to be suspicious of rules which appear to be broadly based. To test that proposition check out the *ratio decidendi* in *Donoghue* v *Stevenson* [1932] AC 562 and then read *Grant* v *Australian Knitting Mills Ltd* [1936] AC 85.

(b)   There is general agreement that the *ratio decidendi* depends upon the choice of an appropriate level of generality. This is the big point made by Stone in his article, 'The *ratio* of the *ratio decidendi*' (1959) 22 MLR 597. The point is illustrated usually by reference to *Donoghue* v *Stevenson* but you ought to be able to work out examples of your own. Think, for instance, of the cases in contract, about the means of communication used to create contractual relations. Is there one rule for all means of communicating acceptance, or is there one rule for instantaneous communication and another rule for communication that is only complete over a measurable period of time? Failing either of these, are there separate rules for each form of communication, say, speech, writing, telephone, telex and electronic mail?

In order to answer such questions and to fix an appropriate level of generality consider the relevance of the facts given to the proposed rule of law. As Professor Zander points out, 'The greater the number of facts in the *ratio*, the narrower its scope; conversely, the fewer or the higher the level of abstraction, the broader the reach of the *ratio*' (*The Law-Making Process*, 4th ed., p. 264). In assigning weight to a precedent, once it is identified, there are several factors to take into account, including the court deciding the case, the existence of dissents, the age of the precedent, the way in which the case has been dealt with in later cases and the general reputation of the case. If a case is strongly disapproved of, this may be a reason for subsequently distinguishing it or attempting to narrow its scope.

From Learning to Practice

The previous two sections have been about learning to recognise binding precedents and being able to predict how they might be used or applied in future cases. Legal method courses usually include some compulsory practice in the techniques of handling cases. Often, you will be referred to a group of cases and you will be asked to demonstrate how the law in those cases developed from case to case, and as a matter of case technique rather than as an exercise in the developing rules of contract or some other subject. There are many groups of cases that may be taken. The development of the rule in *Rylands* v *Fletcher* (1868) LR 3 HL 330, the development of the law on negligent misstatement, the development of the law on the deserted wife's rights in the matrimonial home are just three examples. What is required in exercises of this sort is something like the following:

(a)   To be able to identify the authority which forms the starting-point of the line of cases in question. For example, if dealing with negligent misstatements you could say that the starting-point was the House of Lords approval in *Hedley Byrne & Co. Ltd* v *Heller & Partners Ltd* [1964] AC 465 of Denning LJ's dissenting judgment in *Candler* v *Crane Christmas & Co.* [1951] 2 KB 164.

(b)   To say of each case in the line of cases, whether it merely applied a rule, extended a rule, or reduced the scope of a rule.

(c)   To identify any piece of distinguishing.

(d)   To identify *obiter dicta* which by subsequent approval and adoption become the basis of new decisions and thus obtain an enhanced authority.

There are also *obiter dicta* of such persuasive force that they at once change the law. The statements of principle on negligent misstatement, by the House of Lords in *Hedley Byrne*, come into this category. One sort of exercise is to expose the techniques by which case law is developed, related to a given line of cases or a stated topic. Exercises based on several cases are more suitable for preparation for tutorials or seminar discussion but will sometimes appear on examination papers. Here are two questions that might appear on examination papers. Both can be answered by using the knowledge gained by studying groups of cases such as those mentioned above.

Describe the techniques which judges may use to control the development of the law.

Illustrate the way in which precedent works by reference to the doctrine of promissory estoppel, following the decision in *Central London Property Trust Ltd v High Trees House Ltd* [1947] KB 130.

Comment
The first of the two questions is a general one. The way in which it is worded means that you will have to concentrate on the aspects of case law which make for certainty and orderly development. Those are, the preference of courts for keeping a rule narrow and the possibility of restricting the scope of existing rules by a process of distinguishing. In this case, as in many others, an answer will be so much better if it contains apposite examples. Because this question is framed generally, examples will have to be drawn from more than one group of cases in order to cover as many as possible of the points made. In other words, the emphasis in this question has to be on showing how the various techniques connected with precedent work in practice.

On the other hand, in the second question the examiner is looking for evidence that you can develop an argument to meet incremental changes in factual situations. The argument is built up from case to case and the development of the rule strictly controlled. The second question is undoubtedly a question about case law techniques and not a contract law question. Perhaps the distinction is an unreal one which distorts the way in which things work in practice. The fact remains that many courses do teach legal method separately and, that being so, it cannot simply be 'method' in the abstract that is taught. There must be reference to actual cases. Usually, fair-minded examiners will only use cases that are known to their students as a basis for questions of this sort. It is really rather like the difference between set books and unseen translations in literature examinations. The two create different types of expectation in performance. So, the exercise in question 2 would only be set in an unseen examination in the context of particular groups of cases with which the examiner could expect the students to be familiar from work done during the course.

In this case, an answer would have to show how, beginning with *High Trees House* itself, the doctrine arose and how it was refined and explained in succeeding cases. Once again, it will show the cautious and step-by-step development of English Law.

In the following list of stages to cover in an answer to this question the cases mentioned are all cases with which students studying the law of contract should be familiar.

(a)   In *High Trees House* itself the notion of promissory estoppel was introduced as an *obiter dictum*. That *dictum* was itself based on earlier authorities such as *Hughes* v *Metropolitan Railway* (1877) 2 App Cas 439. A comment may be inserted here that it seems surprising that the idea of promissory estoppel was not discussed in *Foakes* v *Beer* (1884) 9 App Cas 605.

(b)   In the following case of *Combe* v *Combe* [1951] 2 KB 215, in which an attempt was made to found a cause of action on a bare promise unsupported by consideration, the Court of Appeal explained the nature of the doctrine as a form of equitable relief available as a defence or 'shield' only, thus limiting the potential scope of the rule.

(c)   Just a few years later in *Tool Metal Manufacturing Co. Ltd* v *Tungsten Electric Co. Ltd* [1955] 1 WLR 761, the question was whether a promise to forgo strict legal entitlements extinguished those entitlements or merely suspended them, if the promise was accepted as a promissory estoppel. The court found that in the right circumstances the effect would be suspensory only. This was probably an extension of the doctrine.

(d)   ... and so on until the doctrine was mentioned for the first time in the House of Lords, in the case of *Woodhouse A. C. Israel Cocoa Ltd SA* v *Nigerian Produce Marketing Co. Ltd* [1972] AC 741 in 1972. That case was found by the House of Lords not to be a case of promissory estoppel. Therefore, no ruling was given on the doctrine; the House of Lords simply gave notice that it reserved its position on the whole question of promissory estoppel and would review the doctrine comprehensively when the opportunity to do so arose.

In Farrar and Dugdale, *Introduction to Legal Method* (chapters 8 and 14), there are extensive passages discussing the development of a part of the law in this way. There is an even more detailed treatment of this subject in Holland and Webb's *Learning Legal Rules*, chapter 6.

JUDICIAL LAW MAKING

The extent to which new rules of law emerge from, or are directly created as a result of, judicial decision-making is controversial. It is therefore a topic about which, at one and the same time, students should be both enthusiastic and wary. I believe students are enthusiastic about courses and parts of courses which present them with a challenge. On the other hand care has to be taken in handling controversial topics in an academic context. What I propose to do in this section is to point out the various ways in which the judicial role in the law-making process gives rise to debate and opportunity for questions. There are real issues here which determine the outcome of real cases affecting thousands of people. At the same time, this topic provides examiners with ideal material to test the intellectual qualities of examinees. These qualities are the powers of analysis and comparison and the ability to make a reasoned choice between arguments.

This is an area in which there are no final answers. The debate goes on between the judges themselves and between legal theorists about what judges do and what they should do. In so far as judicial opinion goes, it is at least as important for you to note what the judges do as what they say they do.

The contribution which this topic makes to courses on the legal process can be summarised in five questions. The need to answer the last three of these five questions depends upon an affirmative answer to the first question and also, probably, the second question as well. The questions are:

(a)   DO judges make law?
(b)   SHOULD judges make law?
(c)   HOW do judges make law?
(d)   WHY do judges make law?
(e)   WHAT law should judges make?

All these questions are set in the context of the English legal system. Your understanding of English judges' work will be enhanced if you have some knowledge of the judicial role in the United States and the Continental European systems, particularly France and Germany. Cross and Harris, Zander, and Farrar and Dugdale, all have separate sections which will indicate the extent to which it is necessary for you to go in making a comparative study. The influence of Community law also continues to increase. The questions which you will be set in seminar discussions and in examinations will deal with the judges' role in a way that can be related to one or more of the questions set out above. A question that merely asks you to 'Discuss the role of the judge as part of the law-making process', without further detail or instruction, invites superficial treatment and answers. Unfortunately, people who set such questions are rarely satisfied with superficial answers. It is for that reason that you must be able to separate the elements of that all-embracing question and demonstrate how those elements relate to one another. Fortunately such questions are becoming less frequent, but when faced with one, you must first identify the aspect of the topic to which the question refers and marshal the relevant body of knowledge.

In dealing with this topic in a seminar or tutorial situation you should expect to be directed to certain subtopics and specific questions. For example, in a seminar on the judicial role in law making you might expect to be asked to consider such questions as:

(a) What is meant by 'policy' and to what extent can or should judges consider issues of policy?
(b) To what extent should laymen be involved in the process of law making?

Do Judges Make Law?

Not long ago, the common view was that judges favoured the declaratory theory of judging. According to this theory the judge, in announcing his decision, merely declared what the law was, adopting the *fiction* that the law had always been the same. Today, there is a general acknowledgement that at least at the higher levels of the judiciary there is a significant number of decisions to be made in which judges have some choice. The resulting decision at least incrementally represents a new departure in the law and a new rule of law. That this is so is clear from looking at the way in which the law develops and changes through the workings of the doctrine of precedent. Even in other legal systems based on codification, the judicial lawmaker is accepted. In French law, compare the ban on judges laying down general rules in art. 5 of the Civil Code, with the overtly innovatory role of the Conseil d'État in administrative law. In Swiss law, art. 1 of the Civil Code expressly recognises the need for judicial interpretation and development of the Code.

In the English legal system, the debate today is not so much about whether the judges do make law. It is about the proper place of judicial law making.

Should Judges Make Law?

This question should be approached on two levels. In the first place you may ask whether judge-made law is inevitable in any legal system. Your answer must be that it appears so, whenever any degree of regard is paid to past decisions of the courts in reaching new decisions. There is greater scope for judge-made law in those systems which accord most authority to past decisions.

At the second level, your inquiry should be whether the practice of judicial law making as it exists in the English legal system is a proper and acceptable one. This in turn may be broken down into three parts:

(a) a consideration of the practices of the court;
(b) judicial characteristics and behaviour, and
(c) the areas of law within which judicial law making occurs.

I propose to deal with (c) under the heading of the fifth question, What law should judges make? Under (a) comes a critical appraisal of those features of the English legal system which give rise to judge-made law. These are set out in the consideration below of how judges make law.

That leaves a consideration of judicial characteristics and behaviour. This is in itself the subject of full-scale studies such as Professor Griffith's study, *The Politics of the Judiciary*. Such a study begins with a consideration of the social and educational background of members of the judiciary and their selection and training as judges. It must conclude with a study of the extent to which those social and educational factors are reflected in the decisions judges make. Do the decisions which they make support judicial claims of impartiality and loyalty to *legal* values above peer group loyalty and attitudes to contemporary (and sometimes fleeting) issues of policy? As a counterweight to Professor Griffith's views read Lord Devlin's article, 'Judges, government and politics' (1978) 41 MLR 505. (This article is reprinted in Zander, *The Law-Making Process*, 4th ed., pp. 308–11.) The *Modern Law Review* has, over the years, published a number of articles analysing judicial attitudes to different matters; these include, industrial conflict, race relations, and landlord and tenant cases. The information in such articles is the sort of factual base you need to form the opinions you will express in answers to questions on this aspect of judicial law making.

How do Judges Make Law?

The answer to this question is chiefly concerned with the way in which judges have developed the doctrine of precedent in English law. In particular, I would point out to you that the extent of the authority accorded to a single decision is a unique feature of the English legal system. There have been suggestions that this led to the tyranny of the single decision. Judge-made law is also retrospective in its operation and this has much to do with judicial caution in avoiding pronouncements of general principles. Even in appellate courts judgments are sometimes still given in an extempore or 'off-the-cuff' way instead of being reserved. The practice of having multiple judgments also affects the quality of judge-made law with its possibility of more uncertainty in the law. (Compare the collegiate nature and the style of judgments in the European Court of Justice.) The undesirable effects of these features of judicial practice have been mitigated by having more reserved judgments and having single majority judgments, especially in the House of Lords. So far there has been successful resistance to the idea of introducing a system of prospective overruling to counteract the worst consequences of the retrospective effect of judge-made law. There seems to be no practical way of overcoming the need to wait for a suitable case to occur before desirable changes can be brought about by judge-made law.

Why do Judges Make Law?

My reason for asking you to ponder this question is to direct your attention to the debate amongst the judges concerning distinctions between principle and policy. There seems to be agreement that the reason for the acceptance of judicial law making is the need for judges to develop the law in accordance with general principles. You may recall that this is sometimes given as a justification for having a second tier of appellate jurisdiction. Legal principle is concerned with ensuring that decisions conform with an ethical standard which in turn gives rise to those peculiarly 'legal' values identified by Stein and Shand in *Legal Values in Western Society*. These values include impartiality, objectivity, the rules of natural justice and a high degree of certainty and predictability. Not all judges agree that their role extends to deciding policy issues of an economic, social or political nature. Perhaps the key to this dispute lies in the answer to the question, What law should judges make?

What Law Should Judges Make?

I have implied and the question implies that there may be a proper sphere of substantive law for judicial creativity, and that there may be another sphere in which the judges should abstain from an interventionist, creative role. (With reference to criminal law, see *Shaw* v *Director of Public Prosecutions* [1962] AC 220.) The point may be put in another way. Is there a distinction between the type of issues suitable for law making through the process of (a) the courts, (b) the Law Commissions and (c) political debate? (The inclusion of (b) and (c) indicates that this whole topic is bound up with the law-making process generally and that you must be prepared to consider judge-made law alongside other forms of law.)

What guidance is available to help you in deciding this question? As a beginning, perhaps you should recall what you already know:

(a)   The *Practice Statement* by the House of Lords in 1966 clearly set out types of case in which the House would not normally overrule its own previous decisions.

(b)   The judges sometimes disagree amongst themselves about the occasions on which they should intervene.

(c)   Sometimes the policy pursued by the judges is at variance with the social policy as laid down by Parliament.

(d)   There are examples of good and bad judicial decisions in all branches of the law.

As a humble student, what sense can be made, you ask, of such generalised statements? In reply, I suggest that you study the views of Lord Reid. I offer the following, partial summary:

(a)   In property and contract, a degree of injustice should be accepted in order to achieve a fairly high degree of certainty.

(b)   The judges should not extend the criminal law.

(c)   The common law, including the law of tort, is best left to development by the judges.

(d)   The decisions of the courts should be based on common sense and be reasonable.

(e)   Sometimes the law is so clear and strong that the only solution is to rely upon the legislature for reform.

In general terms, where there are wide differences of view on a matter of social or economic policy, the judges are wise to refrain from imposing a solution which appears to favour one view at the expense of another. Such matters are best decided by Parliament.

If you adopt Lord Reid's views as the framework within which to work out an answer to the question, What law should judges make?, you will need to do two things:

(a)   Take account of opposing views, such as the more radical views of Lord Denning.

(b)   Collect examples which illustrate the views expressed by Lord Reid, including examples such as *Knuller (Publishing, Printing & Promotions) Ltd* v *Director of Public Prosecutions* [1973] AC 435, which created uncertainty in the criminal law and was contrary to legislative policy. As an example of (e) in the list of Lord Reid's views, use the case of *Curtledge* v *L. Jopling & Sons Ltd* [1963] AC 758.

Finally, there are two propositions that will always be valid, or so it seems:

(a)   Judges may give decisions which reflect what they think the law ought to be, but in doing so they will content themselves with saying 'This is what the law is'.

(b)   Most judges will go to considerable lengths to avoid being called legislators, naked or otherwise (see *Magor & St Mellons Rural District Council* v *Newport Corporation* [1952] AC 189).

An actual examination question set in a first-year examination on the English legal system was:

'Judges must and do legislate.' Discuss.

The five questions posed at the beginning of this section provide relevant material for an answer to that examination question.

ADVANTAGES AND DISADVANTAGES OF A DOCTRINE OF PRECEDENT

Questions about the advantages and disadvantages of a doctrine of precedent are some of the oldest in the examiners' repertoire. They are often combined with questions about the relative merits of all the various sources of law in our legal system. In addition, knowing the virtues and vices of a doctrine of precedent as found in English law will assist you in making qualitative judgments about, for instance, the way in which our judges make law. Also, knowing the strong and weak points of the system will assist you in evaluating proposals for change. Such an evaluation might also include comment on the way in which some of these proposals actually work in practice in European Community law and other jurisdictions. Let me give two examples:

(a) *A proposal to adopt a system of prospective overruling.* Such a practice exists in the United States Supreme Court, and has been supported by several judges of the House of Lords. It would be designed to overcome one of the disadvantages of our doctrine of precedent, namely, its retrospective effect, which is sometimes responsible for the unwillingness of our courts to overrule previous decisions. The device carries within itself its own disadvantages, not least the fact that the public would have a different perception of the judicial role. The arguments against prospective overruling in English courts are set out in Zander's *The Law-Making Process* in extracts from articles by A. Nicol and Lord Devlin, which originally appeared in 39 MLR, p. 542 and p. 11 respectively.

(b) *Single judgments in appellate cases.* The disadvantage of having multiple judgments in a case relate to the difficulty often found in deciding 'what the case stands for'. There is a price to pay for increased certainty. It is that there must inevitably be some element of compromise in the judgment delivered, as a result of the deliberations of three or five judges (up to 13 judges, with almost as many languages in the European Court).

Before concluding with a note of the claimed advantages and disadvantages of precedent, let me remind you that most qualities have both 'good' words and 'bad' words to describe them. Consider, for example the ideas of 'fat' and 'thin'. If those terms are presumed to be neutral see how different attitudes to the 'fatness' and 'thinness' of a person can be conveyed by using different words.

Neutral word	Approving word	Disapproving word
Fat	Plump	Podgy
Thin	Slim	Skinny

Likewise, the characteristics of precedent and the values promoted by the system of precedent. If taken too far each of the claimed advantages can turn into a disadvantage. The advantages of the system are:

(a)   It creates a high degree of predictability, thus enabling people to settle their affairs with confidence.
(b)   It promotes fair and efficient adjudication.
(c)   It promotes public confidence in the judiciary.

The disadvantages of the system are:

(a)   Over-emphasis on individual decisions.
(b)   Its retrospective action may upset legitimate expectations.
(c)   Bad decisions may stand for many years.
(d)   It is slow to respond to changing conditions.
(e)   There may be uncertainty about what the law is.
(f)   There is attention to detail at the expense of a consideration of policy and principle.

The system gives opportunity for both flexibility and stability. It is for the judges of each generation to maintain an appropriate balance between flexibility and stability. There are, within the system, sufficient leeways to keep the law from becoming rigid and like 'the law of the Medes and Persians, which altereth not'.

A recent examination question which related precedent to other sources of law, was:

How are new rules added to English law? What are the advantages and disadvantages of the various methods?

A NOTE ON LAW REPORTING AND DATA RETRIEVAL SYSTEMS

At the beginning of the section on *stare decisis,* I mentioned the importance of law reports as reliable records of the case. Most textbooks and most courses devote some attention to the question of law reporting.

In a legal system course, law reporting appears for one or more of the following reasons:

(a)   The history of law reporting is an interesting topic in its own right.
(b)   Familiarity with the range of different reports, especially the modern series, is essential in studying the law.
(c)   You need to be aware of the degree of authority accorded by the courts to different series of reports and the reasons for the differences in the

authority so accorded. There is less authority accorded to unreported decisions, for example, and many reports are not revised by the judges before publication.

There is a great number of specialist reports at the present day, and also there are available data retrieval systems. These computerised systems make it possible to conduct elaborate searches for authorities, resulting in some cases in very extensive citation of authorities. Both the House of Lords and the Court of Appeal have taken steps to curtail the citation of unnecessary authorities.

Unless law reporting forms a separate item in your syllabus, a knowledge of law reporting will be chiefly of use in support of your understanding of the doctrine of precedent and the way in which it works. This chapter will finish with an exercise in case analysis.

CASE ANALYSIS EXERCISE

Introduction

Case analysis exercises occur in a number of legal method courses, as already indicated. These exercises may differ in detail but they are all essentially similar in purpose. At the University of Bristol students are required to write a case analysis of about 1,500 words in length and to deal with the case under the following heads:

(a)   A statement of the material facts.

(b)   A statement of the *legal* issues on which the parties are in disagreement.

(c)   The *ratio decidendi* of the case, with an explanation of the choice made.

(d)   Any *obiter dictum,* with an assessment of its significance.

(e)   A summary of the way in which the court treated other authorities and relevant legislation.

(f)   The use made by the court of principle and policy. (At this point students are advised to reread the judgments of Lords Scarman and Wilberforce in *McLoughlin* v *O'Brian* [1983] 1 AC 410.)

(g)   The nature of the legal reasoning used by the court; the use of analogies, and whether the reasoning was deductive or inductive.

(h)   A personal assessment by the student of the decision. Was it good or bad; what is its likely impact on future decisions?

Such an exercise develops the skills of legal research, analysis and drafting.

A Case to Analyse

Here is a case for you to analyse in accordance with the above structure. It is a case with which you are probably familiar. Read *Pharmaceutical Society of Great Britain* v *Boots Cash Chemists (Southern) Ltd*, at first instance before Lord Goddard CJ [1952] 2 QB 795, [1952] 2 All ER 456. When you have read the case write down your own ideas of what should appear under the various headings. Only when you have completed that task, compare your own ideas with the following suggestions. References are to the report in *The Law Reports*.

Material facts

The shop was arranged in the self-service way (an innovation in 1951). The shop sold poisons which, by statute, could be sold only under the supervision of a qualified pharmacist.

Each item in the shop was marked with its price.

The customer selected the goods and presented them to the cashier, who stated the price and received the money.

The pharmacist was positioned near the cash desk and had authority to prevent the removal of drugs from the shop.

Legal issues

This was a special case stated for the opinion of the court on the application of the Pharmacy and Poisons Act 1933, s. 18. The legal issue was whether the procedure adopted by the defendant constituted a sale under the supervision of a qualified pharmacist. In order to resolve that issue, the question to be decided was, in the words of Lord Goddard CJ, 'whether the sale is completed before or after the intending purchaser has passed the scrutiny of the pharmacist and paid his money, or, to put it in another way, whether the offer . . . is an offer by the shopkeeper or an offer by the buyer'.

Ratio decidendi

If a customer picks up a bottle of a controlled substance, marked with the price, from the shelves of a self-service store, and presents it to the cashier near where the pharmacist is stationed, then (per Lord Goddard CJ at p. 802):

(a) that is an offer by the customer to buy;

(b) there is no sale until the buyer's offer to buy is accepted by the acceptance of the price;

(c) such a sale takes place under the supervision of the pharmacist.

The *ratio* is expressed in this way so as to relate closely to the material facts of the case. It is narrow in scope because of the nature of the case, seeking a specific ruling on the meaning of a phrase in a statute. (Refer back to Professor Zander's quote from *The Bramble Bush* on page 187.)

Obiter dictum

At p. 803 Lord Goddard says that if the pharmacist is in a position to forbid the taking of the poison even after the sale is complete, the sale is still effected under the supervision of the pharmacist within the meaning of the Pharmacy and Poisons Act 1933, s. 18.

Use of authority and legislation

This is a case brought to determine whether an agreed factual situation comes within the scope of a statutory provision. It is not a case in which the words in the statute have to be interpreted. Both during the argument of the case and in his judgment Lord Goddard (at p. 801) refers to the case of *Carlill* v *Carbolic Smoke Ball Co.* [1893] 1 QB 256, and the speech of Bowen LJ in that case at p. 269, for guidance on the meaning of an offer. After referring to the opposing arguments of counsel he comes to the conclusion that there is nothing in the facts of this case to bring it within the definition of an offer as explained by Bowen LJ. So there is no reason to reverse the well-established principle that the mere exposure of goods for sale by a shopkeeper indicates to the public that he is willing to treat but does not amount to an offer to sell.

Use of principle and policy

At p. 802, Lord Goddard supports his opinion on the law relating to invitations to treat by reference to 'ordinary principles of common sense and of commerce'. He also refers to the serious results that would follow if 'the exposure of an article is an offer to sell'. He gives examples of those results. The customer could not change his mind once he picked up an article; and the shopkeeper could not stop the customer taking away the article.

Reasoning

There seems in this case to be an argument based on analogies with the practices already existing in other retail trades; for example, booksellers. The deduction is then drawn that this form of trading is no different and that therefore the display on the shelves must be an invitation to treat. Reference to 'serious results' (see above) is an example of a consequential argument.

An assessment of the case

The decision in the case appears to be soundly based on existing authority. On the face of it, it is limited to the application of the Pharmacy and Poisons Act 1933, s. 18, in the context of a self-service system. However, the remarks made at pp. 801 and 802 show that the judge clearly thought that his decision should apply to all sales on the self-service system. From the vantage point of the 1990s we now know that this was the right decision from a commercial viewpoint, seeing that the self-service system is the dominant form of retail trading.

On the specific issue raised by the case, observation of the trading arrangements in Boots and other large stores selling controlled goods (including intoxicants and cigarettes) shows that any disquiet there might have been over the reality of the supervision found in this case to have existed in law has been dispelled by having a separate sales area for these goods. In the 1950s a person reading this case might have found difficulty in choosing the right level of generality; namely, was this decision to apply to all self-service stores or only to chemists?

Conclusion

The example chosen to show you how a case analysis exercise might be approached is a very simple and short case with a single judgment. More elaborate cases from appellate courts will provide significantly more material under each heading. Here is a final question on case law for you to consider.

If a case had decided in 1950 that greengrocery exposed for sale in the self-service manner constituted an offer, do you think that that case might have been distinguished in *Pharmaceutical Society of Great Britain* v *Boots Cash Chemists (Southern) Ltd* in 1952 because of the need for supervision in the sale of controlled medicines and drugs?

FURTHER READING

Cross, Sir R. and Harris, J.W., *Precedent in English Law* (4th edn., Clarendon Press, 1991).

Farrar, J.H. and Dugdale, A.M., *Introduction to Legal Method* (3rd edn., Sweet and Maxwell, 1990).

Holland, J.A. and Webb, J.S., *Learning Legal Rules* (2nd edn., Blackstone Press, 1993).

11 LEGISLATION

Legislation is the most important source of law in the contemporary English legal system. As such it forms an important part of all courses on English legal system and method, although the approach to this topic varies from one institution to another. A study of the syllabuses and examination papers of a number of institutions shows that there is a solid core of material on statutory interpretation which is found in every course. Around that core, institutions build their own requirements. The pattern to be followed in this chapter reflects the content and method of teaching and assessing of a majority of the courses on the English legal system.

The form in which your own course is presented will govern the sort of exercises and assessments which form part of the course. If, for example, your course culminates in a single three-hour examination paper there is a strong possibility that 'legislation' as a topic will figure on that paper in the form of one essay-type question. In the last few years, a favourite subject for that essay question has been the extent to which judges seek out the intentions of Parliament when faced with a problem of statutory interpretation. Very often, the question is set in the context of a quotation from a judge in the course of a judgment. As we shall see later, there are some favourite judges whose judgments are used in this way.

Courses which have an element of continuous assessment are more likely to set assignments in the form of exercises in drafting clauses in Bills and in statutory interpretation, based on either real or fictional statutes. All courses may use these as the basis of tutorial work during the course of the year. As with case law, 'legislation' as a part of a legal system course has two purposes. It is studied for its own intrinsic interest as a vital part of one of the world's major legal systems. It is also explained and demonstrated as an essential 'tool' for the job of learning the law and later practising the law. It falls to the lot of many people teaching English legal system courses to provide both forms of teaching and instruction. It is for that reason that a short passage on legislation was included in chapter 3, on the basic tools for the job. Now is the time to ensure your mastery of that elementary material and to look at one or two short statutes to familiarise yourself with their layout. Statutes such as the Unfair Contract Terms Act 1977 are of about the right length and complexity for such a task.

TEXTBOOKS

As in other parts of a legal system course, you can glean much helpful guidance about the weight to be given to a topic and the approach to it by calculating what proportion of class time is spent on it and which textbooks you are recommended to use. The all-purpose legal system textbooks, such as Dr Ingman's *The English Legal Process* and Smith and Bailey's *The Modern English Legal System,* appear to give equal weighting to legislation with other major topics in the syllabus. In some cases, however, tutors will recommend in clear terms that 'You should have' or that 'It will be useful to have' one or more specialist books on legal method, which deal in equal measure or thereabouts with legislation and precedent. The leading books are, of course, Farrar and Dugdale, *Introduction to Legal Method,* Holland and Webb, *Learning Legal Rules* and Zander's *The Law-Making Process.* Such suggestions are to be heeded, at least to the extent that you prepare to write exercises as coursework, as they will be described later in this chapter, as well as to answer one or two essay-type questions in an examination. Finally, there are the specialist books on this topic with which you should be able to express some degree of familiarity. On legislation as a whole, from its inception to its application, there is *Legislation* by Miers and Page. On the more traditional English legal system course approach there is Cross on *Statutory Interpretation* and Bennion on *Statute Law.* For a wealth of examples of the application of particular rules there is the classic, *Maxwell on the Interpretation of Statutes.* In the case of periodical literature there is the specialist publication, *Statute Law Review.*

In order to understand the thinking which goes into the making of a statute, it is very useful to consult the working papers and reports of the Law Commission. These documents review the current state of the law on a particular matter and make detailed proposals, with draft bills attached, for legislative action. Very often the reports contain alternative proposals and reasoned arguments for preferring a particular set of proposals. You will be referred to some of these documents in any case, in connection with other subjects such as contract and tort. Use the opportunity to reinforce your legal method or legal system work by thinking about them as exercises in the art of legislation as well as thinking about them as proposals for the reform of the substantive law. You might take as examples the Law Commission's published papers and reports leading up to the enactment of the Animals Act 1971 or the Unfair Contract Terms Act 1977. If your course is concerned in any detail with the enactment of legislation and the problems of drafting, choose a piece of legislation that has recently completed all its stages and ask your library for all the documentation it has, from the first publication of the Bill until it emerged in its final form as a fully fledged statute. You will be able to study at first hand both the process of enactment and the effect of textual amendments introduced during the passage of the bill. In the process you will acquire knowledge which will help you to develop drafting skills.

A study of the various syllabuses and methods of assessment in current use suggests that the topic of legislation in an English legal system course now covers the following matters:

(a)   The origins of legislation.
(b)   Types of legislation, including delegated or subordinate legislation.
(c)   The structure of statutes, their presentation and drafting.
(d)   Statutory interpretation.
(e)   Proposals for the reform of statute law and statutory interpretation.
(f)   Law reform generally.
(g)   Community legislation and its interpretation.

The rest of this chapter will deal with each of these matters and conclude with a review of typical questions. In some courses at least, you may expect practical exercises, which may count towards course assessment, in connection with items (c) and (d) in the above list. Such exercises may be based on either actual statutes or fictional proposals for legislation and fictional statutes.

ORIGINS AND PREPARATION OF LEGISLATION

If we take Farrar and Dugdale's *Introduction to Legal Method* and Professor Zander's *The Law-Making Process* as two of the most widely used textbooks which are concerned solely with legal method, it appears that a study of legislation in your sort of course begins with a brief review of the way in which legislative proposals are formulated. That approach is in accord with the thinking that legislation should be studied as a whole and not divided between a legal system course and a constitutional law course. Treatment of the whole within one syllabus also eliminates potential overlaps between two courses. From the point of view of those whose primary interest is in legal systems and legal method it is a useful way of demonstrating how some of the problems of statutory interpretation arise in the first instance. It may also show how the legislative process in its present form will inevitably produce problems for the user of statutes.

Judging by the distribution of types of question on examination papers, it seems that thus far, at any rate, what has just been said represents the use being made of this essentially introductory part of the topic. Although it may be the case that a knowledge of the origins of legislation and the legislative process is regarded as auxiliary and supplementary material in most legal method and legal system courses, you must not disregard it as of no consequence to you in the way you will perform on this course. On the contrary, it appears to me to be a mark of a higher-order skill to be able to show how the problems existing in one sphere of activity are dependent upon what happens in another sphere of activity.

As the legislative process is locked into political debate and the resulting legislation is an expression of the results of that debate it is not surprising that our legislators sometimes seem to pay little attention to making their product 'user friendly'. Such a consideration may be in the forefront of the draftsman's mind, but even there it must compete with other considerations relating to the parliamentary process itself and the requirements of formal debate. It is not always easy or possible to reconcile these competing considerations.

If you are persuaded of the need to know something of the origins of legislative proposals you will be asking two things. What is it that I need to know? and what use should I expect to make of it? In the first instance you should be able to identify the different sources of proposals and their characteristics in their raw state.

Generally speaking the government is in control of the legislative machine. Government controls the parliamentary timetable and the resources of the great Departments of State. Some government-sponsored legislation is clearly based on the political commitments made in election manifestos. Other legislation is required simply in order to carry on the day-to-day business of governing. In either case, the government has the resources of the civil service with which to prepare detailed briefs for the draftsman. Government must also consider the detailed proposals made by such official bodies as royal commissions, departmental committees and the Law Commissions and decide whether to accept the proposals in whole or in part (see, for example, chapter 8, legal aid). Proposals which are accepted are then taken over by the government machine. Private members' Bills are in another category. These bills may be the work of individual members or they may be the result of the member concerned sponsoring the proposals of an outside pressure group. The point for you to grasp here is that unless these bills are taken over or given assistance by the government they often compare unfavourably on a technical level with the products of the government legislative machine. The first section of chapter 1 in Professor Zander's book contains passages which illustrate the complex origins of a single Bill, and the changes that a proposal may undergo before it is ever published as a draft Bill awaiting its first reading.

When you review the actual mechanics of enactment the points to look for are the ways in which the draftsman's work is now at the mercy of the Members of Parliament who may amend it. The watchfulness of the officials in charge of the Bill at the committee stages is all important in keeping the Bill in a form that will result in a user-friendly or even a workable statute.

This way of looking at the origins of legislation and the mechanics of enactment is quite different from the traditional constitutional law concerns with legislation, which concentrate on the relationship between the legal forms of legislative activity and the democratic and political debate. The point is made, for example, in de Smith, *Constitutional and Administrative Law*, that it is exceptional for a Department to introduce a Bill without prior consultation with organisations that will be affected by the legislation. It may be that your course attempts to combine both ways of looking at this topic of legislation.

The sort of work which will benefit from this preliminary look at legislation includes drafting exercises and essays on the deficiencies of statute law. These preliminary considerations may enable you to take a more balanced view and to mitigate the harshness of the judgment you might make without the benefit of these preliminary considerations. Your course may combine what appeared traditionally in a constitutional law syllabus under the heading of legislation, with that which has always appeared in English legal system courses. In that event you may expect an assignment or examination question dealing with the political and policy aspects of legislation and the work of Parliament. If you are at all unsure of the attitude adopted on this by your course, first read the syllabus carefully, then find out what sort of books are recommended. If you are still unsure, ask your subject tutor.

TYPES OF LEGISLATION

In this section, there will be set out several ways in which legislation may be classified. Classification is a form of definition and definitions are only necessary if they are to be of some practical use. Therefore there is set out here simply the different ways in which legislation is classified and the significance of each form of classification. You will easily detect the classifications which are of most significance to legislation in the context of an English legal system course.

The various classifications are these:

Types of legislation	Significance
Public general Acts and private Acts	Indicates procedure by which passed. If an Act is a private Act it applies to a locality or affects the legal position of a defined group of persons or organisation. (*Note*: Be careful not to confuse private Bills and Acts with private members' Bills which result in public general Acts if passed.)
Money Bills and other Bills	Money Bills have special procedures and the powers of the House of Lords are restricted under the Parliament Acts 1911–1949.
Amending, consolidating and codifying Acts	In the case of consolidating Acts, they may be passed by special procedures e.g., under the Consolidation of Enactments (Procedure) Act 1949. This classification also indicates the relevance of particular approaches to construction and interpretation.
Legislation by subordinate or delegated legislation (including by-laws)	Delegated legislation takes a variety of forms, which raises the possibility of applying the procedural *ultra vires* rule. Delegated legislation is also subject to the substantive *ultra vires* rule and, in addition, by-laws are subject to the reasonableness test. Statutory instruments are subject to the controls of the Statutory Instruments Act 1946.

Parliamentary sovereignty entails the position that the validity of an Act of Parliament may not be questioned in an English court. Attempts to challenge the validity of a statute in recent years have failed. These cases include *British Railways Board* v *Pickin* [1974] AC 765, a case involving a private Act, and a claim that the Canada Act 1982 was *ultra vires for* failing to comply with the Statute of Westminster 1931. Both Lord Reid (in *British Railways Board* v *Pickin*) and Lord Scarman (in *Duport Steels Ltd* v *Sirs* [1980] 1 WLR 142) have expressed clear views on the duty of the courts in the field of statute law 'to interpret and to apply the law'. On the other hand the supremacy of European Community law, insisted upon by the European Court in the *Simmenthal* case [1978] ECR 629, has been accepted by the English courts in the *Factortame* cases.

In many courses there is also a requirement to know the types of secondary legislation made by the European Community under art. 189 of the EC Treaty. Regulations and Directives give rise to problems of statutory interpretation both in domestic courts of the member States and in the European Court of Justice.

STRUCTURE OF STATUTES: PRESENTATION AND DRAFTING

It will be clear to you at the stage of your studies when you may be reading this chapter that you are going to spend a great deal of time reading legislation. Knowing the structure of legislation will help you to handle the statute book in an efficient way. For that reason alone it is worth setting out the main parts of the structure of an Act of Parliament. In connection with some of the parts listed I shall state what information you may expect to gain from that part to help you in your capacity as a user of legislation. Not all of the various constituent parts that may be found in the statutes in the statute book are set out. Sufficient of them are set out to enable you to use the information you gain from textbooks and lecture notes more effectively. There is an outline of the main structure of Bills and Acts in Farrar and Dugdale, *Introduction to Legal Method*, chapter 9, and Holland and Webb, *Learning Legal Rules*, chapter 3. There is a more lengthy treatment in Smith and Bailey, *The Modern English Legal System*, chapter 5.

The principal parts of a statute are:

(a) Short title.
(b) Year and chapter number.
(c) Long title.
(d) Date.
(e) Enacting formula.
(f) Sections (divided into subsections and paragraphs) and schedules.
(g) Extent.
(h) Commencement.
(i) Interpretation.
(j) Amendments and repeals.

Of these ten parts of a statute, you should take particular notice of the following three items for they are of importance to users of the statute from an organisational or structural point of view: the long title, sections and schedules, and interpretation.

Long Title

It is the long title which tells you whether a statute is an amending Act, a consolidating Act or a codifying Act. Take the following examples of long titles:

(a) Sale of Goods Act 1893: 'An Act for codifying the law relating to the sale of goods.'
(b) Sale of Goods Act 1979: 'An Act to consolidate the law relating to the sale of goods'.

(c)   Misrepresentation Act 1967: 'An Act to amend the law relating to innocent misrepresentations and to amend sections 11 and 35 of the Sale of Goods Act 1893'.

These three short examples of long titles tell you that the short title may sometimes mislead you in its indication of the Act's subject-matter. The Misrepresentation Act 1967 is more limited in its scope than the short title indicates. It does not deal with fraudulent misrepresentations. Knowing that an Act is an amending, consolidating or codifying statute tells you immediately what attitude to adopt towards existing statutes and cases when construing the Act. Pre–1893 cases are no longer of good authority when construing post–1893 legislation on the sale of goods, but decisions given after 1893 and before consolidation in 1979 are to continue to be accorded authority in the normal way in construing the legislation since 1979. These consequences flow from the nature of codifying and consolidating statutes, respectively.

Sections and Schedules

In addition to your learning about the respective significance of sections, schedules and marginal notes, there is one practical point to watch when reading a section, subsection or paragraph for its meaning. Very often the task is to discover whether a particular factual situation satisfies the elements specified in the section of a statute. The need when reading the relevant parts of the statute is to note whether a number of requirements set out in the statute are cumulative or alternative. Students often make mistakes by failing to bear this in mind when reading. Much depends in this connection on the sense in which the words 'and' and 'or' are used. Here are three examples to make the point clear:

(a)   The definition of a consumer sale (as set out in the Sale of Goods Act 1979, sch. 1, para. 11):

. . . 'consumer sale' means a sale of goods . . . where the goods—

(a)   are of a type ordinarily bought for private use or consumption; and
(b)   are sold to a person who does not buy . . . them in the course of a business.

Here, the two limbs of the definition are cumulative. A consumer sale is always related both to the goods and the buyer of those goods.

(b)   Exclusion of the condition of satisfactory quality in a contract for the sale of goods (as set out in the Sale of Goods Act 1979, s. 14(2)):

. . . there is no such condition—

    (a)   as regards defects specifically drawn to the buyer's attention . . .; or
    (b)   if the buyer examines the goods. . . .

Thus, in this case the condition is excluded if *either* the seller draws the buyer's attention to the defect *or* the buyer examines the goods.

    (c)   The jurisdiction of the Court of Appeal (as set out in the Supreme Court Act 1981, s. 15(2)):

. . . there shall be exercisable by the Court of Appeal—

    (a)   all such jurisdiction . . . as is conferred on it by this . . . Act; and
    (b)   all such other jurisdiction . . . as was exercisable by it immediately
before the commencement of this Act.

This is an example of the use of the word 'and' to indicate that two or more separate possibilities exist. This listing of cumulative or separate requirements often occurs in a number of lettered paragraphs. It may also occur within the continuous text of a section or subsection. An example is the definition of the condition of 'fitness for purpose' in a sale of goods in the Sale of Goods Act 1979, s. 14(3). Find the section and read it, and work out for yourself how many requirements must be satisfied before the condition is implied into a contract for the sale of goods.

Interpretation

In looking at interpretation sections, take particular note of whether the definitions in the section apply to the whole of a statute or only to a particular part of the statute. The opening words of the section will state this. See, for example, the use of interpretation sections in the Unfair Contract Terms Act 1977.

Presentation of Statutes

Comment on the presentation of statutes falls under two heads; the arrangement and presentation of individual statutes and the arrangement of the statute book as a whole.

Individual statutes
The order in which a statute is arranged follows structurally the pattern set out in the books mentioned above. The only major exception is the placing of interpretation sections. The main interest, however, in the arrangement of an

Act is in the arrangement of the subject-matter. A glance at the 'arrangement of sections' in the Supreme Court Act 1981 will show that the subject-matter is arranged in a logical order, dealing with the constitution of the court and its constituents, followed by treatment of jurisdiction and concluding the main part of the Act with practice and procedure. In that sense, the Supreme Court Act 1981 is an unusual Act, for it is a common complaint that statutes are not written in such a straightforward and logical way. With a complex statute, there is often no way of discovering the section you need except by looking through the entire list of sections as set out in the arrangement of sections. This is a practical matter for you to overcome by familiarity with the principal statutes connected with the different syllabuses of your course. It is also a matter to store up in your mind as a point of critical comment on the practice of legislation. The draftsman sometimes has good reason for his arrangement of sections, in the need to get controversial matters debated at a favourable time in the parliamentary legislative timetable. Also, there may be late additions of whole topics, midway through the legislative process. This is a frequent occurrence in the passage of Criminal Justice Bills as there are demands for instant legislation on matters of topical moment. That leads sometimes to bad legislation. It is a reasonable point to make, in critical essays on legislation, whether those political considerations should take precedence over the technical and legal aspects of legislation. It seems that because legislation is a record of parliamentary debate some illogicality in the arrangement of subject-matter is inevitable. In reading statutes which create criminal offences, you should be aware of the practice of defining the offence in one section and setting out penalties in subsequent sections.

The statute book
The arrangement of the statute book as a chronological record stems from the point made at the end of the last paragraph. This was more apparent when statutes were arranged by reference to regnal years and parliamentary sessions, that is, until the change in the method of citation in 1963. It is easier to remember the name of a statute than its chapter number so it is a great help that the volumes of the statutes contain also an alphabetical list of the Acts contained in the volume. You still need to know the year in which the Act was passed.

A more radical point is to ask whether the statute book as a whole could be classified and arranged by subject matter. This is done in the publication known as *Statutes in Force*. This has been done also for the whole of the law, not just statutes, in *Halsbury's Laws of England*. Commercial publishers publish collections of statutes from time to time on particular topics. The selection depends upon the editors and the target market for the publications. The most serious complaint about the state of the statute book as a whole is the difficulty of knowing which statutes are currently in force, the extent to which they are in force and the effects of subsequent amendments and partial repeals. These difficulties are addressed in the work of the Law Commissions, by the use of Statute Law (Repeals) Acts and by consolidation. Publications such as *Current Law* are good starting-points for an investigation into the current state of statute law on a particular matter. If you have access to Lexis and know which statute you wish to consult, Lexis will provide you with the answers to your questions about the state of amendments and whether a statute is in force in whole or in part. It is worthwhile collecting some examples of past and present difficulties in establishing the state of statute law as this is an area coming within the scope of some examination questions on the critical consideration of the state of legislation in this country.

Drafting of Statutes

The drafting of statutes is mentioned in the syllabuses of quite a few institutions. In practical terms, you may expect to have to do one of two types of work in connection with drafting. You may be asked to do some drafting yourself or you may have to write a critical essay on the current state of drafting in English law.

The drafting exercises take various forms. Common ones are: drafting a short bill to achieve a stated objective, and drafting amendments to actual clauses in Bills currently before Parliament. In either case you may expect detailed instructions. Exercises in fictional legislation, although intended to result in short Bills, tend to deal with topics which are deceptive in their simplicity, such as bills to ban smoking in public places or to introduce compulsory screening for AIDS. In such cases it is necessary to pay close attention to clear and tight definitions of the objectives to be achieved. These exercises will also demonstrate the possibility of indirect attacks on a problem. A classic case is the ban on tobacco advertising on television. That is not intended *per se* as a control on advertising but as a public health measure to reduce the amount of smoking by the population at large. In order to undertake a simple drafting exercise or to write critically about drafting you must first understand the nature of the draftsman's task.

The draftsman has a choice of styles and a choice of ways in which the material is structured. The English style has a marked preference for detailed statements of rules over the statement of general principles as found in continental legal systems and EC treaties. A good example of the marked contrast in styles, since both apply in England, is a comparison of the Sex Discrimination Act 1975 incorporating the Equal Pay Act 1970, with the wording of art. 119 of the EC Treaty, which deals with the question of equal pay in a Community context.

There is rather more choice exercised in the selection of structure for the legislative material. The choice is between a statement of a small number of positive rules of relatively broad scope followed by a series of exceptions or to state the whole of the material as far as possible in the form of detailed rules of a positive nature but of narrow scope. The task is similar to the construction of a railway timetable.

Take the case of a timetable to show the movements of all passenger trains in a week from London to Newcastle and assume that the movement of each train is dependent on a provision in a statute entitled the London to Newcastle (Railway Timetable) Operations Act 1995. This could be a very short 'but unworkable' Act. Section 1 could provide, 'Trains shall depart from London King's Cross for Newcastle at hourly intervals between 0600 hours until 2300 hours daily'. The railway system we all know could not operate with such a simple statement only to control its operations. At the other extreme, the Act could, by a separate section for each train, set out the movements of trains in detail. In practice, the draftsman has to choose a position somewhere between those two extremes. In the case of our imagined Act, the draftsman would have to decide what general rules he could lay down and what exceptions would be necessary to take account of variables. If one day's timetable in the week was going to be markedly different, say Sunday, then the Act could immediately make separate provision for 'Sundays' and 'Mondays to Saturdays'. There might be many other variables which would have to be dealt with as exceptions; such as not running certain trains on bank holidays or varying once or twice in the day a regular departure time normally set at the same time during an hour. A decision would be needed also on whether to indicate what refreshment facilities were to be available.

Consideration of these problems of timetabling will show you the realities of how to define objectives and to structure your material to take care of exceptional situations and variables. The particular case of railway timetabling and your own experience of diagrammatic timetables might lead you to question the appropriateness of the prose style of legislation in all cases. United Kingdom legislation has made only tentative experiments with alternative ways of expressing legislative intent. Some few statutes, such as the Consumer Credit Act 1974, use mathematical formulae to prescribe methods of calculation. In EC law, quite elaborate diagrams are incorporated into Regulations on technical matters such as standards of construction for motor vehicles and motor vehicle parts.

A consideration of the state of the art of drafting in UK legislation may conveniently be achieved by looking at the work of two people. Mr Francis Bennion, a one-time draftsman, and Sir William Dale, a senior lawyer-civil servant, who published a report on our drafting, *Legislative Drafting: A New Approach*, in 1977. The work of both is referred to and summarised in the main textbooks and cases and materials books. Mr Bennion's work is a source for you of analysis of the work of the draftsman in terms of objectives and the constraints on the draftsman. These may be found in what he termed 'drafting parameters' in his book *Statute Law*. Some of these relate to the process of enactment, preparational parameters, and some to the ultimate operation of the enactment, operational parameters. The most important parameters are: procedural legitimacy, timeliness and legal effectiveness. They often take priority over comprehensibility and legal compatibility. A more complete list and explanation of these parameters may be found in Smith and Bailey, *The Modern English Legal System*, pp. 250–1.

Sir William Dale identified the following points of criticism of drafting in the United Kingdom:

(a) Long involved sentences.
(b) Much detail, little principle.
(c) An indirect approach to the subject-matter.
(d) Subtraction, as in 'Subject to . . .', 'Provided that . . .'.
(e) Poor arrangement.
(f) Too many schedules and too long schedules.
(g) Too much reliance on cross-references.

A study of Mr Bennion's operational parameters, such as legal effectiveness and legal compatibility, will show you the link between drafting and statutory interpretation. All lawyers from time to time have to draft documents as well as to interpet them. For that reason alone, drafting exercises as part of your English legal system course are very worthwhile, as well as giving an opportunity, seldom offered to law students, to be creative. Chapter 7 in Holland and Webb, *Learning Legal Rules*, deals with the subject of drafting in some detail, with many good examples.

STATUTORY INTERPRETATION

Remember that the rules of statutory interpretation are not merely a part of an English legal system syllabus; they provide the tools that should be employed in any legal subject area where statutory materials appear. The other parts of the subject feed into the practice of statutory interpretation and its problems. This is supported by the fact that examiners still have two favourite questions. One is based on the theme that it is the task of judges to discover and apply the intentions of Parliament. The other is one of several variations on the theme of the supposed dichotomy between the literal approach and the purpose-based approach to the interpretation of statutes. Even if your examiner sets traditional questions in these forms you may, to your advantage, adopt a broader approach. This is becoming easier to achieve now that textbook writers such as Smith and Bailey have begun to develop an alternative form of exposition of the subject compared with the standard traditional treatment. That standard treatment was to set out the various rules, with examples, and to pay only minor attention to the way in which the whole subject worked as a unified whole. It became a mystery to know why a single judge sometimes adopted the literal rule and sometimes the mischief rule in quite similar cases. A favourite pair of cases were the decisions of Lord Parker CJ in *Bryan* v *Robinson* [1960] 1 WLR 506 and *Smith* v *Hughes* [1960] 1 WLR 830. Neither case appears in the list of cases in any of the books on the legal system by the following authors: Farrar and Dugdale, Ingman, Miers and Page, Smith and Bailey or Zander. Teachers and writers have begun to catch up with the way in which judges work in practice. Two writers in particular may be credited with this movement: F.A.R. Bennion and Professor Sir Rupert Cross. These two writers have made it possible for you to be able to write critically in an integrated way about statutory interpretation and to practise the skills of construction and interpretation in a methodical way and not merely to stick labels on well-established examples of the rules. If you have a choice between writing about interpretation and 'having a go' at interpretation, I would say that the practice is more satisfying but it may still be easier to score high marks by writing a good critical essay. There are many worked examples of statutory interpretation in Holland and Webb's *Learning Legal Rules*, chapters 8 and 9.

The respective contributions of the two writers I have mentioned, to the learning of the skills of interpretation and their critical exposition are as follows. The 'conditions of doubt' identified by Bennion in his book, *Statute Law*, are in fact an explanation of why statutes (and other documents) need interpretation. Similar points are made by Twining and Miers in their book, *How To Do Things with Rules*. Some of the 'conditions of doubt' are inevitable consequences of the use of language as a means of communication. Others are deliberate devices adopted by the draftsman. There are five conditions of doubt: ellipsis, the use of broad terms, politic uncertainty or deliberate ambiguity, unforeseen developments during the lifetime of the statute, and inadequacies such as printing errors and errors by the draftsman. The use of broad terms is also referred to by Professor Hart in his writings as the 'penumbra effect', that is, many words have a core meaning and a range of subsidiary meanings within an area of influence cast like a shadow by the core meaning. So, Bennion and others may be referred to in the opening paragraphs of an essay on statutory interpretation in explanation of why the process is needed at all. For an amusing and cogent example of the need for proper interpretation of rules, see the case in Twining and Miers, *How To Do Things with Rules*, of the small boy for whom rules are made to regulate his eating habits between meals. When you come to the next paragraph bear in mind that the too literal interpretation of the rules by the small boy just referred to, resulted in the boy's father, presumably the rule maker, losing his fresh salmon salad tea to the family cat. Forbidden to enter the pantry the boy simply stood and watched as the cat entered the pantry and ate the father's tea, which had been set out on a plate and left in the pantry.

Professor Cross has provided one possible methodology for those who wish to make sense out of the process of statutory interpretation. Such a methodology was badly needed by students faced with the task of predicting possible judicial interpretations of complex statutory provisions. The reason lay in the fragmented nature of the subject, which consisted of:

(a)   Three general approaches to statutory interpretation.
(b)   Textual or internal aids to interpretation.
(c)   Rules of language.
(d)   External aids to interpretation.
(e)   Presumptions of legislative intent.

The chief difficulty lies in the choice made between the three general approaches, known as the literal rule, the golden rule and the mischief rule. You all know that our judges, with some notorious exceptions, have a preference for the literal rule. There is a strong and vocal group of judges who wish to give more prominence to the mischief rule or the purpose rule. Which rule judges choose on a particular occasion appears sometimes to be a matter of caprice. One writer said, 'A court invokes whichever of the rules produces a result that satisfies its sense of justice in the case before it'. Unfortunately for students, tutors in seminars and examiners do not accept very readily the student's instinctive sense of justice not based on authority. Examiners tend to condemn such answers in this subject, saying that they are based on guesswork. For that reason it is helpful to adopt Professor Cross's unified contextual approach, however tentative it may be. It has two merits for the student. It provides a framework for thinking through problems until you can develop a 'feel' for the subject and it has the support of dicta in some recent decisions of the House of Lords.

Because all three general approaches have a part to play in Professor Cross's scheme you should begin by learning the meaning of each of the three and be able to distinguish examples of the application of each of them. All the textbooks do this admirably, with well-chosen examples designed to stick in the student's mind. You are then in a position to adopt Professor Cross's model as a step-by-step approach to any task of interpretation which you may be given. In some cases, of course, both teaching examples and actual cases will need detailed consideration of only one of the steps in the procedure; maybe the application of a rule of language or the application of a provision in the Interpretation Act 1978.

The procedure which I suggest you follow in exercises of statutory interpretation is based on the unified contextual approach which Professor Cross suggests is the method followed by the judges themselves:

(a)   Read the statute as a whole to establish its context. This includes its historical context and indications of the scope of the subject-matter.

(b)   If words are given a technical meaning by the statute itself, apply that meaning.

(c)   In all other cases consider first the ordinary dictionary meaning of the words.

(d)   If the ordinary meaning would produce absurd results which cannot reasonably be supposed to have been the intention of the legislature, apply the words in any secondary meaning which they are capable of bearing.

(e)   Only read in words if they are necessarily implied by words which are already in the statute. Only add to, alter or ignore statutory words in order to prevent a provision from being unintelligible or irreconcilable with the rest of the statute.

(f)   In applying these rules you may resort to the rules of language and grammatical construction and presumptions. Presumptions are especially valuable in applying the rules at stage (d).

The principal rules of language are those known by their Latin names. They are:

(a)   *Ejusdem generis*, where general words follow a list of particular words; the general words may take their meaning from the class created by the particular words.

(b)   *Noscitur a sociis*, where words derive their meaning from the context in which they appear.

(c)   *Expressio unius est exclusio alterius*, where mention of one or more things of a particular class, excludes all other members of the class.

The principal presumptions are:

(a)   Against changes in the common law.
(b)   Against ousting the jurisdiction of the courts.
(c)   Against interference with vested rights.
(d)   Against retrospective operation.
(e)   Against binding the Crown.

You should note the attitude of the courts to internal aids to interpretation, such as the long title to an Act.

The principal external aids to interpretation and to establish the context of a statute are:

(a)   Historical setting.
(b)   Dictionaries and other literary sources.

(c)   Practice, commercial and social.
(d)   Other statutes *in pari materia*.
(e)   Legislative antecedents.
(f)   Government publications.
(g)   International treaties.

..One of the most important developments in recent years in relation to external aids to interpretation is the admissibility of Hansard as such an aid. This was established by the House of Lords in *Pepper* v *Hart* [1992] 3 WLR 1032 and changed the practice established in an earlier House of Lords opinion in *Davis* v *Johnson* [1979] AC 317. It is instructive to read the leading opinion of Lord Browne-Wilkinson and the dissenting opinion of Lord Mackay to discover the reasons for and against the use of Hansard in the interpretation of a statute. In essence the argument is, on one side, that of principle, i.e., access to parliamentary words may throw light on the mischief behind a statute or the legislative intent, as opposed to, on the other side, considerations of cost, uncertainty in the parliamentary words themselves and problems of access to Hansard.

Clearly an assignment or examination question could revolve around an evaluation of above arguments. Remember there are no right answers, after all in the space of 13 years the House of Lords was persuaded by each of two opposing arguments!

Another approach to this aid to interpretation is to look at the limits of the rule, that is, Hansard may be used only where a statute is ambiguous or the literal meaning leads to an absurdity, the parliamentary material clearly indicates the mischief or legislative intent, and the parliamentary words are those of the minister or other promoter of a bill. Then you may be asked to consider how this rule has been used in subsequent cases. See the interesting questions posed by Zander in *The Law-Making Process*, pp. 153–7.

Lastly, in approaching a general problem of statutory interpretation, which may involve a fictional Act of Parliament and a series of questions asking how the Act may be applied to factual situations, there may be an opportunity to state the rule in *Pepper* v *Hart* and to apply it to the problem.

In writing critically about statutory interpretation and in doing exercises in the interpretation of statutes there are two things you must remember:

(a)   The rules of statutory interpretation are judge-made, are guidelines only and may be modified by the judges themselves.

(b)   The aids to interpretation set out above are sometimes in conflict with one another. In any case, their respective application is based only on presumptions in their favour. Like all but conclusive or irrebuttable presumptions, these rules will not be applied if there is good reason for not doing so.

Before finishing this section I must deal with the effect of following the unified contextual approach on the two traditional questions mentioned at the beginning of the section.

Explain what the judges mean when they say that in the interpretation of legislation they seek out and apply the intention of Parliament.

The approach I have suggested does not preclude a discussion of the practical difficulties of establishing the common intentions of a body of 600 and more persons. Those difficulties relate both to the physical movements of the members of the legislature and their individual states of mind at the time that they voted for a particular legislative measure. Those difficulties are dealt with in detail by Smith and Bailey, *The Modern English Legal System*, pp. 320–1. If, on the other hand, following Lord Reid, we believe that the judges are not seeking the intentions of a collective entity called Parliament but are restating the problem of finding the true meaning of the words used by Parliament, then the model suggested in this chapter is designed to do just that: to establish the meaning of the text. The various stages in the procedure based on that model may be referred to as showing the way in which the meaning of the text can be made to shine through its surface obscurity.

Explain the Law Commissions' reasons for saying that the 'mischief rule' is a rather more satisfactory approach than the other two established 'rules'.

In this form the second question emphasises the technical aspects of the three 'rules'. In so doing, the implied claim is made that the 'mischief rule' approach should be given more prominence, given that it is common knowledge that there is a preference for the 'literal rule'. Although Professor Cross's model does not go so far as to adopt the proposals for giving statutory precedence to the mischief rule (as in New Zealand), it does require a preliminary review of the entire piece of legislation in question to establish the context. In *Attorney-General* v *Prince Ernest Augustus of Hanover* [1957] AC 436 at p. 461, Viscount Simonds had defined the context in these words:

I conceive it to be my right and duty to examine every word of a statute in its context, and I use 'context' in its widest sense, which I have already indicated as including not only other enacting provisions of the same statute, but its preamble, the existing state of the law, other statutes *in pari materia*, and the mischief which I can, by those and other legitimate means, discern the statute was intended to remedy.

Note the correspondence between Viscount Simonds's list and the list of external aids to interpretation set out above.

Also, Lord Scarman's position is illustrative of the cautious approach to change in this area. Although he said in a lecture that no one would dare to choose the literal rule rather than the purposive construction of a statute he has also said in *Akbarali v Brent London Borough Council* [1983] 2 AC 309, at p. 348, that the purposive approach can only be adopted if the judges 'can find in the statute *read as a whole* [emphasis added] . . . an expression of Parliament's purpose or policy'. Furthermore, clause 2(a) of Lord Scarman's Bill of 1980, based on the Law Commissions' proposals, merely said that a construction 'which would promote the general legislative purpose underlying the provision in question is to be *preferred* [emphasis added] to a construction which would not'.

Therefore, to summarise the position it may be said that the unified contextual approach (a) does not deny the shortcomings of the literal rule; and (b) endorses the rather cautious proposals to give greater emphasis to legislative purpose when setting about the task of statutory interpretation.

European Community Legislation

Most English legal system courses now contain references to the institutions of the European Community and Community law as a further source of English law. The question arises how far the interpretation of that law in legislative form differs from the practices of the English courts. Occasionally examiners set a question on some aspect of Community legislation. Also, your knowledge can be used to good effect as the source of comparisons with English practice, where there is a direct link between the two items being compared. Section 3 of the European Communities Act 1972 requires English courts to apply and take judicial notice of Community law.

There are two aspects of Community legislation for you to grasp. First, there is the form and content of such legislation and secondly there is the approach to be taken to its interpretation. The legislation consists of the Treaties and secondary legislation in the form of Regulations and Directives. Points to note about the form and content of this legislation are:

(a) The Treaties are drafted in the form of broad statements of principle. Many important concepts are not defined.

(b) Regulations and Directives may be drafted with more particularity but even they are not as detailed as English legislation.

(c) The Treaties embody a statement of their own objectives. See, for example, arts 2 and 3 of the EC Treaty.

(d) Secondary legislation (i.e., Regulations and Directives) must state objectives in terms of the objectives laid down by the Treaties (EC Treaty, art. 189).

(e)   As a consequence of (d), the jurisdiction to question the validity of Community legislation (EC Treaty, art. 173) is an active one.

You must consider two separate jurisdictions in looking at the interpretation of Community legislation: the Court of Justice of the European Communities and the courts of the member States.

Interpretation by the CJEC
The European Court is perhaps a little more willing than English courts to consider the context and purposes of a legislative provision. The avowed purposes of the legislation will appear on the face of secondary legislation by reason of the EC Treaty, art. 189. In the case of the interpretation of the Treaty provisions, reference may be made to arts 2 and 3 of the EC Treaty to establish the Community purpose on which a legislative act is based. Where the different language versions of the legislation differ because of translation, the court will adopt the meaning in the language which most closely represents the overall purposes of the Treaties. This is also the approach of English courts in construing the provisions of a Treaty with an authentic text in English and another, foreign language (see *Fothergill* v *Monarch Airlines Ltd* [1981] AC 251 and *Rothmans of Pall Mall (Overseas) Ltd* v *Saudi Arabian Airlines Corporation* [1981] QB 368). The latter case presented the court with a choice between two English-language versions, an American one and an English one, of a translation from French.
   The court adopts a robust approach in order to uphold the claims of Community law when in conflict with the laws of member States.

Interpretation by English courts (and the courts of other Member States)   In all the member States, the prime consideration is to ensure that Community law is interpreted consistently throughout the Community. The use of the preliminary reference provided for by the EC Treaty, art. 177, ensures that this is done to a degree. In English courts a different stance is adopted compared with the usual standards of statutory interpretation in English courts. The cases from *H. P. Bulmer Ltd* v *J. Bollinger SA* [1974] Ch 401 onwards demonstrate that this is so. In that case, Lord Denning MR said, at p. 425: 'Beyond doubt the English courts must follow the same principles as the European Court'. That means not examining words in meticulous detail and not applying a strict literal interpretation. The case of *R* v *Henn* [1978] 1 WLR 103 and [1981] AC 850 is a neat illustration of the point. The Court of Appeal had held that a total ban on imports was not a restriction of a quantitative nature within art. 30 of the EC Treaty. The House of Lords was spared the embarrassment of having to decide that a total ban (or zero) was not a quantitative restriction. Finally, the supremacy of Community law is well established and accepted in principle by the courts of member States (see page 207).

Although there is a degree of inconsistency in recent decisions of the House of Lords, it seems that a more purposive approach to statutory interpretation is being adopted in English courts; at least where the legislation is based on the need to implement Community legislation. Usually, the legislation will be a Community Directive. This approach is seen most clearly in *Litster* v *Forth Dry Dock & Engineering Co. Ltd* [1990] 1 AC 546. You need to be aware of the problems of interpretation in relation to domestic law, where there is a Directive which is not implemented or not given full effect by domestic law (see *Marleasing SA* v *La Commercial Internacional de Alimentacion SA* [1992] 1 CMLR 305 and *Webb* v *EMO Air Cargo (UK) Ltd* [1993] 1 CMLR 259). There is a good exposition of European legal method in English courts in Holland and Webb's *Learning Legal Rules* at pp. 228-31 (and note, particularly, pp. 261–5). There is a shorter treatment of the same topic in Smith and Bailey, *The Modern English Legal System* at pp. 367-8. Therefore, in considering problems on statutory interpretation do not forget to include a consideration of whether the legislation in question was enacted specifically to implement a piece of Community legislation.

PROPOSALS FOR THE REFORM OF STATUTE LAW AND STATUTORY INTERPRETATION

The defects in English statute law have been sufficiently indicated in previous sections of this chapter. As long ago as 1970, the then newly formed Statute Law Society published a report entitled *Statute Law Deficiencies*. In their summary of conclusions the authors of the report said, 'The procedures by which statute law is made and officially promulgated should be governed by the needs of the user'. Another important report was that of the Renton Committee on the Preparation of Legislation in 1975. Some of the deficiencies identified have been remedied in the intervening years. For example, there are now alphabetical indexes of the statutes in each annual volume. There has been an increase in the availability of statutes in their up-to-date and current form. However, in 1977 Sir William Dale's report, *Legislative Drafting: A New Approach,* found many of the same deficiencies.

The 1990s have seen the publication of the Hansard Society's *Report on the Legislative Process (Making the Law)*, which seeks to address many 'old' problems with new (and sometimes 'radical') solutions. It is essential reading in the present context.

There have been continuing complaints about the way in which the courts interpret statutes in a restrictive 'literalist' way. The reform of statute law and the reform of statutory interpretation are inevitably linked together. The draftsman and the judge both adopt defensive tactics to guard against the excesses of the other. The danger of the draftsman indulging in excessive recourse to open-ended wordings giving rise to the possibility of wholesale abuses of power by the executive is remote. Equally remote is the prospect of the judges using a purpose-based approach to interpretation to extend the scope of legislation in a way which would impose unlooked-for and unacceptable burdens on government. Therefore you should consider the remainder of this section as a whole, although it is set out as two separate summaries of the principal proposals for the reform of the statute book and the reform of the rules of statutory interpretation. In any event, these are the principal points for inclusion in essays on the current state of our statute law and its interpretation. Essay titles and examination questions on this part of the syllabus fall into two categories of generality:

(a) Those seeking comment on the state of statute law generally.

(b) Those seeking comment on *either* the state of statute law, including drafting and presentation, or proposals for change in the approach to statutory interpretation.

The higher the level of generality the less detail it is possible to expect of you in an answer. That is more than made up for by the degree of skill you must demonstrate in selecting and classifying the issues involved, so as to produce a single coherent piece of work and not just a list.

Proposals for the Reform of the Statute Book

Proposals fall into two categories:

(a) Improvements in supervision of the drafting process.

(b) Further improvements in the format and accessibility of legislation, including delegated legislation.

In line with the conclusion of the Statute Law Society concerning giving priority to the needs of the user, Sir William Dale proposed the establishment of a Law Council to advise the government on draft Bills. The 'users' of legislation would have significant representation on this body. It has been suggested also that greater use should be made of subject experts rather than relying on the expertise of draftsmanship. There should be more attention paid to style and logical ordering of the subject-matter. Principles should be expressed first, followed up by detail. To an extent the Health and Safety at Work etc. Act 1974 follows this pattern. There should be improved arrangements for prompt publication of legislation, especially delegated legislation. The Renton Committee made many detailed proposals regarding the wording used in statutes. More training should be given to draftsmen and their number should be increased. One proposal which has a direct bearing on the proposals for the reform of statutory interpretation is that statutes should be prefaced by an explanatory statement of purpose. The Hansard Society's Report did not consider this to be helpful.

Attempts at reform of statutory interpretation have included proposals that judges should take such statements into account. This has some connection with the use of 'travaux préparatoires' in French law. These statements should be sufficiently extensive to be meaningful and useful, and much more than an enlarged long title.

Underlying all these arguments about the nature of the statute book is the large question of *codification*. Farrar and Dugdale, *Introduction to Legal Method*, has an entire chapter on this matter. Their comments on the operation of the Sale of Goods Acts deserve careful study. The Law Commissions produced further proposals (Cm 137, 1987) for the amendment of the law on implied terms on the quality of goods sold and supplied. Further need for amendment of the provisions was felt to be necessary both in relation to the meaning of the implied terms and the remedies for breach of those terms. The short draft Bill included in the Law Commissions' report was intended to work by a process of incorporation of the new proposals into the existing legislation. The change has been brought into force by the Sale and Supply of Goods Act 1994. The report opened by saying that it did not 'recommend a codification of those areas of the law of sale covered by the Law Commission's terms of reference'. The rest of the section entitled 'The background to this Report' gave the views of the Commissions on the codification of the law relating to the sale of goods and the Commissions' role in any future exercises in codification of this branch of the law. By implication those views may be extended to the prospects for codification of other branches of the law.

I would add only this to what you may read elsewhere about codification: the requisite political conditions for extensive codification of the law do not appear to exist in the United Kingdom. There seem to be three situations which result in large-scale and successful codification in modern times:

(a)   A basic change in the legal order of a State following a revolution, as in France in 1789. This produced the French Civil Code in the first decade of the 19th century.

(b)   A need to use law as a means of bringing about unification of a number of sovereign States, as in the Germany of the 19th century; the German Civil Code was promulgated in 1900.

(c)   A need to provide for a uniform body of law where there are separate jurisdictions within one political unit. This applies within the United States. The Uniform Commercial Code may be, but need not be, adopted by the individual states of the union.

None of this is to deny that codification of English law might be beneficial. It is simply a judgment on the political prospects for large-scale codification in the United Kingdom. Looking at the treatment of codification in textbooks such as Ingman, *The English Legal Process*, and Smith and Bailey, *The Modern English Legal System*, leads me to the conclusion that a knowledge of the pros and cons and methods of codification will be of incidental value only in most of your courses. Incidental, that is, to discussions of legislation generally and not forming a topic in itself.

Proposals for the Reform of Statutory Interpretation

There are a number of proposals to consider under this heading. The principal features of these proposals are set out in Table 9.1. Do not forget to read them together with the comments in the previous paragraphs on proposals for the improvement of the statute book. The material covered in this chapter under the headings, types of legislation, structure and drafting of statutes and proposals for change, constitutes what you should know and be able to deploy in answer to questions, at any level of generality, on the state of statute law in this country at the present day.

Table 9.1   Reform of rules of statutory interpretation: Aids to interpretation

Criticism of the English approach to interpretation voiced as long ago as 1932 by Professor H. Laski in a note appended to the Report on Ministers' Powers (Cmd 4060).

In 1969, the Law Commissions produced a report, *The Interpretation of Statutes*.

This was followed by the Renton Report (Cmnd 6053) in 1975. Para. 81 of the Law Commissions' report signals a proposed new approach: 'a limited degree of statutory intervention is required in this field . . . to clarify, and in some respects to relax the strictness of, the rules which . . . exclude altogether or exclude *when the meaning is otherwise unambiguous*, certain material from consideration' (emphasis added).

See Farrar, *Law Reform and the Law Commission*, pp. 47-55. Also pp. 55-7 on the form of legislation. Should or need statutes depend upon a purely literary form? Can diagrams and/or flow charts be used, for example, to express statutory intentions?

Statutory reform suggested by Law Commissions for four purposes:

(a)   To clarify and relax the strict rules as to context.
(b)   To emphasise the importance of:

(i)   general legislative purpose; and
(ii)   fulfilment of international obligations.

(c)   To indicate whether there is a remedy for breach of statutory obligation. (See the Health and Safety at Work etc. Act 1974, s. 47).

(d)   To encourage the preparation in selected cases of explanatory material for use by the courts.

The Renton Committee wanted a *new Interpretation Act* to incorporate such of the Law Commissions' proposals as are accepted.

The presumption in criminal law in favour of the requirement of *mens rea* should continue. Any reform should be left to those working on the reform/codification of the criminal law.

Lord Scarman introduced a Bill in the House of Lords in 1980, based on the Law Commissions' draft clauses. This was withdrawn and a new Bill introduced in 1981 in a more restricted version. That bill was rejected on second reading in the House of Commons. The 1981 Bill is printed in Miers and Page, *Legislation*.

The Interpretation Act 1978 was merely a consolidating Act, consolidating the Act of 1889 and some other enactments. It did not address issues of statutory interpretation.

The material in the section of this chapter on statutory interpretation is designed to assist in work of the sort represented by the sample question at the end of the chapter, whilst that section and the last part of this section are to be combined as the source of material for questions in the form of critical essays on statutory interpretation.

LAW REFORM

In this section I shall deal with the subject of law reform in the context of first-year law syllabuses that have an item devoted to law reform. These items often come at the end of a course and at the end of textbooks. They are not to be ignored for that reason. Questions occur with some frequency on the subject of law reform.

For the purpose of this section I understand law reform to be the conscious considered change of the law by legislation; with the intention that the changes will be improvements. I do not overlook the fact that the judges have it within their power to carry out reform of the law. Their power to do so, however, is limited and has its drawbacks. It is, for instance, in the nature of judge-made law to be retrospective and to depend upon the accidents of litigation. Lord Hailsham of St Marylebone never did get the opportunity he promised the House of Lords in *Woodhouse A. C. Israel Cocoa Ltd SA v Nigerian Produce Marketing Co. Ltd* [1972] AC 741 in 1972 to examine thoroughly the idea of promissory estoppel.

For examination purposes a consideration of legislation as a source of law reform should be conducted under the following heads:

(a) A brief résumé of the history of law reform.
(b) Consideration of methods and techniques in legislating.
(c) The work of law reform agencies.
(d) An evaluation of the results of law reform.

Such treatment of the topic places it firmly in the context of legal method and leaves out of account the substantive issues of law reform. In this part of the subject, substantive measures of law reform are to be used as illustrations of how law reform works.

Historical Résumé

Law reform as we know it today began in the 19th century, under the impact of the changes wrought by industrialisation and Benthamite thinking. The idea of 'utility' and that mankind could, by a rearrangement of its affairs, better itself by increasing the sum of human happiness was a powerful stimulus to law reform. Much, but not all, of the energy devoted to law reform in the 19th century went into modernising and improving our legal institutions. The main agencies of law reform were a series of royal commissions culminating in the report of the Judicature Commission, which led to the establishment of the Supreme Court by the Judicature Acts. There is a wealth of material from which you may obtain examples of both structural and institutional reforms and reforms of the substantive law in Manchester's *Sources of English Legal History*. The latter half of the century witnessed substantial reforms in criminal and commercial law. Property law too received constant attention from the reformers from the 1830s right up to the legislation of 1925. The reforms of property law and conveyancing are a good example of the use of a particular method in a programme of law reform. That method is to introduce a number of reforming pieces of legislation of limited scope. The process is then completed by large-scale consolidation, as with the 1925 property legislation consisting of: Law of Property Act 1925, Settled Land Act 1925, Land Registration Act 1925, Land Charges Act 1925, Administration of Estates Act 1925 and Trustee Act 1925.

Methods and Techniques

The type of legislation chosen will depend upon the scale of the reforms being carried out. I have just indicated the method adopted in the case of the law of property. Company law is a recent example of the same kind, where the Companies Act 1985 is the large-scale consolidating measure. The initial choice is between amendment, consolidation or codification of the law. The next stage is to decide whether all of the necessary detail can be included in an Act of Parliament. Should detailed provisions which are likely to require frequent change be put in the form of delegated legislation? A comparison of the first post–1945 national insurance legislation with later social security legislation will show that the later legislation makes greater use of delegated legislation. This change in itself is a type of reform of the format of legislation.

The reference to technique in the heading of this section is a reference to technique in the sense used in Professor Summers's article, 'The Technique Element in Law' (1971) 59 Calif L Rev 733. This article is used as the basis of a chapter in Farrar and Dugdale, *Introduction to Legal Method*, on methods of social control through law. One example can be taken to illustrate how the choice of technique can affect the effectiveness of a measure of law reform. Following the Zeebrugge ferry disaster in the winter of 1987, a decision was made to strengthen the law so as to promote higher standards of safety at sea for the users of roll-on roll-off ferries. In theory the lawmakers had a choice of techniques. They could change the law on the liabilities of ferry operators to pay damages to victims of accidents (the grievance remedial technique). They could require ferry operators to pay a tax on vessels not conforming to specified standards (the fiscal technique). They could impose penalties on ferry owners and crews for defined offences (the penal technique). In the event, the Merchant Shipping Bill when it was introduced adopted the penal technique. In some cases a combination of techniques is used. It is a question of judgment which technique will most effectively achieve the objective of the legislation. Learning to make such judgments is part of the skill to be learned in doing drafting exercises.

Law Reform Agencies

At the present time there are two kinds of law reform agencies:

(a)   *Ad hoc* bodies such as royal commissions and departmental committees. Controversial issues of the day which merit the attention of law reformers are often referred to these bodies. That was so, for example, in the cases of trade unions (Donovan 1969) and the provision of legal services (Benson 1979). Times have changed for trade unions since 1969 and in chapter 8 we saw what has happened to the proposals of the Benson Royal Commission on Legal Services about legal aid. That may not be untypical. The use of royal commissions was thought to be in abeyance until the appointment of the Royal Commission on Criminal Justice in 1991.

(b)   Permanent law reform agencies. Some of our permanent law reform committees date back to the 1930s. The idea of a permanent agency to consider questions of law reform arises out of the difficulty of finding time in the parliamentary timetable for the reform of 'lawyer's law'. This was especially true of the origins of the Law Commissions. The Law Commissions were largely the response to a pressure group of lawyers who produced a book in the early 1960s called *Law Reform Now*. This book drew attention to many inadequacies and injustices in the then state of the law. The Law Commissions for England and Wales and Scotland were established by the Law Commission Act 1965. The Commission for England and Wales is under a duty to keep the whole of the law under review and to prepare programmes for reform. Its working methods involve consultation with lawyers and other interested parties. It has had considerable success. The difficulties it faces include: problems in finding time for the enactment of its proposals; slow or no progress on its proposals for codification; keeping clear dividing lines between its work and the work of other law reform agencies, both *ad hoc* and permanent. The other principal permanent law reform agencies are the Criminal Law Revision Committee and the Law Reform Committee.

Evaluation

The success of law reform may be measured in several ways. One obvious measure of the success of a law reform agency is the success it has in getting its proposals enacted into law. The permanent agencies seem to be more successful on this score than the *ad hoc* agencies.

To try to discover how well the law works following its reform is another measure of success but one which it is difficult to quantify. Take the example of the law relating to the wearing of seat belts in motor cars. Which of the following do you think is the best measure of the success of the law?

(a)   The number of successful prosecutions for not wearing a seat belt.

(b)   Observation of a statistically accurate sample of occupants of motor cars at a number of check-points.

(c)   The fact that since the introduction of the law there have been fewer accidents involving injury to front-seat passengers and drivers of motor cars.

(d)   Automatic reductions for contributory negligence in damages awards where the plaintiff was not and should have been wearing a seat belt.

Each of these four items is defective as a measure of the success of the law. If success is measured merely in terms of compliance with the law, then item (b) is the most satisfactory measure. If success is to be measured in terms of achieving a stated objective, then item (c) is the most satisfactory measure, provided that the nature of the injuries is taken into account and other reasons for the reduction in the number of injuries can be excluded — that, for example, there has been no reduction in the number of accidents.

Instead of measuring compliance with the law it may be sufficient to show that the number of disputes arising under the new law is much less than under the law it replaced. This may be shown by the lack of litigation on the new law. In some situations, however, lack of litigation may be evidence merely that the law is being evaded or ignored and that people are basing their arrangements on other standards. In spite of these difficulties in measurement there is often a shared consensus that grows up that a particular law is working badly or working well. It is only after some time has elapsed that these judgments can be made. Experience shows that the solution of one problem leads to the creation of new problems. The definition of theft in the Theft Act 1968, replacing the Larceny Act 1916, is a good example of that situation.

A QUESTION OF STATUTORY INTERPRETATION

Section 1(1) of the Guard Dogs Act 1975:

A person shall not use or permit the use of a guard dog at any premises unless a person ('the handler') who is capable of controlling the dog is present on the premises and the dog is under the control of the handler at all times while it is being so used except while it is secured so that it is not at liberty to go freely about the premises.

Is an offence committed under the Act if:

(a)   a dog is left chained on the premises; and
(b)   there is no handler on the premises at the time the dog is left chained.

Give reasons for your answer.

Comment

As it happens there was a case decided on this very point: *Hobson* v *Gledhill* [1978] 1 WLR 215, [1978] 1 All ER 945. In a case stated by the Huddersfield Magistrates, the Divisional Court was asked 'Whether by virtue of s. 1(1) of the Guard Dogs Act 1975 where a guard dog is used on premises it is necessary for a person capable of controlling the dog to be present on the premises *at all times* whilst the dog is being so used notwithstanding that the dog is secured so that it is not at liberty to go freely about the premises'.

Assume the facts are as in the case of *Hobson* v *Gledhill*, where three dogs were left chained on premises consisting of a yard and buildings. None of the dogs was on a chain of more than 13 feet in length or could get within two feet of the gate. At the material time there was no person on the premises. Peter Pain J gave the leading judgment. His judgment is a good illustration of the interpretation process where there is an ambiguity in the statute.

(At this point look back at what was said on page 216 about Professor Cross's model of statutory interpretation.)

Before going through Peter Pain J's argument (which is quite short), you should study carefully the words of the section to discover for yourself the source of any possible ambiguity. Good! You have spotted it. It is a common structural difficulty, found in many legislative provisions. You have to decide whether an exception or proviso applies to the whole of a paragraph or only to that part to which it is adjacent; and without the benefit of punctuation to help you. In order to be quite clear about the difficulty I shall set out the paragraph in an alternative way which will make clear the nature of the difficulty. The paragraph as written is logically capable of bearing two meanings, neither of which is better than the other at first sight. Those meanings are:

(a)   There is no offence if there is always a handler capable of controlling the dog, on premises where a dog is being used;
AND the dog is under the control of the handler unless the dog is secured.

(b)   There is no offence if there is a handler capable of controlling the dog on premises where a dog is being used and the dog is under the control of the handler;
OR the dog is secured.

For meaning (a), the words in the paragraph, 'except while it is secured so that it is not at liberty to go freely about the premises' apply only to the words in the paragraph beginning, 'and the dog is under the control of the handler at all times while it is being so used'.

Whereas for meaning (b), the words beginning 'except while it is secured' apply to the whole paragraph.

Alternatively the paragraph could be set out in the form of shorter propositions, thus:

Equivalent to   (a)   If a dog is used on premises as a guard dog,

(i)   a person capable of controlling the dog shall be on the premises, and

(ii)   the dog shall be under the control of the handler or secured so that it is not at liberty to go about the premises.

Equivalent to   (b)   If a dog is used on premises as a guard dog,

    (i)   a person shall be on the premises in control of the dog, or
    (ii) the dog shall be secured so that it is not at liberty to go about the premises.

(*Note*: In the second version, equivalent to (b), the words 'capable of controlling the dog' as found in the actual paragraph of the Act are rendered superfluous. As Parliament is presumed to intend to give meaning to all the words used in an Act, this would indicate a preference for meaning (a). However, it is time to see how Peter Pain J dealt with the problem.)

The Judgment of Peter Pain J

It was agreed that the subsection gave rise to ambiguities, and prosecution authorities wished to know whether it required a handler to be present at all times that a dog was being used. There is evidence in the judgment that the whole context of the Act was considered. There is reference to the possibility of taking judicial notice 'of the fact that a number of fairly small premises do protect themselves by the use of guard dogs'. And that, 'If a handler always had to be on the premises with the guard dogs, the economic burden on persons using those premises would be very heavy indeed'. There is also reference to other parts of the Act dealing with the dogs' welfare in answer to the question whether a person could leave the dog tied up indefinitely without attention.

Having recognised the ambiguity and explained the significance of it, the judge then 'comes to the *rule* that a penal statute, where there is an ambiguity, should always be construed in favour of the citizen who may find himself the subject of the penalty' (emphasis added).

(The judge refers to the rule, whereas textbook writers refer to this proposition as a *presumption*).

Having taken into account that rule, or presumption, the judge expressed the opinion that the restricted duty 'does *meet the mischief* which Parliament was seeking to provide against because, provided the dog is properly secured, the person who may come on the premises, whether lawfully or not, is in a position to remove himself from the ambit of the dog's teeth' (emphasis added). To the question set out above, as propounded by the justices, the judge then said that it was not necessary for the handler to be present at all times.

Conclusion

Comments in a supporting judgment by Lord Widgery CJ illustrate the fact that the judges apply the meaning of the words used by Parliament and do not guess the intention of Parliament. In the words of Lord Widgery:

> ... there is a good deal to be said for the view that it would be desirable to take the reform further and to abolish ... the conception of a dog alone on the premises, even when it is tied up. But for the reasons which have been given, I am quite unable to say which of the solutions canvassed was the intention of Parliament, and the right course ... is to favour the citizen. ... If we are wrong, and we have chosen a solution which is contrary to the wishes of Parliament, it will not be very difficult for Parliament to put that right in a suitable statute hereafter.

FURTHER READING

Cross, Sir R., *Statutory Interpretation* (3rd edn., Butterworths, 1995).

Farrar, J.H. and Dugdale, A.M., *Introduction to Legal Method* (3rd edn., Sweet and Maxwell, 1990).

Holland, J.A. and Webb, J.S., Learning Legal Rules (2nd edn., Blackstone Press, 1993).

Ingman, T., *The English Legal Process* (5th edn., Blackstone Press, 1994).

Miers, D. and Page, A., *Legislation* (2nd edn., Sweet and Maxwell, 1990).

12 LAWYERS, JUDGES AND LAY PEOPLE IN THE LEGAL SYSTEM

Many of the current English legal system courses include a special part devoted to the role of professional judges in the legal system. It is often coupled with a discussion about the part played by lay people in the administration of justice. Something has been said already in chapters 3, 6 and 7 about the various judicial offices found in the legal system. This final chapter is the place to bring that information together and to look at the judges and their work as a whole. It will be convenient also to consider the part played by professional lawyers in the administration of justice together with some of the problems facing the professions at the present time.

These are matters which produce a steady stream of examination questions. These questions may be of a technical legal nature, concerning, for example, judicial immunities. It is more likely that they will fall into the 'law in action' category and require a critical appraisal of the judiciary or the professions, as the case may be. For the last time in this book, I shall say that critical appraisal is most effective when soundly based on empirical knowledge.

So far as the judiciary are concerned, the bare facts of their offices, tenure and conditions of service are set out in the table in chapter 3. A similar knowledge base for the rules relating to the professions can be found in most of the standard textbooks on the English legal system. The rules referred to here need further amplification before they can be presented as part of a critical appraisal. You need some information of a statistical rather than an anecdotal nature about these aspects of the judiciary and the professions which you set out to appraise. For the judiciary, the sort of information you require can be found in such books as Griffith's *The Politics of the Judiciary* and other smaller surveys published from time to time. Look out for those published by the Labour Research Department. In looking at sets of statistics about the judiciary and the legal professions, it is well to remember that like all statistics, whether from an official source or not, they may be subject to a variety of interpretations. It is still useful to know, however, that in 1987 all the Law Lords except one had been appointed by the Thatcher administration. It might be making a different sort of statement to say that all but one of them have been appointed since 1979. Other useful supplementary reading about the judiciary includes Paterson's book, *The Law Lords.* Equally enlightening are the books written by the judges themselves about being judges. Lords Hailsham and Denning have been prolific writers. The well-known writer of legal entertainments, Henry Cecil, was less well known as Judge Leon, a county court judge. Under his pen name of Henry Cecil he gave a series of Hamlyn Lectures on 'the English judge'. They are a good antidote to the realism of books such as *The Politics of the Judiciary.* In 1987, Judge Pickles published a book about his experiences on the circuit bench, entitled *Straight from the Bench.* Read one or more of these books as a complement to your textbook and statistical studies. It may be the closest you will come to sharing the personal experiences of a judge.

For additional information about the professions, delve into the Report of the Royal Commission on Legal Services. Don't neglect either the literature footnoted in your textbooks or occasional reading of the biographies of great lawyers of the past, in order to develop a deeper understanding of the legal professions.

LAWYERS AND THE ENGLISH LEGAL SYSTEM

It is said that one of the characteristics of the common law is that it is a practitioner's law. What does this mean, and what other sorts of law may there be? The first part of that question may be answered by reference to the origins and development of the common law itself. All that there is space to do here is to point out one or two salient features of the common law system, which will help to explain the present-day status of judges and lawyers in the English legal system. The features which identify the English common law as a practitioners' law include:

(a)   The lack of a body of doctrine laid down by lawgivers and administered principally by bureaucrats.

(b)   The acceptance of decisions arrived at after argument as the basis of the law.

(c)   The monopoly which the practitioners obtained over judicial appointments.

(d)   The regulation by the (ex-practitioner) judges and practitioners of legal procedures in the courts.

(e)   Self-regulation by the practitioners of professional affairs.

Of course, it took a very considerable number of years for all of these features of the legal system to become established. At the present day, one of the controversial issues in the law is whether or not the law can be wrested from the hands of the practitioner and be placed in the safe keeping of 'demos' as the 'people's law' or a democratic law. That issue, I believe, lies at the root of many of the contemporary controversies involving the judiciary and the legal professions. It is certainly implicit in what you will read and learn about the proper role of the judge as lawmaker. The judges and lawyers have the leading parts in the drama of the law. It is time to review their perfomance.

THE JUDICIARY

What do the judges want you to believe about themselves? The English judiciary claim for themselves the benefit of several virtues. These are: independence of the executive and legislature; impartiality in decision-making; respect for the integrity of the common law; and adherence to the declaratory theory of judging. If these claims are well founded, it should be possible to identify their foundations in the rules of the legal system and to determine, by looking at the 'law in action', whether the judges do in fact practice the virtues made possible by the rules. The practice and existence of these virtues does not rule out the possibility of independent vices. The principal questions set in examinations appear to concentrate on a small number of issues, such as the independence of judges and the overall quality of the judiciary in the context of the present system of appointments. Within those two main areas there is scope for discussion of many smaller but related issues. For example, in the context of a discussion about the quality of the judiciary you could include points relating to the eligibility of solicitors for appointment to the High Court bench. This is now possible as a result of the Courts and Legal Services Act 1990. In the light of this information about the main sorts of question asked about the judiciary, I am going to suggest an approach to dealing with the judiciary as part of your syllabus, based on a consideration of the claims to virtue set out at the beginning of this section.

If you take each of the principal claims in turn you can establish the foundations of the claim in the rules and practices of the legal system. Then you can compare the effects of the rules and practices 'in action' with their supposed objectives. At the end of that process you will be able to formulate answers to questions asked about judicial independence, the quality of the judiciary and, in addition, the judicial role in the law-making process.

Independence of the Executive and Legislature

The formal independence of the higher judiciary has been secured since the Act of Settlement of 1701. It rests now on the provisions of the Supreme Court Act 1981. The salaries of the judges are large and since 1786 have been a charge on the Consolidated Fund. Judges are unable to hold any other paid appointments and few do so even after leaving office. This does not apply to the same extent to Lord Chancellors who are political appointees. Judges are disqualified from being MPs and judges with a seat in the House of Lords confine their contributions to technical questions of a legal nature. It is not unknown for judges to have been MPs before their appointment to the bench. In modern times, there is no convention whereby the Attorney-General has a claim on the office of Lord Chief Justice. The office of Lord Chief Justice is now a non-political appointment. The most controversial connection between the executive and the judiciary is the frequent use of judges of all levels as the chairmen or members of royal commissions, departmental committees and tribunals of inquiry. Some of these activities are politically controversial. One of the best known of these was the report by Lord Denning after his inquiry into the Profumo scandal in 1963. More recently Lord Justice Scott chaired the inquiry into sales of arms to Iraq.

Another aspect of judicial independence lies in the fact that the judges have judicial immunity from being sued in connection with the exercise of their jurisdiction. The limits of this immunity were explored in the case of *Sirros* v *Moore* [1975] QB 118.

Absolute privilege, for the purpose of the law of defamation, attaches to the statements made by judges in the course of their judicial office. The existence of these immunities is the price paid for the independence of the judiciary. Occasionally there are instances of judicial behaviour which give rise to concern. In such cases, the Lord Chancellor may rebuke the judge privately, and in extreme cases (being caught smuggling, for example) be required to resign.

On the issue of independence, see the situation which developed between Lord Mackay and Wood J, President of the Employment Appeal Tribunal ((1994) 144 NLJ 527).

Impartiality in Decision-making

In a formal sense, one of the rules of natural justice, the rule against bias, secures the impartiality of decisions given by judges. The leading case is *Dimes* v *Grand Junction Canal Proprietors* (1852) 3 HL Cas 759 in which decrees granted by the Lord Chancellor were set aside. The decrees were in favour of the canal company, in which the Lord Chancellor held shares. The rule of natural justice which gives entitlement to a fair hearing is also relevant on occasions to judicial impartiality. There have been successful appeals in criminal cases where the presiding judge has interfered too much with the progress of the case by asking an inordinate number of questions from the bench. The rules of natural justice are technical rules of administrative law. As such, they do not reach those areas of prejudice connected to the social and political background of judges. It is claimed by some writers and commentators that the social and political background of the judges predisposes them to favour certain sectional interests in the community and to be out of sympathy with other interests. In particular, it can be shown that judges have given more decisions against trade unions than for them, and that they incline towards individual interests at the expense of collective interests. The case of *Bromley London Borough Council* v *Greater London Council* [1983] 1 AC 768 is said to be such a case. The question of social antecedents of judges is also relevant to the larger question of the part judges play in the law-making process, because it is said that the areas in which the judges are most prepared to be judicial activists are linked to the judges' social background. The judiciary are not representative of all social classes within the community and there are few women judges. Making solicitors eligible for appointment to the High Court might over a long period enlarge the social base of the judiciary. In the meantime the continued narrow social base of the judiciary may be a function of the appointments system operated by the Lord Chancellor's Department. This system depends heavily on the personal knowledge of advocates by the judiciary, who pass on this knowledge to the civil servants in the department. It is unlikely that promotion prospects for judges will affect the impartiality of their decisions. There are proposals from time to time for the appointment of a judicial appointments commission on the lines of the civil service commission.

There is another matter which is relevant to the perceived impartiality of judges, although it is also wider in scope. That is the extent to which judges may be subject to discipline and criticism for their behaviour both in and out of court. The pressures on judges to amend their ways are informal, although they may end in the judge being interviewed by a more senior judge and ultimately by the Lord Chancellor. There are lengthy descriptions, from the judges' point of view, of these informal procedures, in Judge Pickles's book, *Straight from the Bench*. The pressure for a formal complaints procedure is not strong at the present time. Note also the possibility of judges speaking extra-judicially about their work and the 'guidance' given to this by the Lord Chancellor and his press office (see *Guardian*, 12 April 1994, p. 18 of the tabloid section).

The above matters are representative of the matters that may affect your judgment about the independence and impartiality of the judges. Before going on to the next question, you might consider what lessons may be learned from the practice in other legal systems regarding the selection and appointment of judges. In the USA there is a mixture of selection by appointment and election, whereas in France there is a career judiciary which is part of the civil service. A recent change in the UK in the appointment of circuit and district judges was the advertisement of some posts and the publication of criteria for appointment.

Respect for the Integrity of the Common Law

The judges are the upholders of the common law, which at one and the same time is seen as the bulwark of the subjects' rights and as the guarantor of the safety of the realm. It must be remembered that as the originators of the common law the judges are largely the masters of their own house. In the constitution of the United Kingdom there is no single source of final authority before which public and political actions may be called to account. By reason of their independence and their control of the use of civil force, the judicial view of what the law requires is extremely powerful. In respect of their claims to be the guardians of the common law and occasionally of 'public morals' you may encounter the question: Who is the guardian of the guardians themselves? (*Quis custodiet ipsos custodes?*) The answer seems to be that we all rely on judicial self-restraint and the ability of Parliament to lay down the law in clear unambiguous terms.

For, although the judges are the guardians of the common law, they recognise the supremacy of Parliament in passing legislation. Judicial attitudes to legislation have been mentioned already in chapter 11. At this juncture, it is sufficient to recall two facts. The rules of statutory interpretation are themselves almost exclusively judge-made; the judges presume that Parliament knows the common law and only abrogates a rule of the common law by using clear words. Thus it appears on occasion that the judges undermine carefully constructed legislative schemes by restrictive interpretation, as, for example, with the interpretation of the Factories Acts. There is a tendency for decisions to reflect individualist values at the expense of collective values, although there are signs that this tendency is becoming less pronounced in the area of taxation. This tendency can also be detected in those parts of the law which are based on case law.

It is probably through the law of contempt that the judges have the greatest opportunity to protect the integrity of the common law as an institution, including of course the integrity of the judicial role itself. Therefore, much of the material in the first part of chapter 8 can be used in connection with commentaries on the judiciary. Two matters deserve mention: judicial findings of contempt in situations where the reputation of the law as such is questioned and cases where the court or judge has to balance the public's 'right to know' against the requirements of confidentiality. In these sorts of case, the attitudes of the judges towards their role as guardians of the law becomes very apparent, as for example in the *Spycatcher* case.

Adherence to the Declaratory Theory of Judging

The 'declaratory theory' of judging was expounded by Blackstone in his *Commentaries on the Laws of England*. It was the dominant theory throughout the late 19th century and the first half of the 20th century. Chapter 10 deals with the present position. Since about 1955 the Law Lords have accepted that they have a limited law-making function. However, the Law Lords' recognition of themselves as lawmakers has not taken place in the courts but in the lecture room and the study. Lord Reid acknowledged the position of the judges as lawmaker in a lecture given in 1972, whereas the limits of judicial activism were indicated by Lord Scarman in *McLoughlin v O'Brian* [1983] 1 AC 410.

If you have to tackle this topic in an examination question about the judiciary you should relate to it your knowledge of both the workings of precedent and statutory interpretation, after making a basic point. Remember too, the fear sometimes expressed that judge-made law may be less certain than legislation in its application. The basic point is this. There is no formal doctrine of the separation of powers in the British constitution. Because of this, the judges are keenly aware that public opinion can all too readily misinterpret their function in a democratic society. In order, therefore, to secure their independence they must adopt a low profile as lawmakers, avoiding as far as possible controversial issues of policy. It is to be expected that judicial law making will be more active and apparent in the areas of law not normally affected by controversial issues of the day.

In conclusion, it is worth stating that the position of the judges (in common with other forms of authority) is made more difficult at the present time by the increased attention paid to the work of the judges, by the press and television. Examples abound of calls for inquiries into serious criminal cases that have been heard in the courts, including cases of alleged too lenient sentencing. Also, so long as the government of the day pursues radical Conservative policies that are a mixture of highly individualist and centralising policies similar in kind to the long-established mixture of judicial values referred to above, it is hardly surprising that some of the decisions of the courts at the higher level will appear to be 'pro-executive' or even politically partisan.

LAY PEOPLE AS JUDGES

Lay people are the decision-makers in the vast majority of cases decided in the legal system. They are involved as magistrates and as members of tribunals, as well as sitting on juries.

In this section I propose to point out one or two matters which crop up from time to time during an English legal system course. These matters relate both to magistrates and their work and to the work of tribunals.

Magistrates

You will be familiar already with the work of the magistrates in connection with your study of the criminal process. At this stage of your course you will be thinking about magistrates as a group of lay people called upon to share in the administration of justice. If you need to do so, revise thoroughly the facts about the method of appointing magistrates, retirement and removal, disqualification, legal liability and training of magistrates.

The issues that you will go on to consider as likely material for essays and examination questions include:

(a)   The reasons for relying on lay magistrates to try the vast majority of criminal cases by summary trial.

(b)   The special needs of courts dealing with children and young offenders and domestic proceedings.

(c)   The principles governing selection of magistrates in attempting to have a representative mix of political opinion and social classes on the bench.

(d)   The need for training and the difference between expertise and experience.

(e)   The role of the clerks to justices as advisers of the magistrates and as manager. See the Scrutiny Report, published in 1989.

This last point may well be a small sub-topic in its own right. As such it is worthwhile spending a little time on studying the changing views about the role of the justices' clerk. The emphasis has shifted from the need to ensure that justice is seen to be done to seeing that the magistrates receive proper professional advice. The basic requirements are set out in *Practice Direction (Justices: Clerk to Court)* [1981] 1 WLR 1163.

Tribunal Chairmen and Members

Since the reforms introduced after the Franks report in 1957, many tribunals have legally qualified chairmen. A glance back at chapter 8 will remind you of the great diversity of functions, style and procedure of tribunals that exists within the English legal system. The concern of this section is with the people who constitute those tribunals, and in particular the contribution of lay people. The most common legal form which is used for the settlement of disputes between the State and its subjects is the tribunal. In such cases, there seems to be general acceptance of the advantages to be gained by having a legally qualified chairman. Many tribunals, however, work in highly specialised fields of endeavour and others deal with the problems of ordinary people in their capacities as employees or benefit claimants. The membership of tribunals, apart from their chairmanship, reflects these facts. Some tribunals' members are chosen for their expertise in the relevant subject-matter. In other cases, the members are chosen for their representative qualities, as the representatives of the employing or employed interest, for example.

If you get a question on the composition of tribunals you should illustrate your answer by reference to appropriate examples of the various points just made. Seek out examples of legally and non-legally qualified chairmen and the different ways of making up the membership panels of tribunals. Public transport, VAT, income tax, rating and valuation are all examples of sectors of public administration with their own tribunals. Within the area of social security you can find examples of the following:

(a)   Tribunals where it has been found advantageous to have a legally qualified chairman to control the procedural aspects and to ensure impartiality in decision-making.

(b)   Tribunals with members representing the employed, self-employed and employing interests.

(c)   Tribunals with members chosen for their expertise.

The distinction which explains the differences between (b) and (c) is that tribunals with a representative membership are concerned generally with issues of fact arising out of claims to benefit, whereas tribunals with an expert membership, usually doctors, are tribunals which are concerned solely with medical issues arising out of claims for benefit.

As a broad generalisation covering all tribunals, you might say that experts are used as members of tribunals where the principal issues for decision are ones in respect of which an expert witness would be called in litigation before the courts.

There is one further important contribution of the non-legally qualified person of which you should take account. That is the use of lay arbitrators for arbitrations. Here, of course, the parties in dispute will often choose to go to arbitration because they are able to select the arbitrator themselves. The choice of arbitrator will be governed in many cases by the selection of an expert in the relevant field. Quite apart from questions which raise issues about arbitration and arbitrators directly, you may find it useful to compare the role of the professional judge with that of the arbitrator when discussing either:

(a)   The qualities of judges as decision-makers, or
(b)   The desirability of setting up specialist courts (see chapter 7).

THE LEGAL PROFESSION

I have pointed out already that English law is a practitioners' law. Therefore, every student of the law must know something about those who practise the law. It is more especially important for those students who intend to go on to become practitioners themselves. The nature of legal practice influences the substance of the law and the way in which it develops. Let me give two examples: one from long ago and one from the present day. The law of personal property is much less well-developed and known in English law than is the law of real property. This is partly attributable to the much later incorporation into the common law of the law of commercial transactions. Modern-day lawyers are often ignorant of whole branches of the law such as social security and the impact of EC membership on English law. Those matters develop outside the experience of most practitioners and will continue to do so for as long as the professions can manage without knowing about them. It may be that you will decide that that time has gone. Solicitors can continue to manage without knowing much about the EC, social security, consumer credit, public housing law and a host of other subjects so long as there is a sufficiency of clients for conveyancing, probate, family work and commercial matters, who can pay the fees demanded. A useful supplementary income may be obtained from doing legally aided accidents work and criminal cases. The position of the barristers may be somewhat less secure already.

Potentially, therefore, the legal professions face a number of challenges. Some of them may be of their own making. Those challenges provide scope for discussion within the English legal system syllabus of the present condition of the legal professions. Before you can engage in such discussions you must know the basic facts about the professions. In this section I shall indicate how you should organise your knowledge about the profession so as to make an effective contribution to discussions about the problems facing the profession today. Most of the principal textbooks have chapters devoted to either 'personnel of the law' or 'the legal professions'. In order to understand something of the way in which the present-day professions are organised you should know a little about their origins and how there came to be two professions of barristers and solicitors. This is covered briefly but adequately in Smith and Bailey, *The Modern English Legal System*, and Walker and Walker, *The English Legal System*. Thus you will be introduced into the world of the Inns of Court and the origins and predecessors of the Law Society, and learn how barristers came to enjoy a monopoly of appointments to the bench and rights of advocacy in the superior courts. Likewise, you may learn how the solicitors became sufficiently powerful to acquire a statutory monopoly over conveyancing. Knowing the details of the way in which the professions are organised will enable you to evaluate proposals which are designed to make the professions more efficient without them having to undergo any fundamental change. Some improvements in efficiency can undoubtedly be achieved by adjustments to the rules of practice which restrict the ways in which lawyers of both branches of the profession conduct their business. Over the past 20 years or so the Bar has in fact removed several restrictive practices.

There is another and more fundamental consideration for you to appreciate before embarking on a discussion of the professions' present condition. That is, to understand that there are two opposing views of the concept of professionalism and that these two views may both be applied to the law. The following account of these opposing views is adapted from Smith and Bailey's introductory section to chapter 3 of *The Modern English Legal System*.

The Royal Commission on Legal Services (Cmnd 7648) assumed that all professions had five main characteristics:

(a)   Central organisation, a governing body with powers of control and discipline.

(b)   A primary function of giving advice or service in a specialised field of knowledge.

(c)   The restriction of admission to those with the required standard of education and training.

(d)   A measure of self-regulation by the profession.

(e)   A paramountcy of the duty owed to the client. In the case of the legal professions this last is subject only to a duty owed to the court.

Another view of professionalism is taken from a book by M.S. Larson, *The Rise of Professionalism*:

(a)   Professionals are the producers of special services.

(b)   They create and control a market for their expertise.

(c)   They assert collectively a special social status.

(d)   They have the ability to be upwardly socially mobile.

Chapter 6 of Cotterell's book, *The Sociology of Law*, contains a useful summary of a variety of views about the professional status of lawyers.

The professionals' view of themselves is that the public interest requires a strong and independent profession, with high ethical standards and a high level of skilled expertise. These things can be secured only by accepting restrictions and giving the profession high rewards. All of this applies to lawyers. However, during the 1980s the opposing view of professionalism has received more notice. This is connected with the movement towards deregulation of services generally; this movement has included the bus industry, the provision of spectacles and the 'big bang' in the City in 1986, with the restructuring of the legal framework of financial services. This has accentuated some old issues in the legal profession and created some new problems as well. The time when legal services were all controlled by the profession with a clear demarcation between the work of barristers and solicitors has gone. It may be more accurate to say that the legal profession may be losing control over the provision of legal services but that the demarcation between barristers and solicitors is still in place for those parts of the legal services still controlled by the profession. The following matters continued until recently to be sources of friction between the two branches of the legal profession:

(a) The possibility of fusion, or partial fusion, whereby all professional lawyers would qualify initially as solicitors and only those choosing to specialise in advocacy would later qualify as barristers.

(b) Rights of audience for solicitors in the High Court.

(c) The possible appointment of solicitors to the High Court bench.

(d) Relaxation of restrictions on the type of work done by employed barristers.

The issues in (b), (c) and (d) have been resolved to a greater or lesser extent by the Courts and Legal Services Act 1990. Whilst solicitors are now eligible for rights of audience in the higher courts, the question remains of how many will achieve such rights.

Some of the new problematic conditions created by the deregulation of services generally include:

(a) The abolition of the solicitors' conveyancing monopoly.

(b) The relaxation of the rules about advertising.

(c) The possibility of partnerships between solicitors and other professionals such as accountants, surveyors and architects.

(d) The creation of very large firms as a result of mergers between leading firms of solicitors.

The first of these conditions was brought about by an amendment to the Solicitors Act 1974 introduced by the Administration of Justice Act 1985. This has led to the appearance of a new body of licensed conveyancers, who are entitled to conduct conveyancing transactions for a fee. Building societies and banks will be able to provide 'one-stop' services in connection with house purchase.

In addition to being aware of these contemporary issues facing the legal professions, there are at least two other matters which continue to provide material for students' work on an English legal system course. These are: questions of professional discipline, complaints and redress of grievances; and the quality of practitioners, their education and training. Each branch of the profession retains control over the discipline of its members and sanctions for professional misconduct. The Solicitors' Practice Rules 1987 have the force of law, being made under the authority of the Solicitors Act 1974, s. 31(1) but the professional conduct of barristers is regulated by the profession itself. Of particular note is the office of Legal Services Ombudsman introduced by the Courts and Legal Services Act 1990. In the case of both barristers and solicitors you should be careful to distinguish differing degrees of professional misconduct from cases of professional negligence. The former are matters to be dealt with by the disciplinary procedures of the professions themselves. Professional negligence, involving liability to the client, is a matter for the courts. There is a compulsory insurance scheme for all practising solicitors and it is a case of professional misconduct for a barrister not to have a professional indemnity insurance.

On grounds of public policy, barristers were held to be immune from being sued in *Rondel* v *Worsley* [1969] 1 AC 191. The limits of this immunity were defined in *Saif Ali* v *Sydney Mitchell & Co.* [1980] AC 198. In this case it was held that the immunity extended only to pre-trial work 'intimately connected with the conduct of the cause in court'. Solicitor advocates enjoy the same immunity. Subject to professional rules to be made by the Bar Council barristers may enter into contracts with their clients (Courts and Legal Services Act 1990, s. 61).

The 1990 Act introduced new arrangements for solicitors' and barristers' disciplinary and complaints procedures. The professions retain the right to make their own rules, subject to overall control by the Lord Chancellor's Advisory Committee on Legal Education and Conduct. The Committee includes a substantial proportion of non-lawyer members.

In addition to the changes already mentioned you should take account of the effect on the professions of Directive 89/48/EEC on the mutual recognition of professional qualifications, as a result of which UK lawyers will be able to qualify readily as lawyers in any other member State and vice versa.

The practical reason for including a reference to the education and training of professional lawyers in the curriculum is because of the light this sheds on the make-up of the professions and their backgrounds. The training of lawyers is firmly based in literary skills and it is therefore no surprise to learn that a majority of law students come from professional and managerial backgrounds; but the bias towards students with a middle-class background is reinforced by the costs involved in the lengthy education and training necessary before qualification. You may gain further insights into the profession by considering the proposals which were made for the reform of professional legal education and the implementation of a changed education for solicitors which occurred in 1993 and the end of the monopoly enjoyed by the Inns of Court School of Law over the education of barristers.

One of the main issues for the legal profession in the 1990s and beyond is the financing of cases. We have already seen (in chapter 8) that the legal aid scheme potentially has entered a new phase of reform, and 1995 has seen the approval of the Conditional Fee Agreements Order. Both developments have important implications for the way in which the legal profession operates.

In addition to the new-style licensed conveyancers mentioned earlier you must also take into account the work of legal executives in solicitors' offices. The most significant point for you to remember about the work of sub-professional workers in the law is the important role that they have in providing alternative legal services. These alternative legal services have been mentioned in connection with the civil process and the provision of legal services to meet otherwise unmet needs (see chapter 8). Just a reminder. These sub-professionals can be found at work in Citizens Advice Bureaux, trade unions, trading standards offices and the motoring organisations. Take note also of the fact that the new arrangements for legal aid will make more use of these specialist advice agencies. It remains to be seen what effects such changes will have on the legal profession as a whole. Could a situation arise in which professional lawyers may be excluded in reality from doing certain sorts of legal work? What price, then, the much vaunted legal values which are claimed as the special preserve of lawyers?

CONCLUSIONS

At the beginning of this chapter it was suggested that, up to the present time, English law has been a practitioners' law. Some of the features of English law and the English legal system which support this point of view were described. In looking at some of the problems currently facing the judiciary and the legal professions it seems that there may be some evidence that this is ceasing to be so. The whole of the comments on the judiciary and the legal professions in this chapter must now be read in the light of the statutory objective in s. 17 of the Courts and Legal Services Act 1990, namely, 'the development of legal services . . . (and in particular the development of advocacy, litigation, conveyancing and probate services) by making provision for *new or better ways* of providing such services and a *wider choice of persons* providing them' (emphasis added).

The principal consequences of implementing this objective are:

(a)   the opening up of the services named to persons and bodies other than professionally qualified lawyers;

(b)   the control of those persons and bodies, including lawyers, providing the services by a new regulatory framework;

(c)   the creation of a hierarchy of 'rights of audience' for those providing advocacy services;

(d) to tie eligibility for appointment to judicial office to having the appropriate 'right of audience' (see the table in chapter 3).

These changes raise the issue of the extent to which the practice of law may become de-professionalised.

The lawyers' view of the legal system is no longer the only view that is taken into account. It may be that it has been decided that law is too serious a matter to be left to the lawyers. As Cotterell puts it in *The Sociology of Law*, there may be a process of 'rationalising' and 'bureaucratising' of the law in a 'modern society' (p. 190). Certainly there is some contemporary evidence for such a view. Two major issues dealt with in this book, the reform of the civil process (see chapter 7) and the reform of legal aid (see chapter 8), will result in some shift of control from the 'professionals' to the 'bureaucrats'.

On the first issue, the judges were openly critical of many of the major proposals coming out of the Lord Chancellor's review of civil procedure. The profession as a whole is apprehensive about the power to be given to the new Legal Aid Board.

What exactly is at stake? The profession is in both cases defending its view of what the public interest requires: a strong independent judiciary and a strong independent body of practitioners. The opposing view is that the public interest requires the rooting out of entrenched bastions of privilege masquerading behind a smoke-screen of professional and ethical standards. Complaints by the judiciary about the potential loss of the long vacation and an extended working day can easily appear to be special pleading to maintain a privileged position with no more merit in it than any trade unionist's protection of overmanning in industry and commerce.

Ultimately it is for you to decide, on the basis not only of the evidence put before you in classes and in books but also your own observation of judges and lawyers 'in action', whether the claims of the profession are founded in reality or are purely bogus.

Even when all the criticisms of the judges and the legal profession have been proved, I believe that your aspirations, mentioned at the beginning of chapter 2, will continue to include elements of wanting to join a community of lawyers, imbued with the service ideal, and acting as the professional guardians of the law.

EXAMINATION QUESTION

In accordance with the SWOT tradition, this chapter will end with a look at sample questions that may be asked in examinations. A sample of 10 recent examination questions from several institutions reveals the following distribution of subject-matter:

Judges	3 questions	Judicial independence	2
		Quality of judges and the appointments system	1
Lay justices	1 question		
Legal profession	6 questions	Rights of audience in the High Court	1
		Professional monopolies	1
		Restrictive practices at the Bar	1
		Fusion of the professions	1
		Work done in law centres	2

As an example of these questions let me suggest that you consider the following:

Compare the services provided by a private firm of solicitors with the services provided by a publicly funded law centre.

Comment

In answering this question, the following main points might be made:

(a)   In all comparisons, care must be taken to have a proper basis for comparison. That means generally comparing like with like. Therefore:

(b)   Point out the great diversity of types of private firm, ranging from sole practitioners to the great new mega-firms of the City. But:

(c)   There is no reason why any private firm should *not* do any of the types of work done by law centres.

(d)   The differences between the two types of practice are to be found in the ethos of each, rather than in difference of type of work, type of client or location.

(e)   Even firms which are doing mostly legal aid work, are constrained by the individualist approach to doing the best for a particular client. The legal aid scheme itself and procedural rules impose this and difficulties arise in coordinating the claims of large groups affected in the same way; for example, claimants with claims arising out of the Zeebrugge ferry disaster or the King's Cross Underground fire.

(f)   On the other hand law centres are more issue and problem centred in their work. Whilst they do much work on behalf of individuals they can also seek ways of tackling prevalent problems in their areas. These problems include bad housing conditions under the control of one or a number of landlords; local employment problems, such as mass redundancies; and problems about local authority services, such as problems relating to educational provision. Some of these problems are not suitable for individualist treatment although they are undoubtedly problems of a legal nature.

P.S.

Having come to the end, may I wish you SWOT!

FURTHER READING

Smith, P.F. and Bailey, S.H., *The Modern English Legal System* by S.H. Bailey and M.J. Gunn (2nd edn., Sweet and Maxwell, 1991).

Walker and Walker, *English Legal System* by R. Walker and R. Ward (7th edn., Butterworths, 1994).

Zander, M., *Cases and Materials on the English Legal System* (6th edn., Butterworths, 1992).

BIBLIOGRAPHY

Allen, Sir C.K., *Law in the Making*, 7th ed. (Oxford: Clarendon Press, 1964).
Atiyah, P.S., *Pragmatism and Theory in English Law* (Hamlyn Lectures 39) (London: Stevens & Sons, 1987).
Baker, J.H., *An Introduction to English Legal History*, 3rd ed. (London: Butterworths, 1990).
Bennion, F., *Statute Law*, 2nd ed. (London: Oyez Longman, 1983).
Blom-Cooper, L., & Drewry, G., *Final Appeal: A Study of the House of Lords in Its Judicial Capacity* (Oxford: Clarendon Press, 1972).
Cane, P., *An Introduction to Administrative Law*, 2nd ed. (Oxford: Clarendon Press, 1992).
Cecil, H., *The English Judge* (Hamlyn Lectures 22) (London: Stevens & Sons, 1970).
Clinch, P., *Using a Law Library* (London: Blackstone Press, 1992).
Committee on Contempt of Court (Chairman: Lord Justice Phillimore), *Report* (Cmnd 5794) (London: HMSO, 1974).
Committee on the Preparation of Legislation (Chairman: Sir David Renton), *Report* (Cmnd 6053) (London: HMSO, 1975).
Cotterrell, R., *The Sociology of Law: An Introduction*, 2nd ed. (London: Butterworths, 1992).
Cross, Sir R., & Harris, J.W., *Precedent in English Law*, 4th ed. (Oxford: Clarendon Press, 1991).
Cross, Sir R., *Statutory Interpretation*, 3rd ed. by J.S. Bell & G. Engle (London: Butterworths, 1995).
Dale, Sir W., *Legislative Drafting: A New Approach* (London: Butterworths, 1977).

David, R., *Major Legal Systems in the World Today*, transl. and adapted by J.E.C. Brierley, 3rd ed. (London: Stevens & Sons, 1985).

de Smith, S.A., & Brazier, R., *Constitutional and Administrative Law*, 7th ed. by R. Brazier (Harmondsworth: Penguin, 1994).

Denning, Lord, *The Discipline of Law* (London: Butterworths, 1979).

Derrett, J.D.M. (ed.), *An Introduction to Legal Systems* (London: Sweet & Maxwell, 1968).

Farrar, J.H., *Law Reform and the Law Commission* (London: Sweet & Maxwell, 1974).

Farrar, J.H., & Dugdale, A.M., *Introduction to Legal Method*, 3rd ed. (London: Sweet & Maxwell, 1990).

Fisher, Sir H., *Report of an Inquiry into the Circumstances Leading to the Trial of Three Persons on Charges Arising out of the Death of Maxwell Confait and the Fire at 27 Doggett Road, London SE6* (HC (1977-8) 90) (London: HMSO, 1977).

Gardner, G., & Martin, A. (eds), *Law Reform Now* (London: Gollancz, 1963).

Goodhart, A.L., *Essays in Jurisprudence and the Common Law* (Cambridge: Cambridge University Press, 1931).

Griffith, J.A.G., *The Politics of the Judiciary*, 4th ed. (London: Fontana Press, 1991).

Hansard Society, *Report on the Legislative Process (Making the Law)* (London: Hansard Society for Parliamentary Government, 1992).

Harding, A., *A Social History of English Law* (Harmondsworth: Penguin, 1966).

Hazlitt, W., *The Spirit of the Age, or Contemporary Portraits*, ed. E.D. Mackerness (Plymouth: Macdonald & Evans, 1975).

Holdsworth, Sir W., *A History of English Law*, vol. 1, 7th ed. by A.L. Goodhart & H.G. Hanbury (London: Methuen, 1956).

Holland, J.A., & Webb, J.S., *Learning Legal Rules*, 2nd ed. (London: Blackstone Press, 1993).

Home Office, *An Independent Prosecution Service for England and Wales* (Cmnd 9074) (London: HMSO, 1983).

Home Office & Lord Chancellor's Office, *The Distribution of Criminal Business between the Crown Court and Magistrates' Courts* (Report of an Interdepartmental Committee; Chairman: Lord Justice James) (Cmnd 6323) (London: HMSO, 1975).

Ingman, T., *The English Legal Process*, 5th ed. (London: Blackstone Press, 1994).

Jackson, R.M., *Jackson's Machinery of Justice*, ed. by J. R. Spencer (Cambridge: Cambridge University Press, 1989).

Kenny, P., *Studying Law*, 3rd ed. (London: Butterworths, 1994).

Kiralfy, A.K.R., *The English Legal System*, 8th ed. (London: Sweet & Maxwell, 1990).

Larson, M.S., *The Rise of Professionalism: A Sociological Analysis* (Berkeley, Calif; London: University of California Press, 1977).

Law Commission & Scottish Law Commission, *Sale and Supply of Goods* (Law Com. No. 160; Scot. Law Com. No. 104; Cm 137) (London: HMSO, 1987).

Law Commission & Scottish Law Commission, *The Interpretation of Statutes* (Law Com. No. 21; Scot. Law Com. No. 11; 1968-69 HC 256) (London: HMSO, 1969).

Lawson, F.H., *Remedies of English Law*, 2nd ed. (London: Butterworths, 1980).

Lee, S., & Fox, M., *Legal Skills*, 2nd ed. (London: Blackstone Press, 1994).

Llewellyn, K.N., *The Bramble Bush: On Our Law and Its Study* (New York: Oceana, 1951).

Lord Chancellor's Department, *Legal Aid: Efficiency Scrutiny* (London: Lord Chancellor's Department, 1986).

Lord Chancellor's Department, *Legal Aid in England and Wales: A New Framework* (Cm 118) (London: HMSO, 1987).

Maitland, F.W., *The Forms of Action at Common Law* (Cambridge: Cambridge University Press, 1936).

Manchester, A.H., *A Modern Legal History of England and Wales 1750–1950* (London: Butterworths, 1980).

Manchester, A.H., *Sources of English Legal History: Law, History and Society in England and Wales 1750–1950* (London: Butterworths, 1984).

Maxwell, Sir P.B., *Maxwell on the Interpretation of Statutes*, 12th ed. by P. St J. Langan (London: Sweet & Maxwell, 1969).

Miers, D.R., & Page A.C., *Legislation*, 2nd ed. (London: Sweet & Maxwell, 1990).

Milsom, S.F.C., *Historical Foundations of the Common Law*, 2nd ed. (London: Butterworths, 1981).

Paterson, A., *The Law Lords* (London: Macmillan, 1982).

Pickles, James, *Straight from the Bench* (London: Phoenix House, 1987).

Potter, Harold, *Potter's Historical Introduction to English law and Its Institutions*, 4th ed. by A.K.R. Kiralfy (London: Sweet & Maxwell, 1958).

Renton, Sir D., *The Preparation of Legislation* (Cmnd. 6053) (London: Sweet & Maxwell, 1975).

Royal Commission on Assizes and Quarter Sessions (Chairman: Lord Beeching), *Report* (Cmnd 4153) (London: HMSO, 1969).

Royal Commission on Criminal Procedure (Chairman: Sir C. Philips), *Report* (Cmnd 8092) (London: HMSO, 1981).

Royal Commission on Legal Services (Chairman: Sir Henry Benson), *Final Report* (Cmnd 7648) (London: HMSO, 1979).

Smith, P.F., & Bailey, S.H., *The Modern English Legal System*, 2nd ed. by S.H. Bailey and M.J. Gunn (London: Sweet & Maxwell, 1991).

Snell, E.H.T., *Snell's Equity*, 29th ed. by P.V. Baker & P. St J. Langan (London: Sweet & Maxwell, 1990).

Starke, J.G., *Introduction to International Law*, 11th ed. (London: Butterworths, 1994).

Statute Law Society, *Statute Law Deficiencies* (London: Sweet & Maxwell, 1970).

Stein, P., *Legal Institutions* (London: Butterworths, 1984).

Stein, P., & Shand, J., *Legal Values in Western Society* (Edinburgh: Edinburgh University Press, 1974).

Stephen, H.J., *Stephen's Commentaries on the Laws of England*, 21st ed. (London: Butterworths, 1950).

Twining, W., & Miers, D., *How To Do Things with Rules*, 3rd ed. (London: Weidenfeld & Nicolson, 1991).

Walker, R.J., & Walker, M.G., *The English Legal System*, 7th ed. by R.J. Walker (London: Butterworths, 1994).

Zander, M., *Cases and Materials on the English Legal System*, 6th ed. (London: Butterworths, 1992).

Zander, M., *The Law-Making Process*, 4th ed. (London: Butterworths, 1994).

INDEX

TITLES IN THE SERIES